Cauleen Smith

Cauleen Smith

Institute of Contemporary Art, University of Pennsylvania

Give it
or
Leave it

Contents

Foreword

There is so much to like about Cauleen Smith's work—the generosity and beauty of her cinematic installation, *Give It or Leave It*,
binds us with awe. It's truly a gift, in line with the giving grace
of the figures around which the project oscillates: Shaker eldress
Rebecca Cox Jackson, the Combahee River Collective, Noah Purifoy,
Simon Rodia, and Alice Coltrane Turiyasangitananda. Over the
past few months, I've watched babies become dazzled by the disco
ball's turn, and Black, Latinx, Asian, and White women bask
in the CCTV live feed under gelled skylights. In the company of
a capacity audience, I followed the voices and movements of Helga
Davis and Justin Hicks through a spellbinding tour of three rooms.
If we replaced consumption with another idea, what would the
world look, sound, and feel like? dismantles the proposition that
black cultural production is only taken, stolen, or appropriated.
Instead Smith's project looks to what the spirits of generosity might
offer in opposition to strife and adversity.

It has been an honor to see this work develop, and the best kind
of wonderful to see it live, travel, expand, contort, and adapt, all
while it was visited, appreciated, acknowledged, questioned, and
loved. For everything, I thank Cauleen Smith. Daniel and Brett
Sundheim Chief Curator Anthony Elms deserves recognition for
his deft organization and extended thoughtfulness. I also must
recognize an installation team of Philadelphia artists led by Paul
Swenbeck, Robert Chaney, and Kate Abercrombie. It should go
without saying that the ICA's entire staff makes all things possible
with heart and care. I am humbled to work alongside each and
every one of them.

Meditating upon Smith's vision, ICA has benefited from gestures that both extended and also reflected her openness and
generosity. I am grateful to Helga Davis and Justin Hicks for their
awe-inspiring performance, an experience which was intimately

woven throughout ICA's galleries. Rhea Anastas remained a valuable collaborator and conversationalist as Smith's work developed, continuing to focus her attention through the duration the exhibition and, of course, the catalogue. Though it may be obvious only to the lucky few who were able to visit both, it's worth nothing that *Give It or Leave It* builds upon Anastas's 2016 exhibition, *The Warplands*. It was also a pleasure to welcome Rodney McMillian back to ICA—this time as an author, in conversation with Smith about the wider and deeper trajectories of her work. We also thank Kimberly Varella, who has done a wonderful job with her book design, as well as Talia Heiman, whose early research helped to track down locations and facts as filming developed. Again, thank you to all.

We appreciate the support Corbett vs. Dempsey and Kate Werble Gallery have given to Smith, throughout this process. As the exhibition moves forward, it is our great fortune to be able to work with our colleagues at the Institute for Contemporary Art, Richmond, and the Frye Art Museum to tour *Give It or Leave It*.

At the University of Pennsylvania, I must acknowledge the arts leadership of Vice-Provost for Faculty Anita L. Allen, Provost Wendell Pritchett, and President Amy Gutmann. I further offer my heartfelt gratitude to ICA's Board President Stephen R. Weber and the entire Board of Overseers.

Finally, we must thank Stacy Tenenbaum Stark and the Foundation for Contemporary Arts. It is a great honor to have received the inaugural Ellsworth Kelly Award for *Give It or Leave It*. The support the FCA has long shown for contemporary art, and in particular, the artists who make it, stands as a model for many.

——————Amy Sadao
Daniel W. Dietrich, II Director

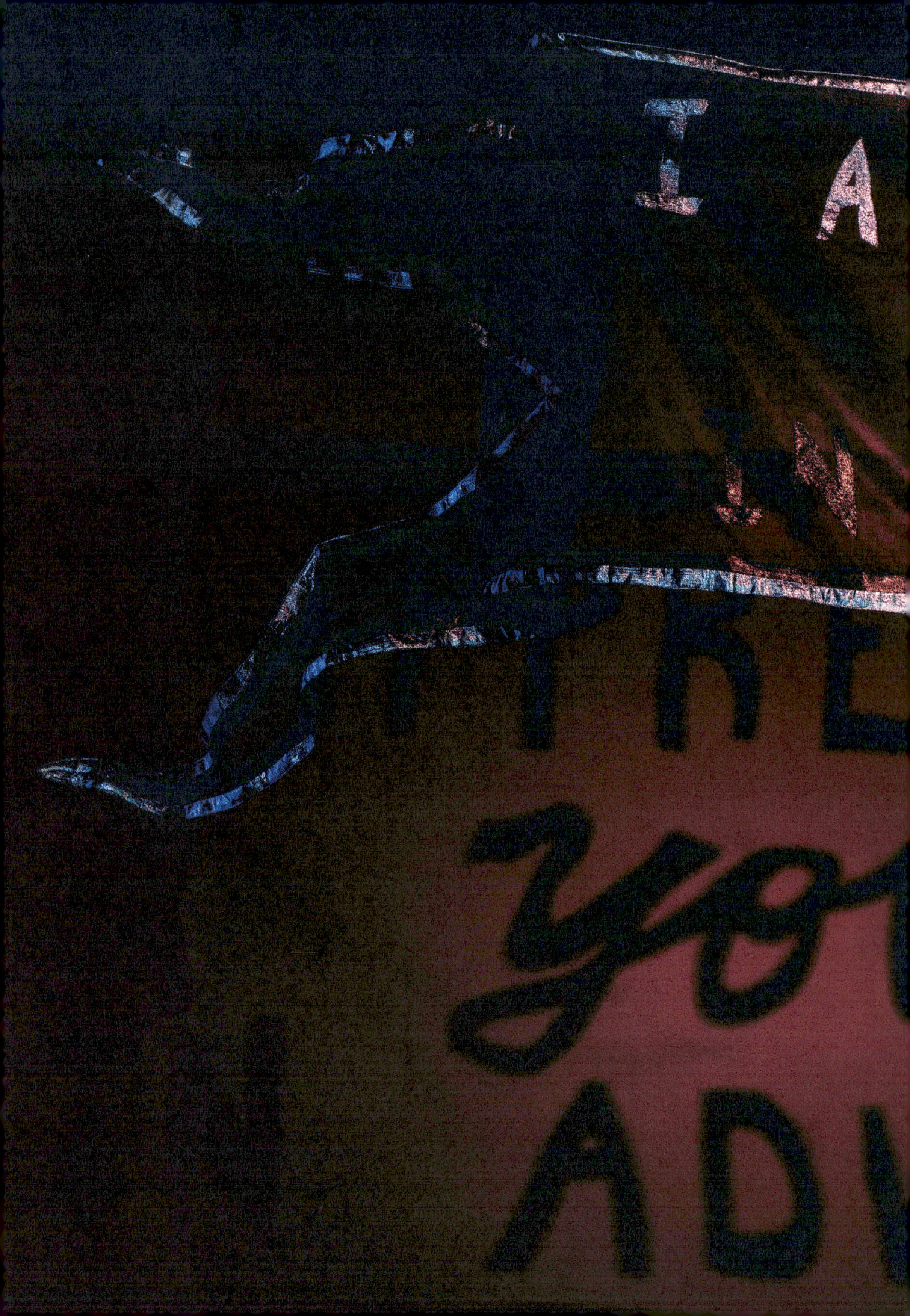

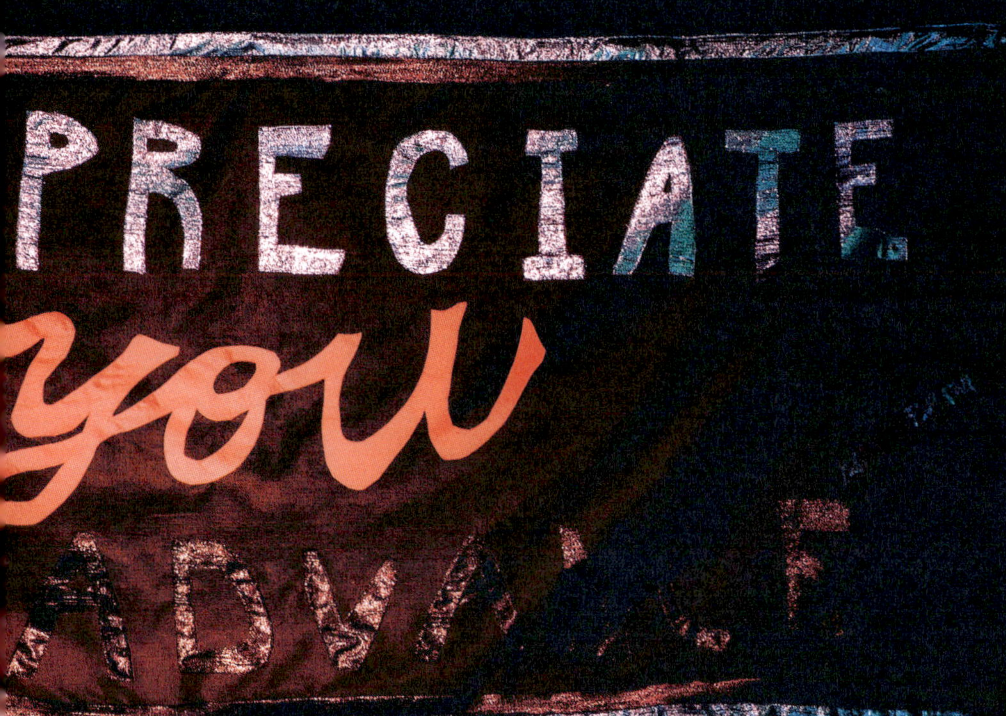
PRECIATE
you
ADVA

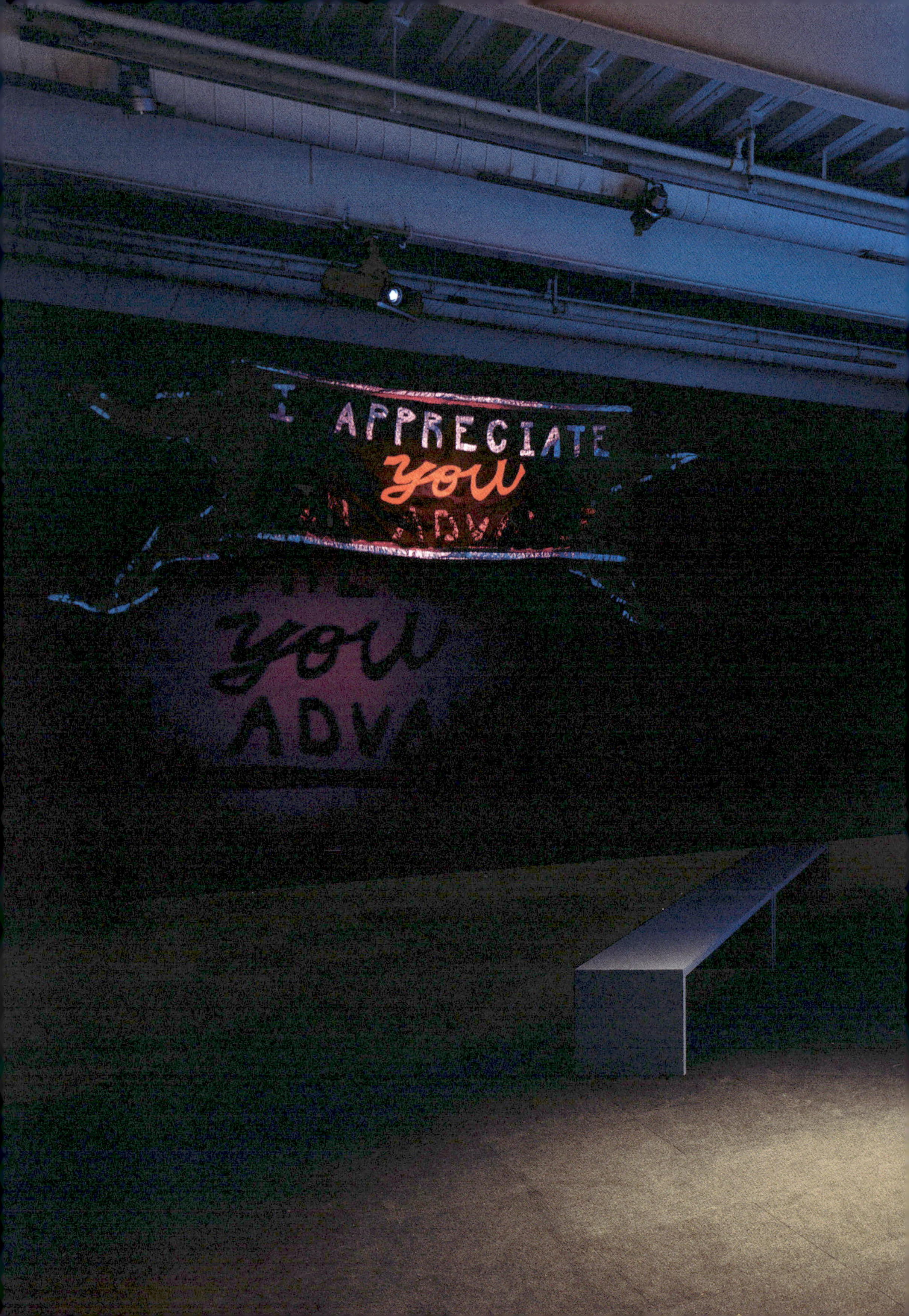
I APPRECIATE
you
YOU
ADV

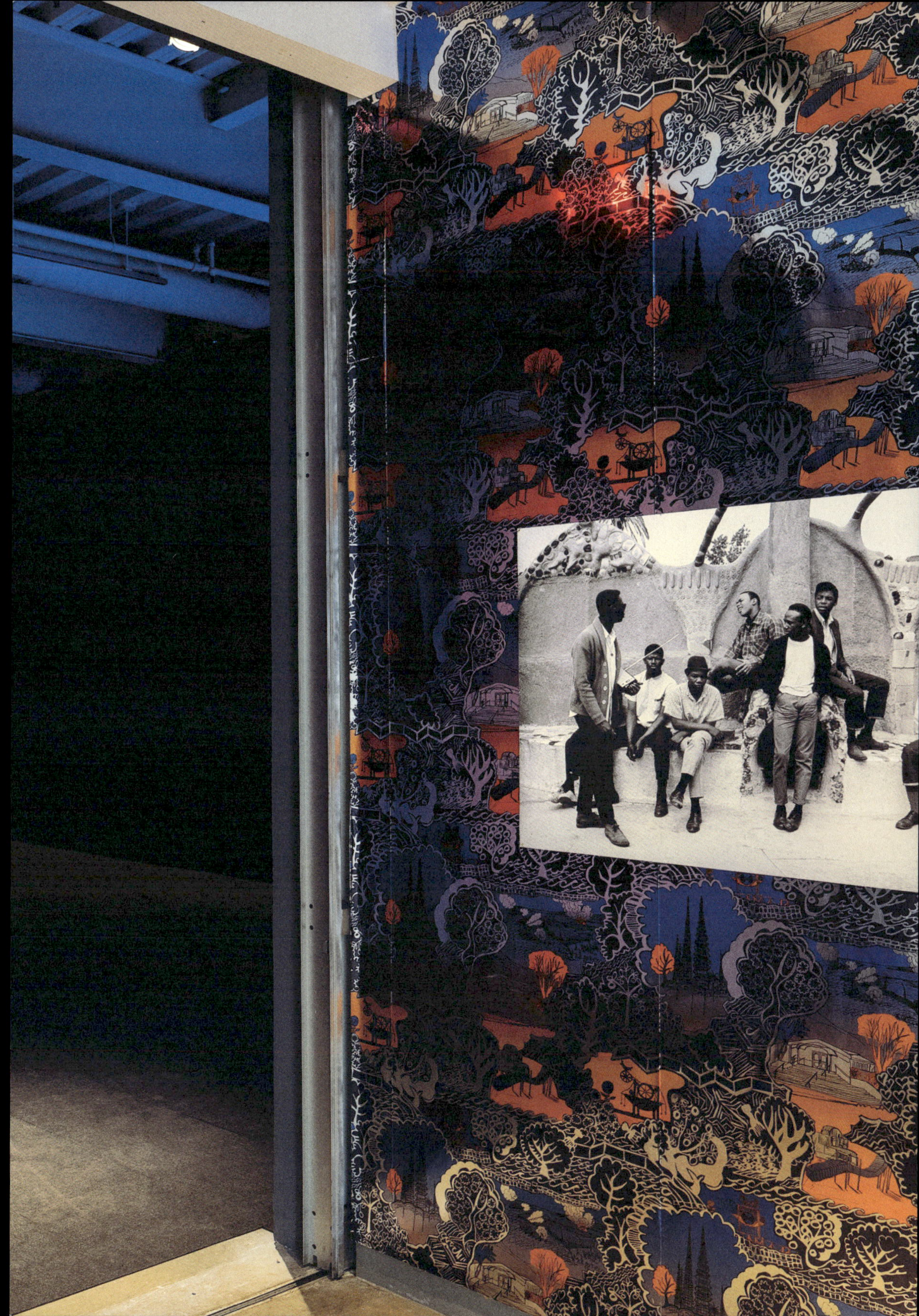

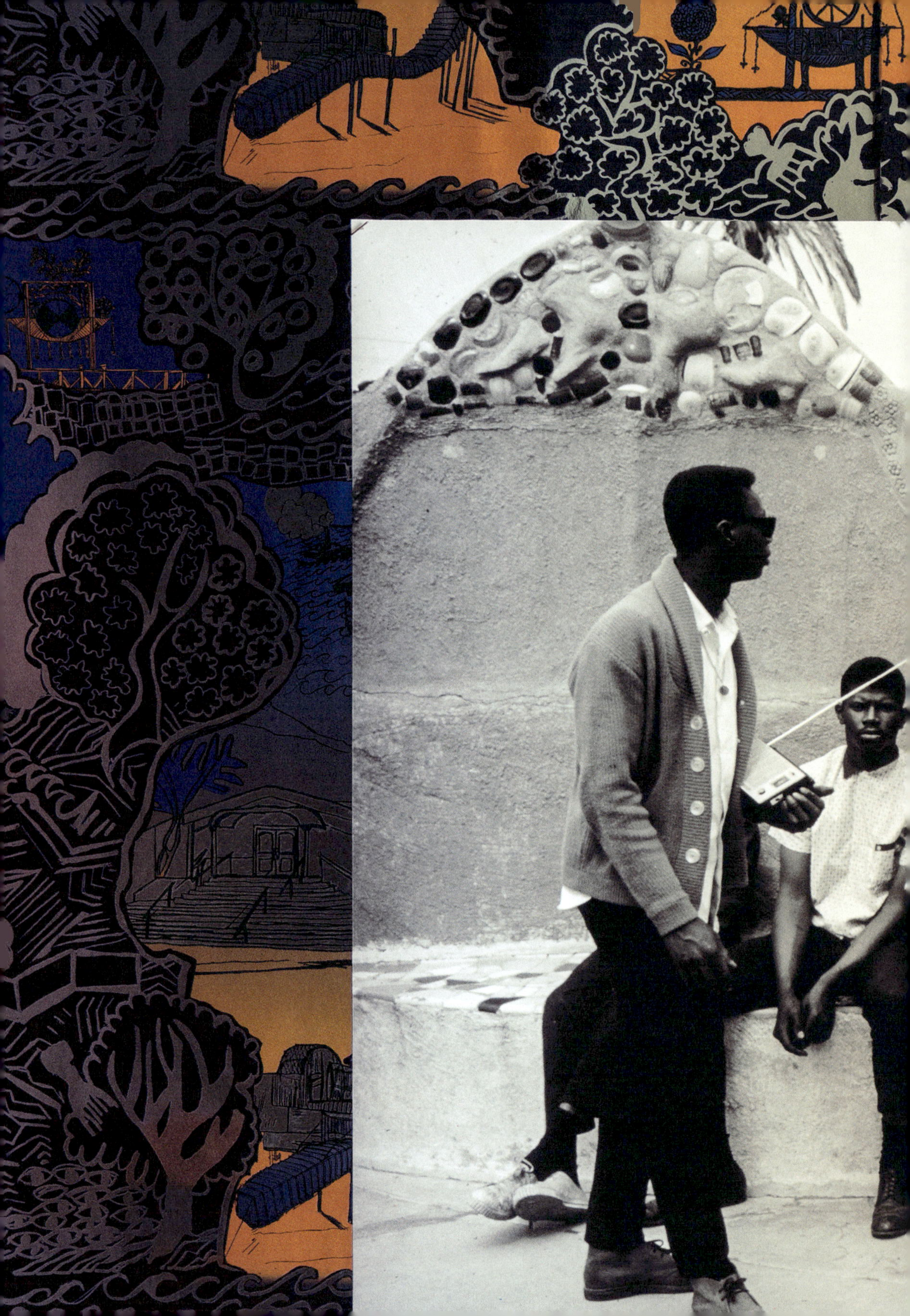

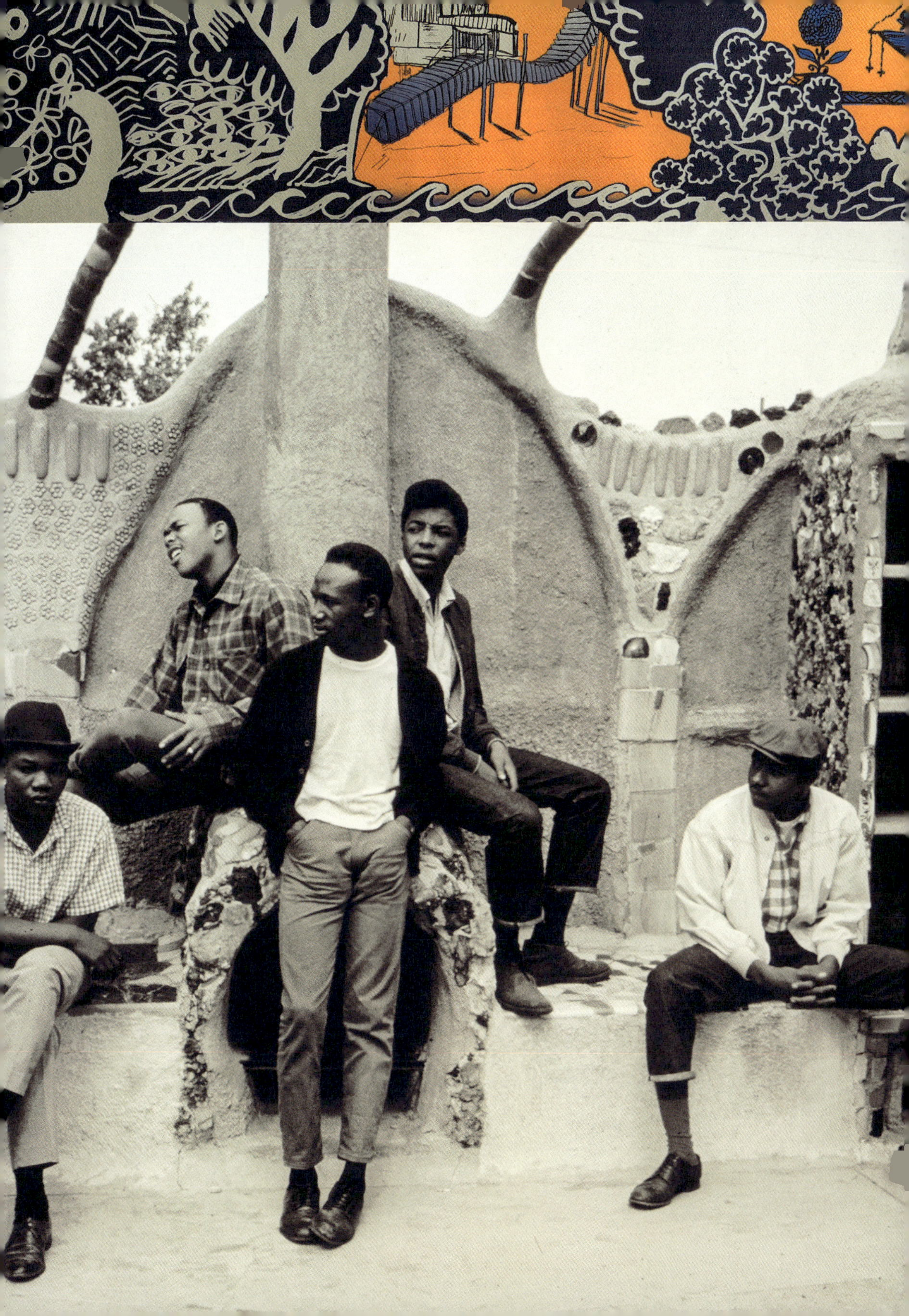

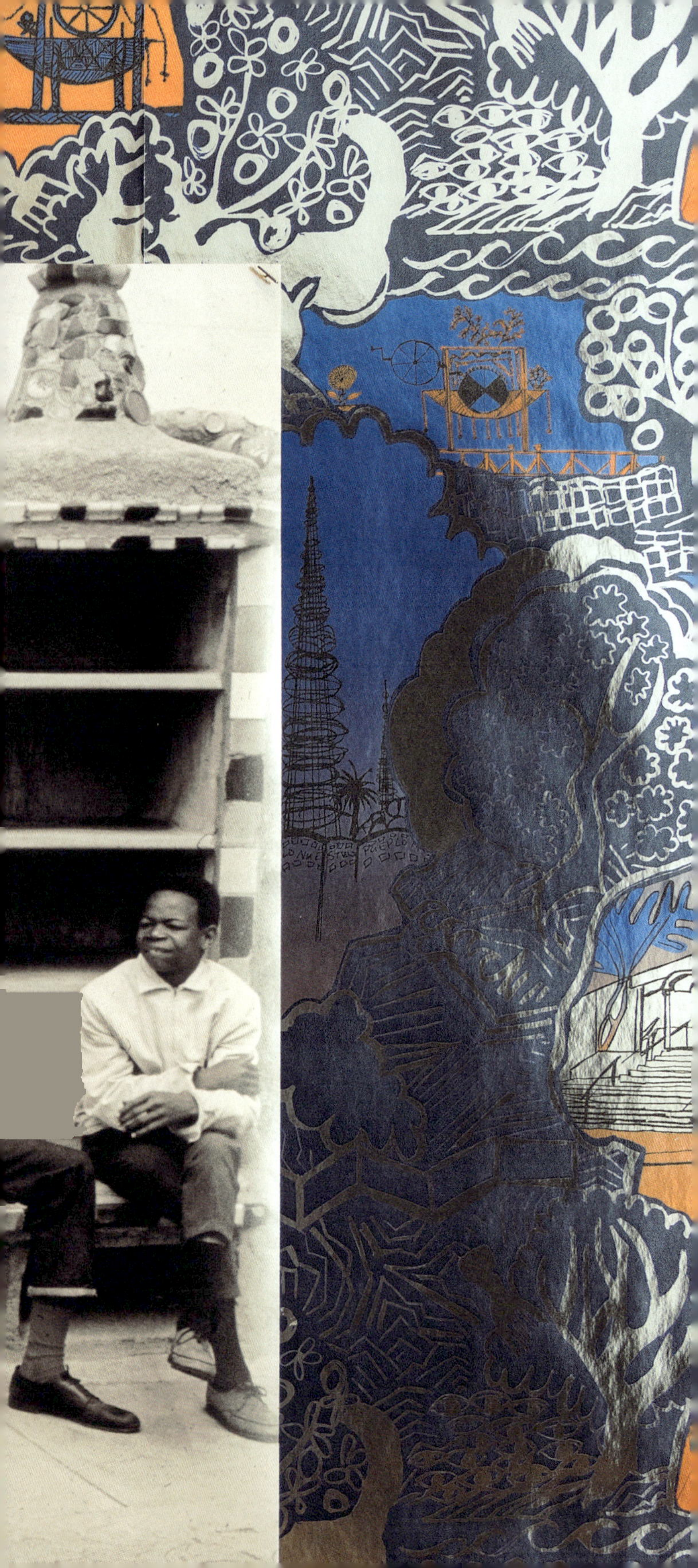

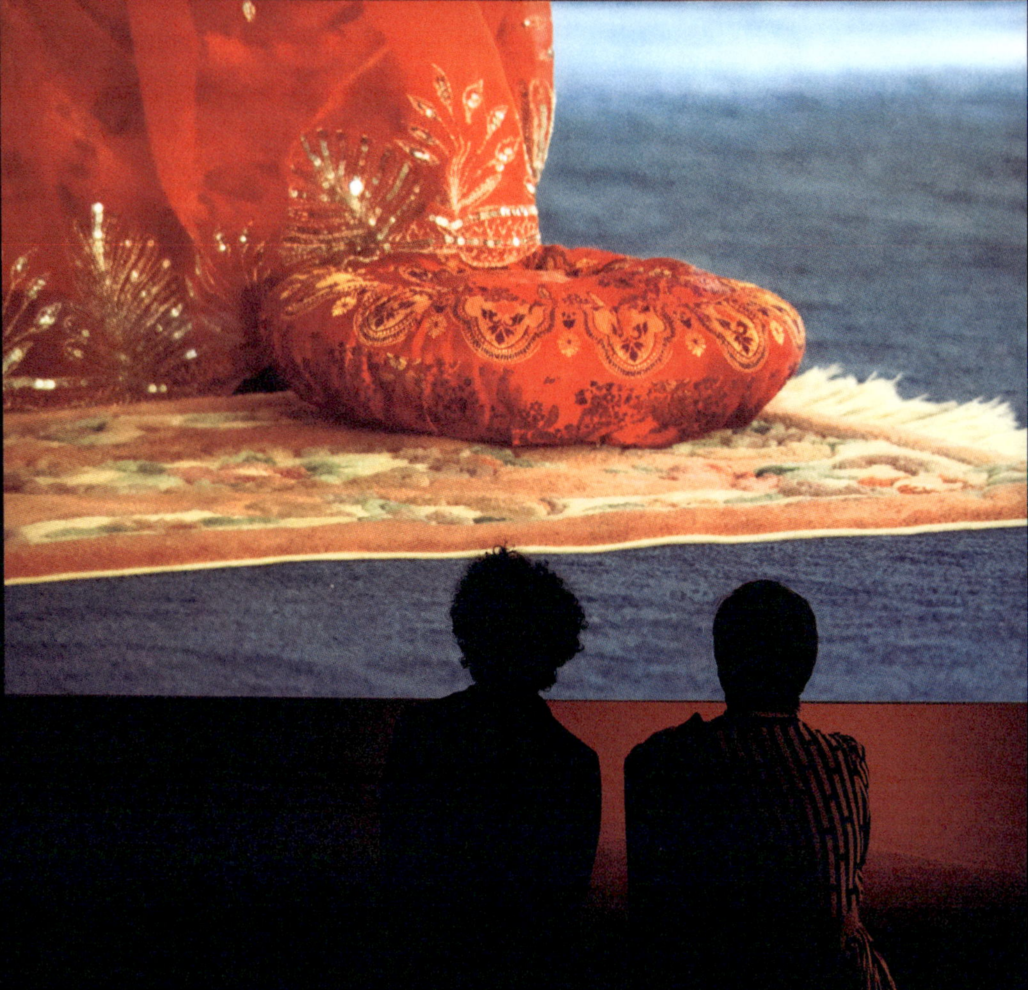

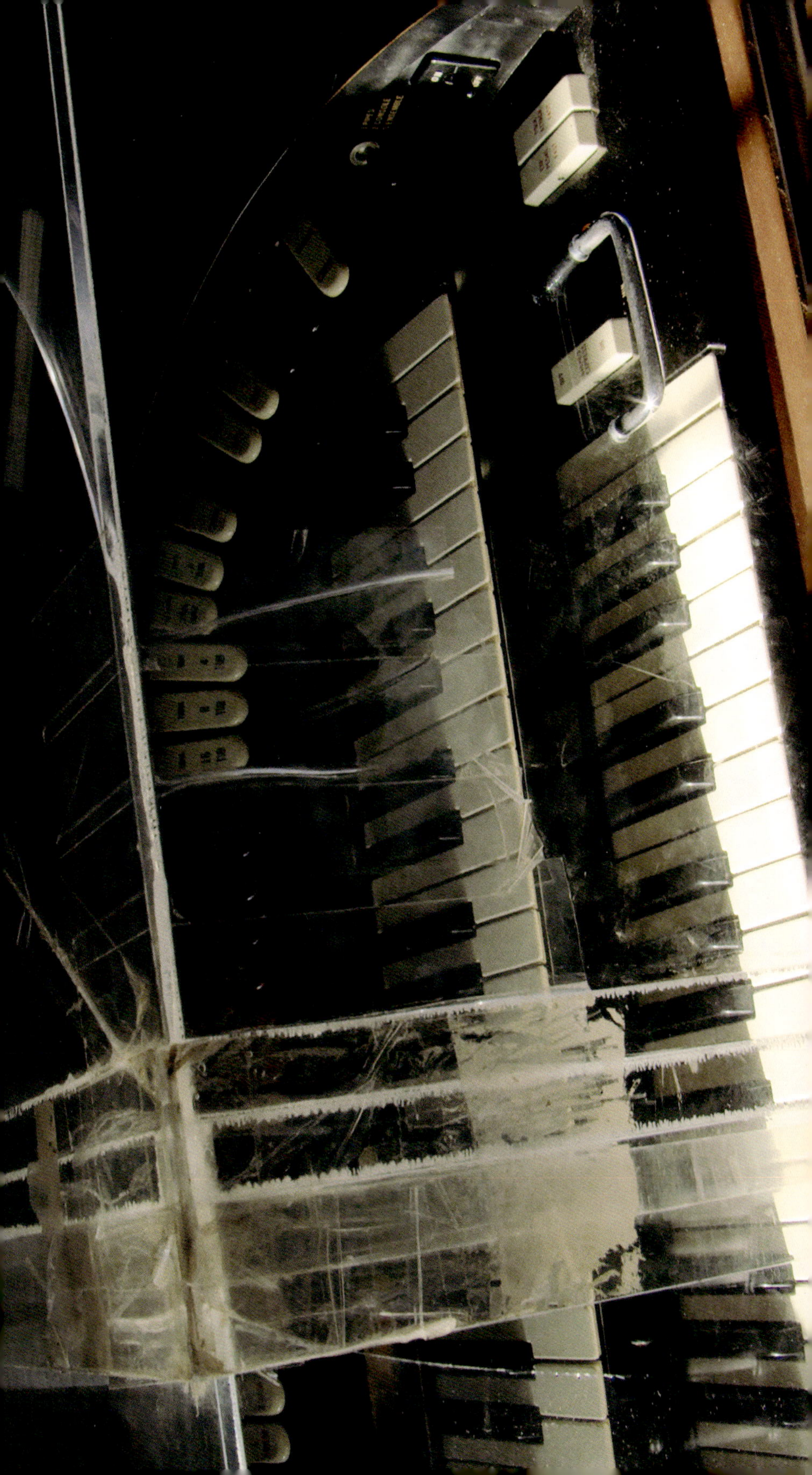

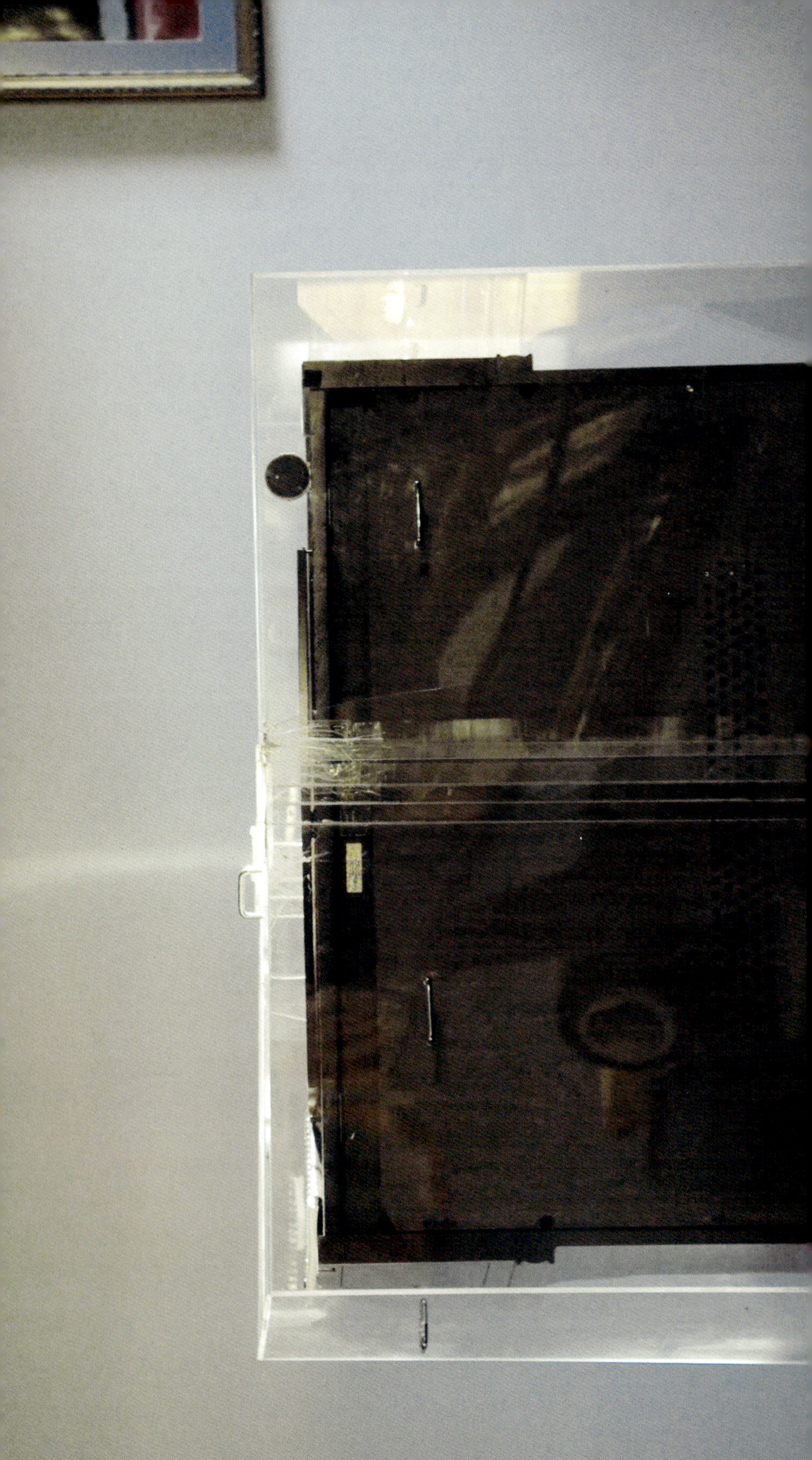

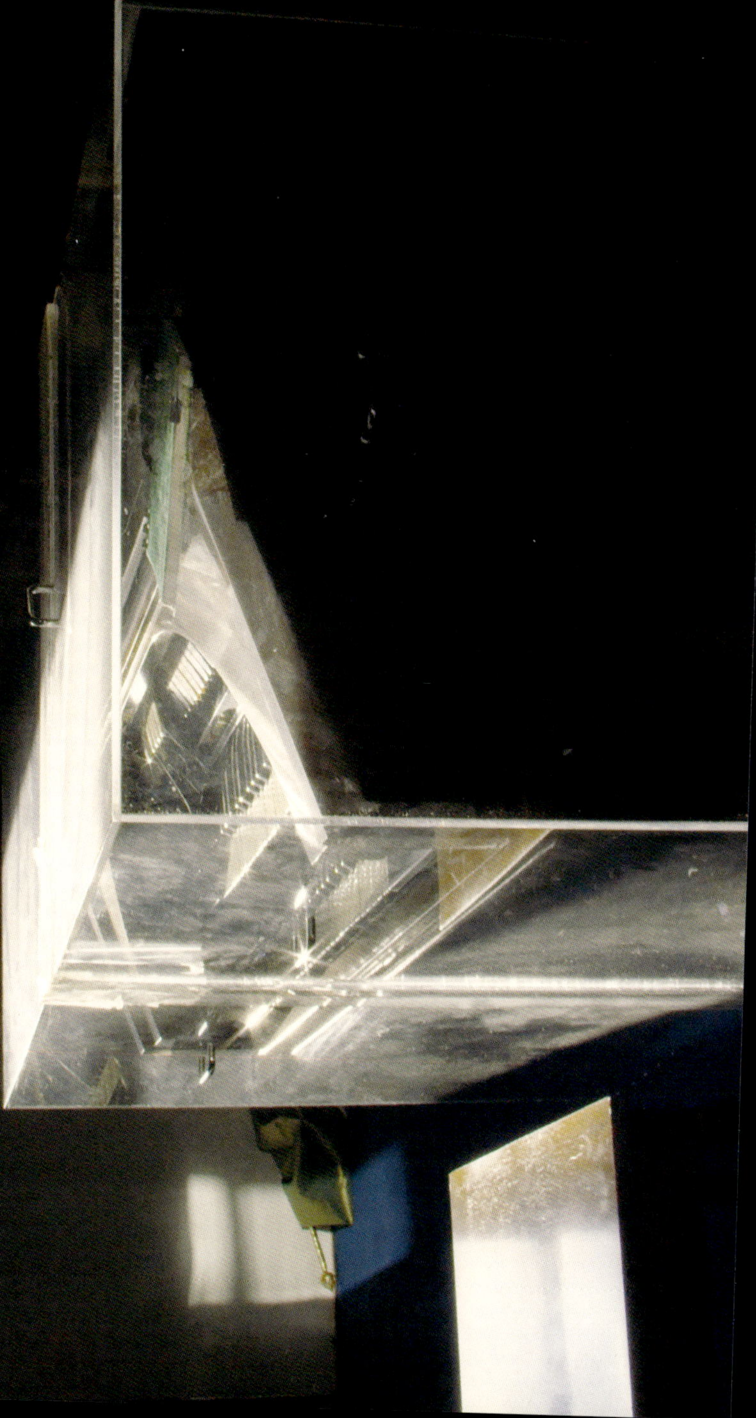

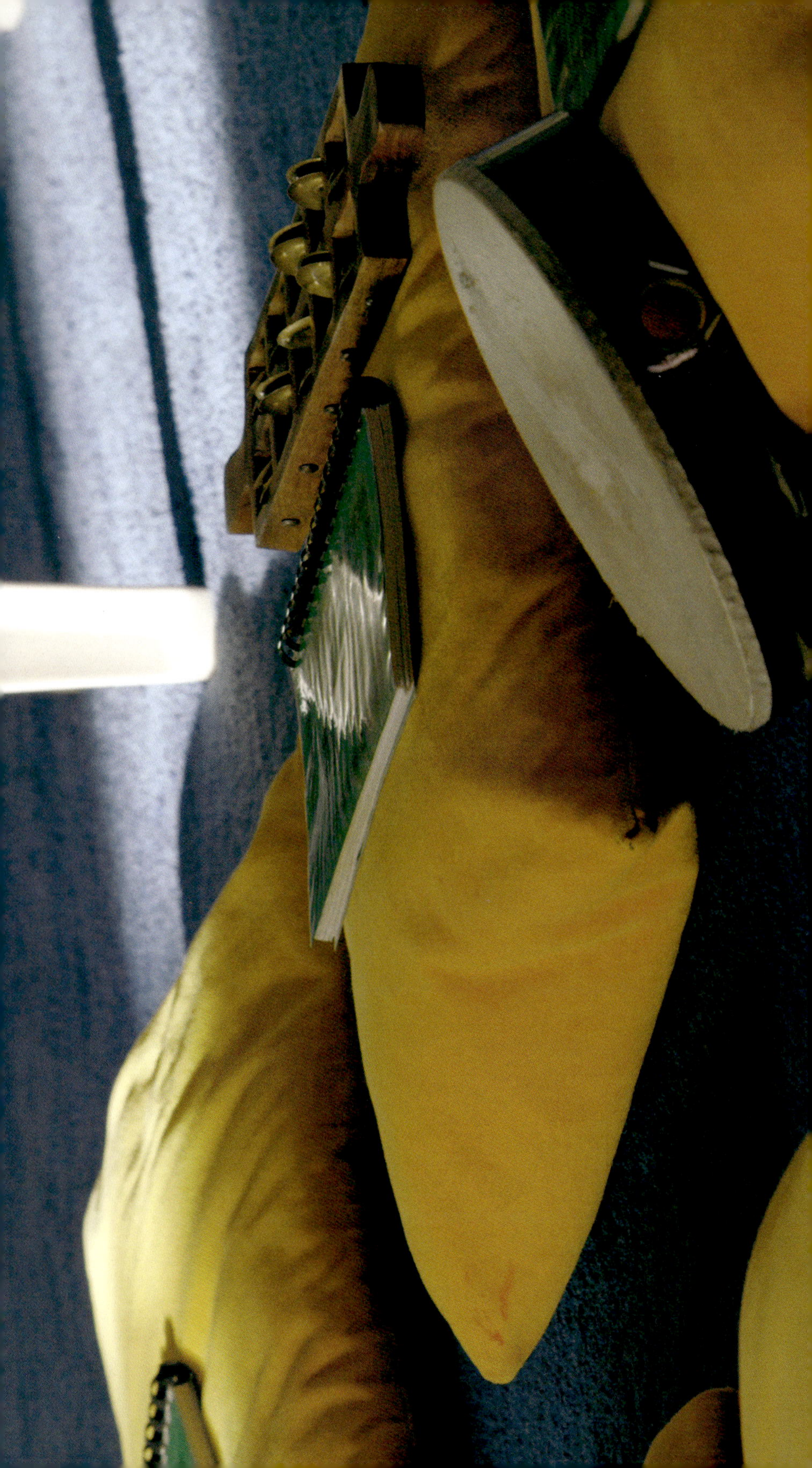

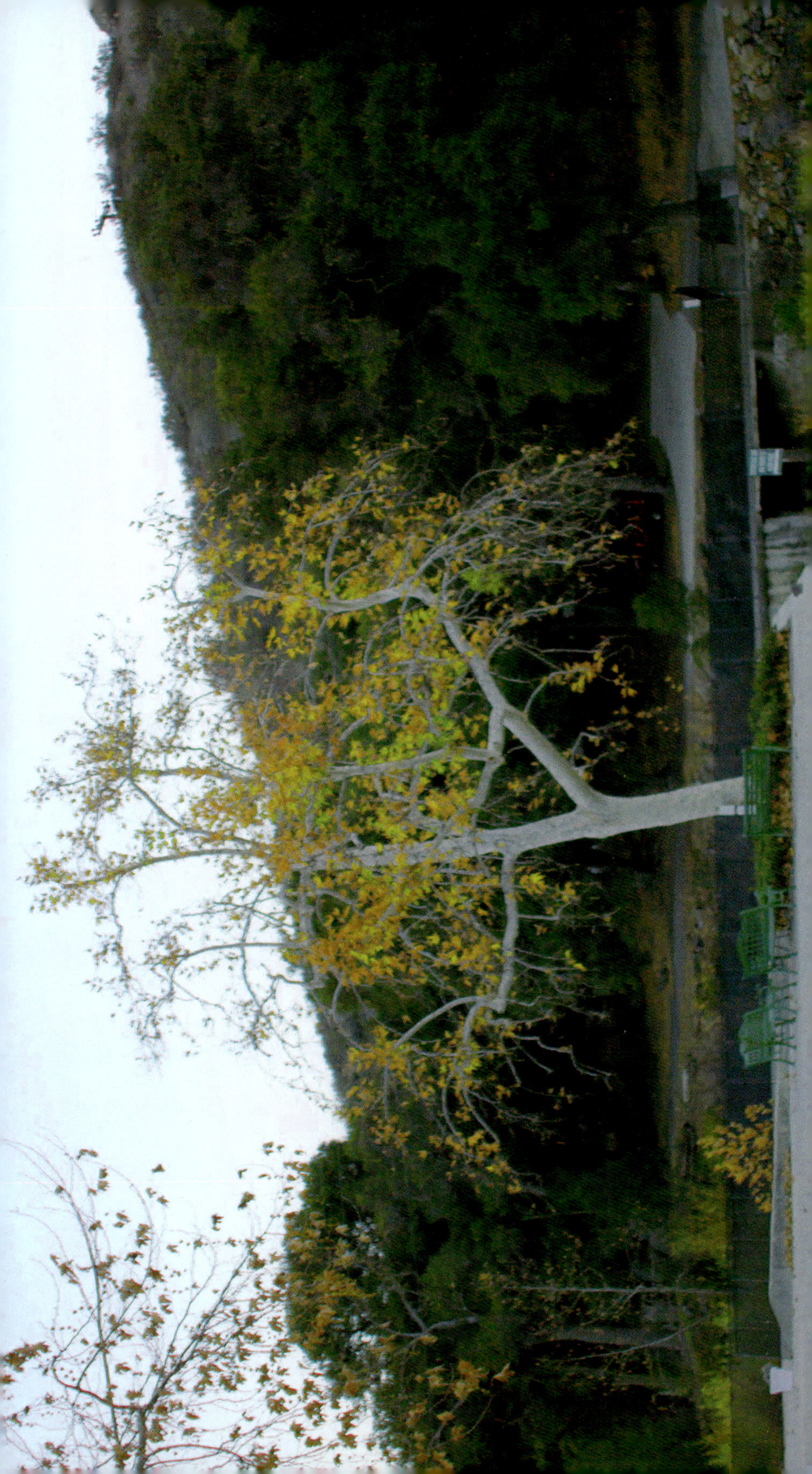

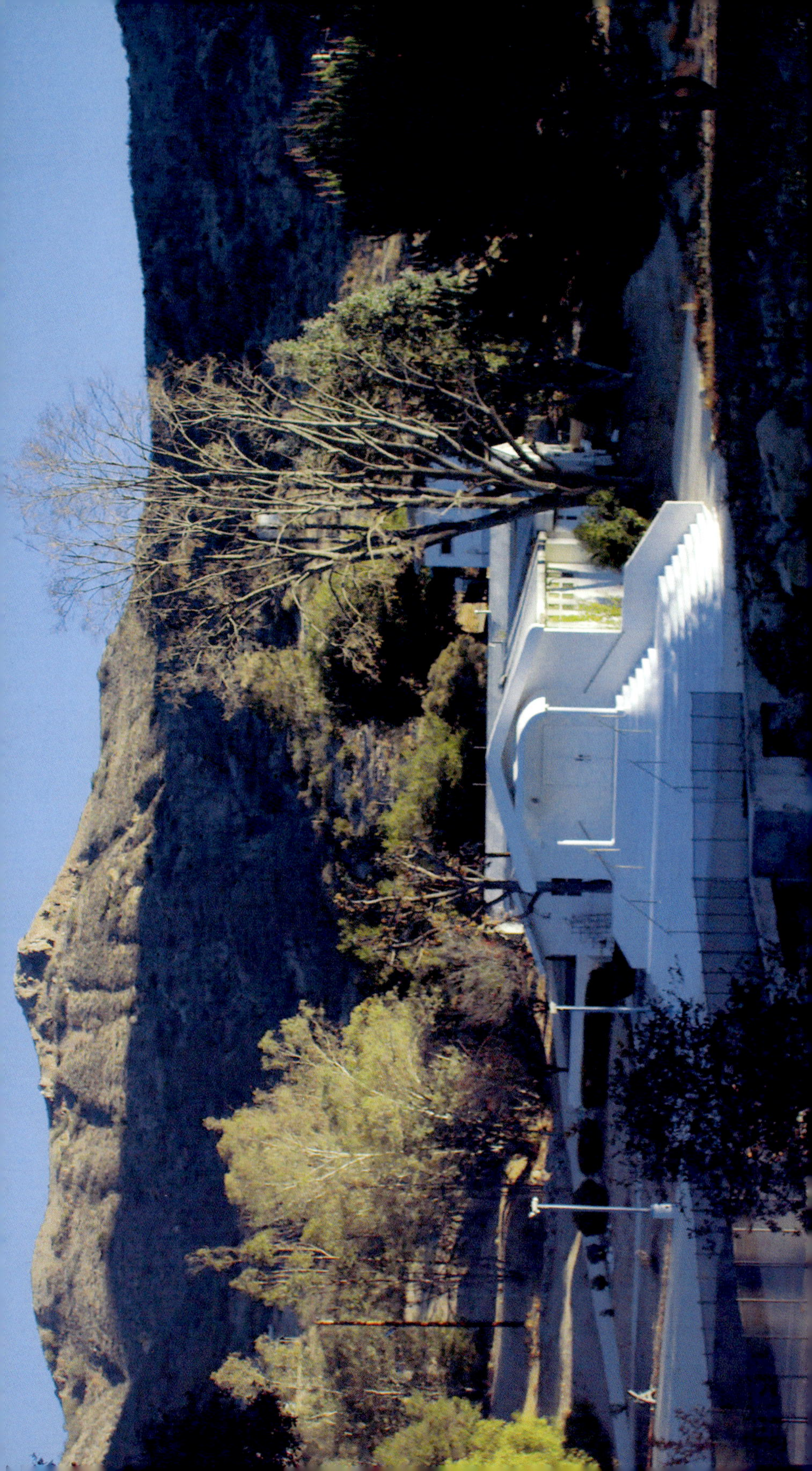

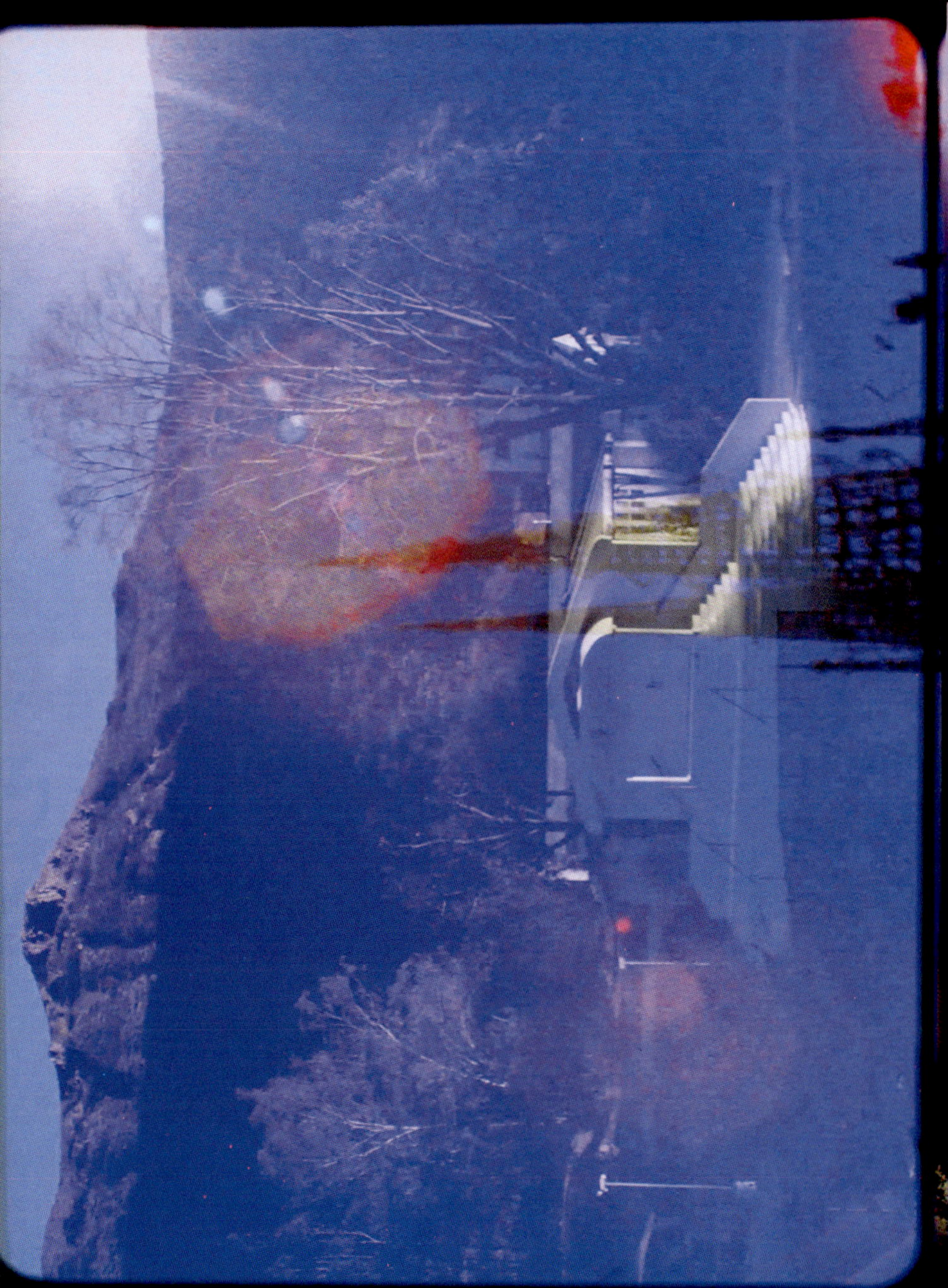

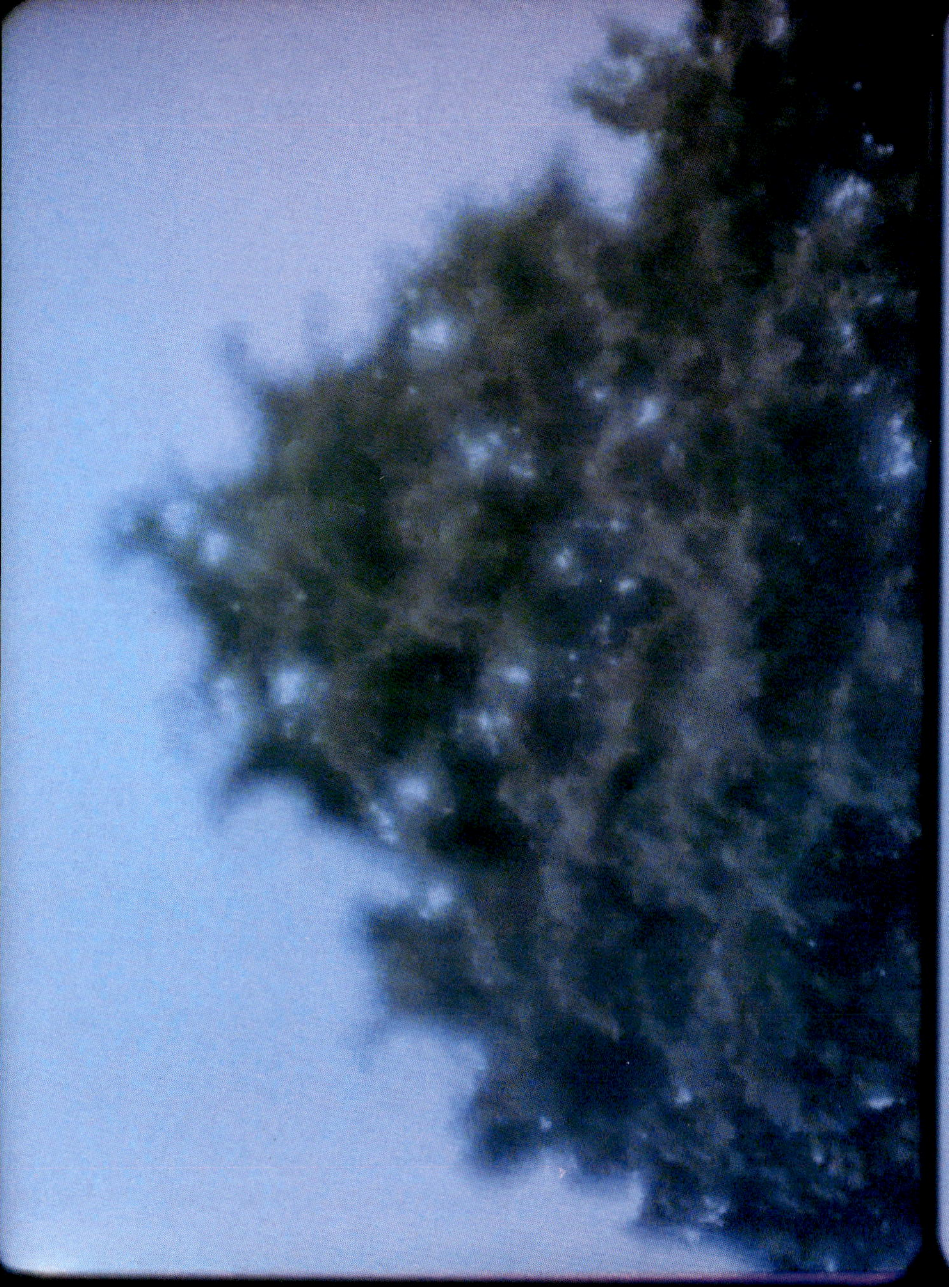

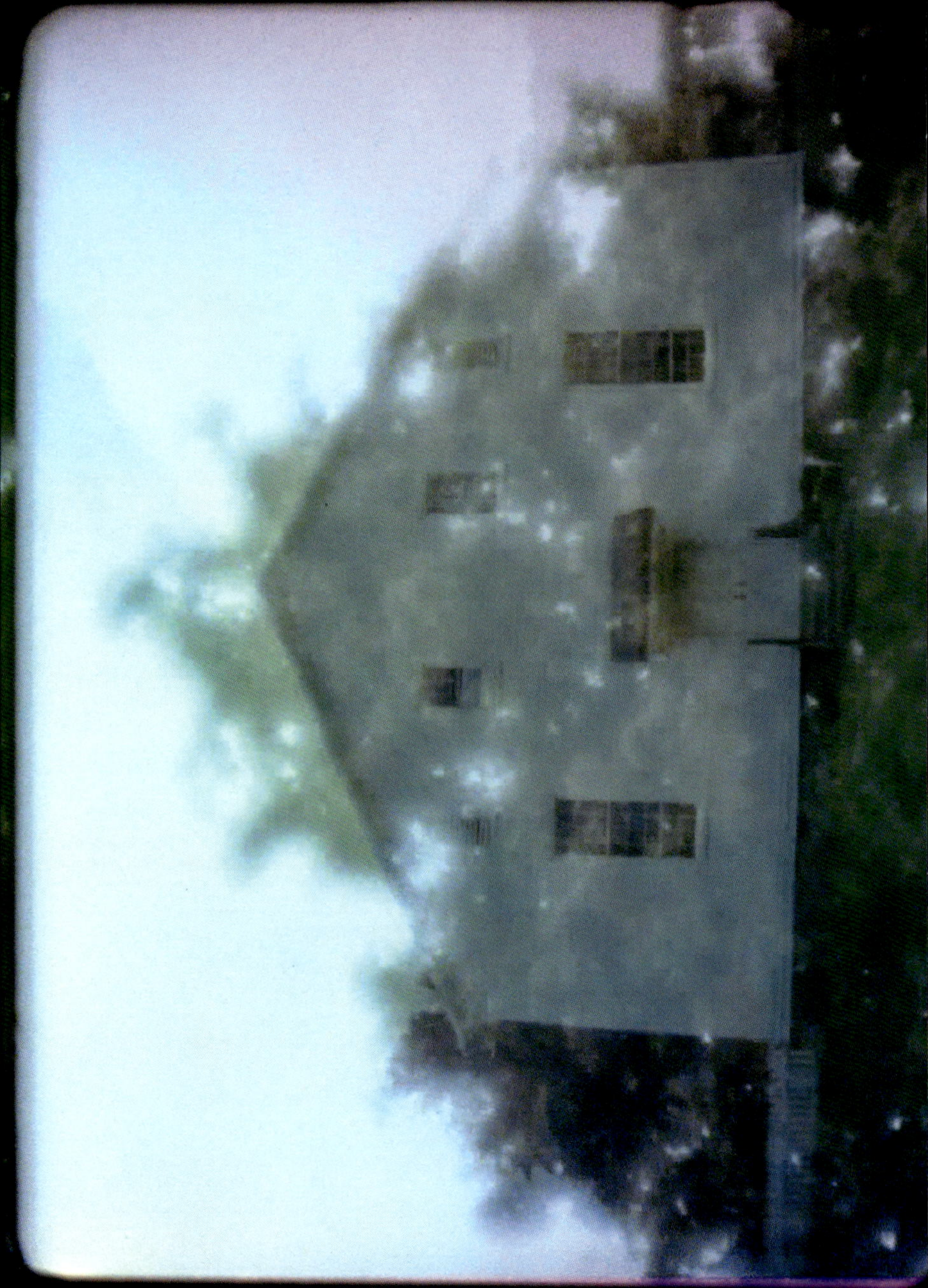

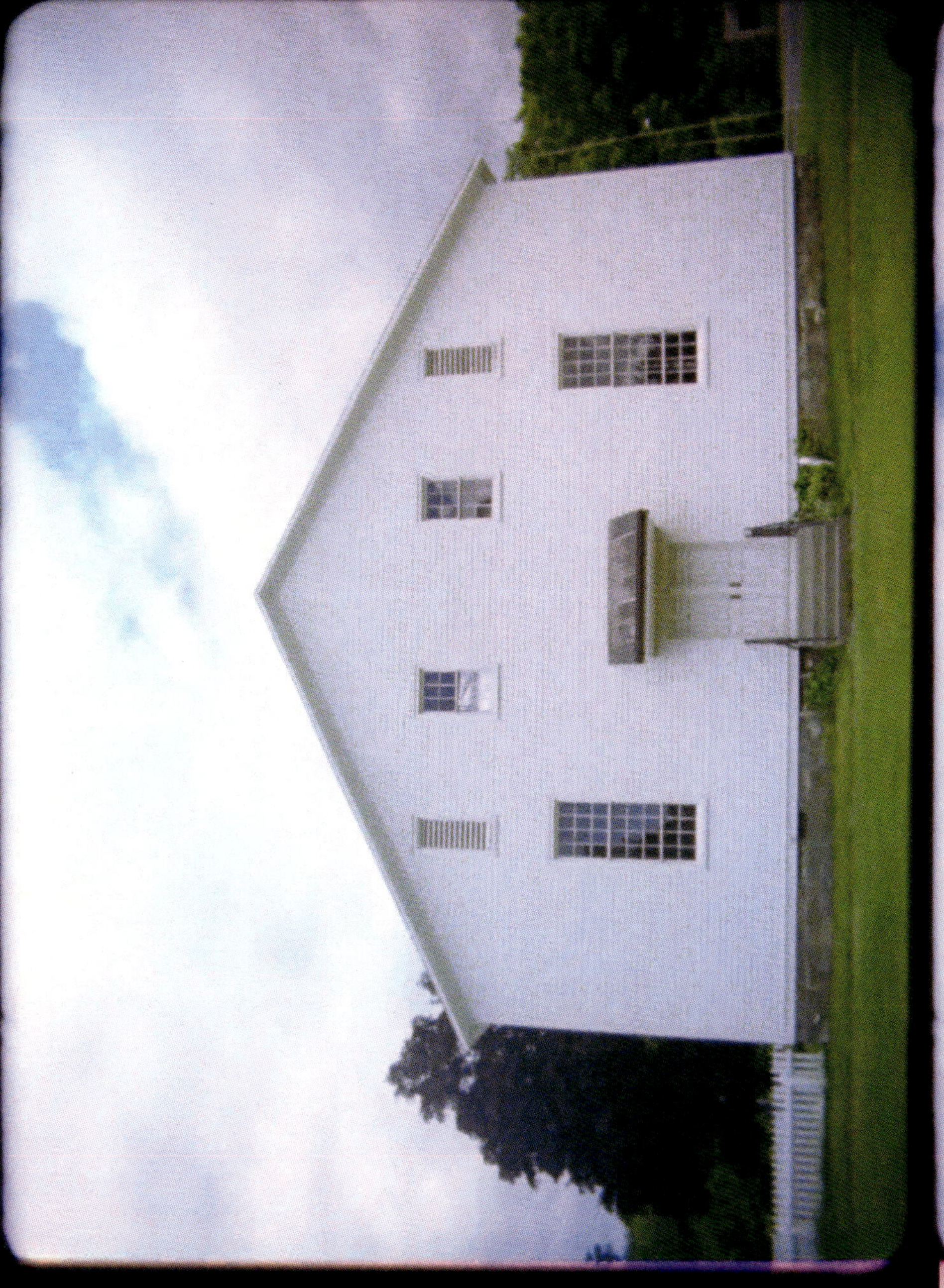

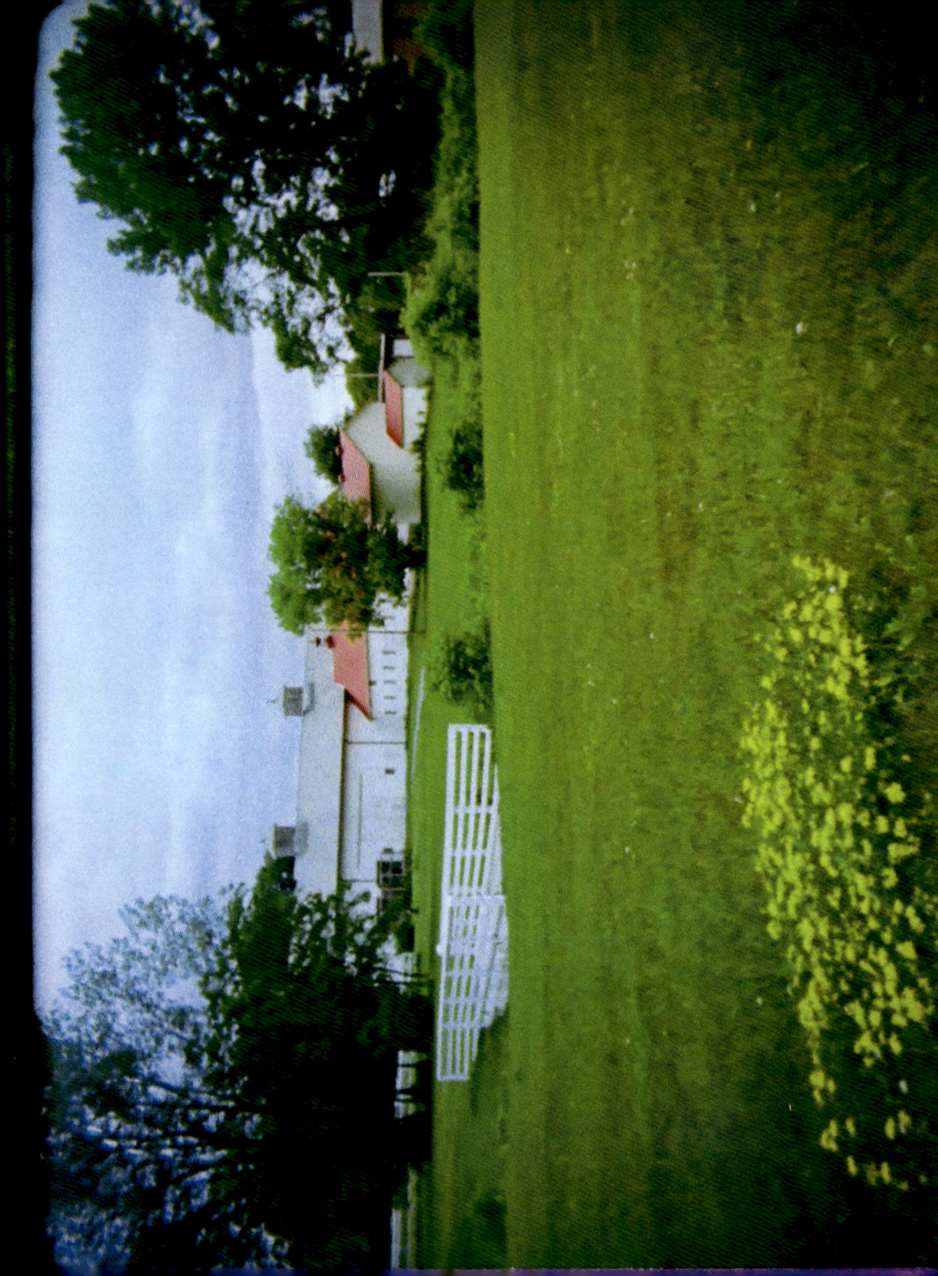

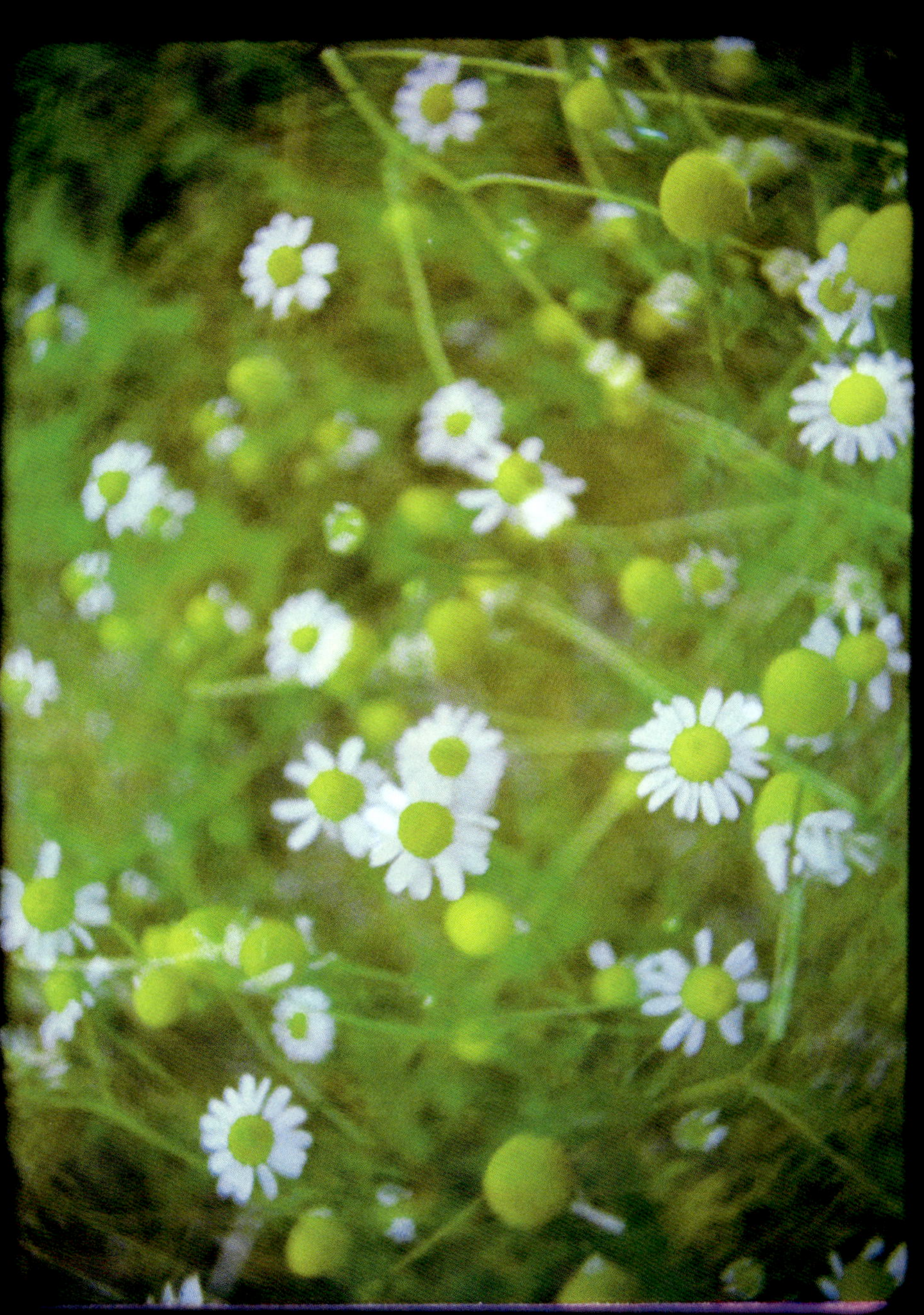

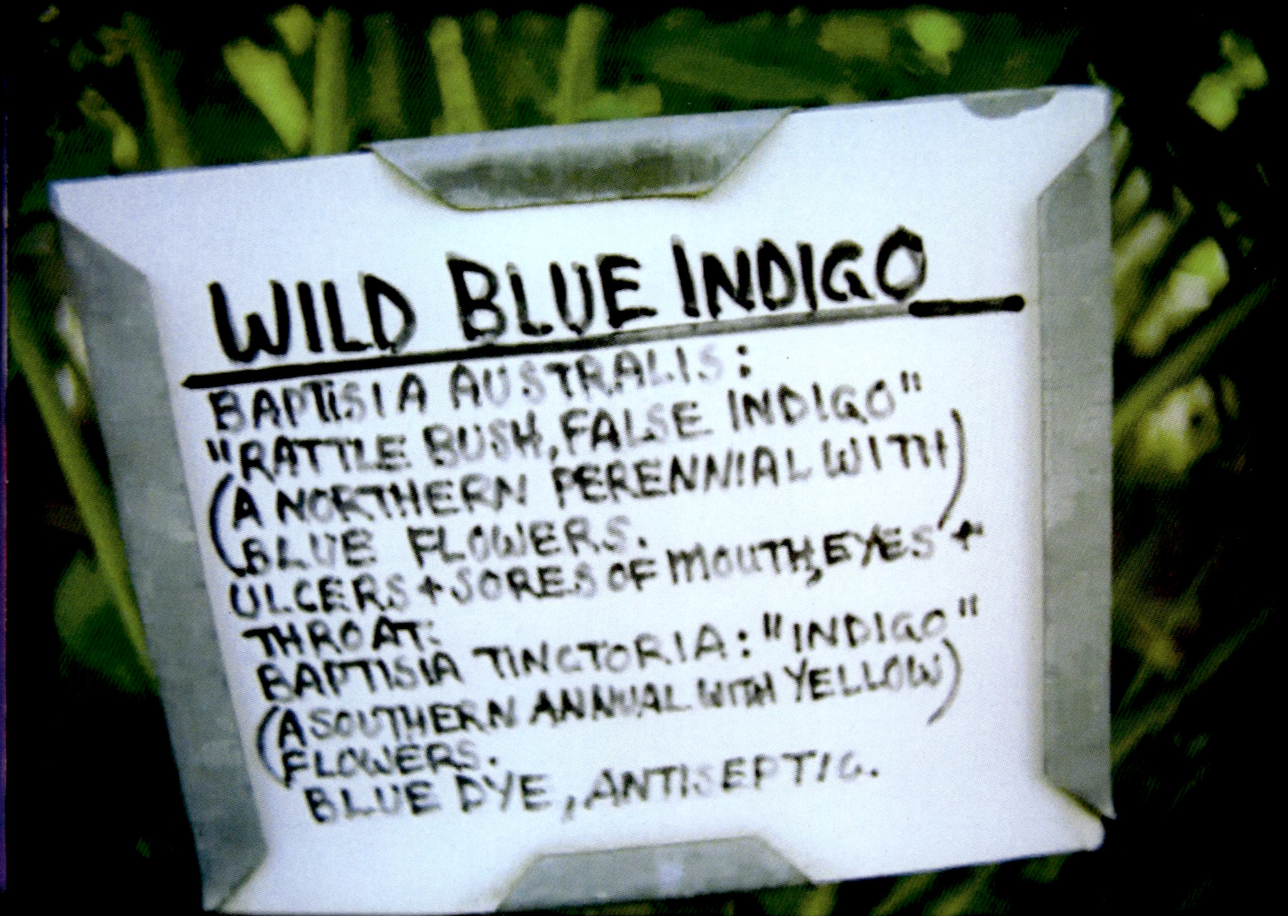

WILD BLUE INDIGO

BAPTISIA AUSTRALIS:
"RATTLE BUSH, FALSE INDIGO"
(A NORTHERN PERENNIAL WITH)
BLUE FLOWERS.
ULCERS + SORES OF MOUTH, EYES +
THROAT.
BAPTISIA TINCTORIA: "INDIGO"
(A SOUTHERN ANNUAL WITH YELLOW)
FLOWERS.
BLUE DYE, ANTISEPTIC.

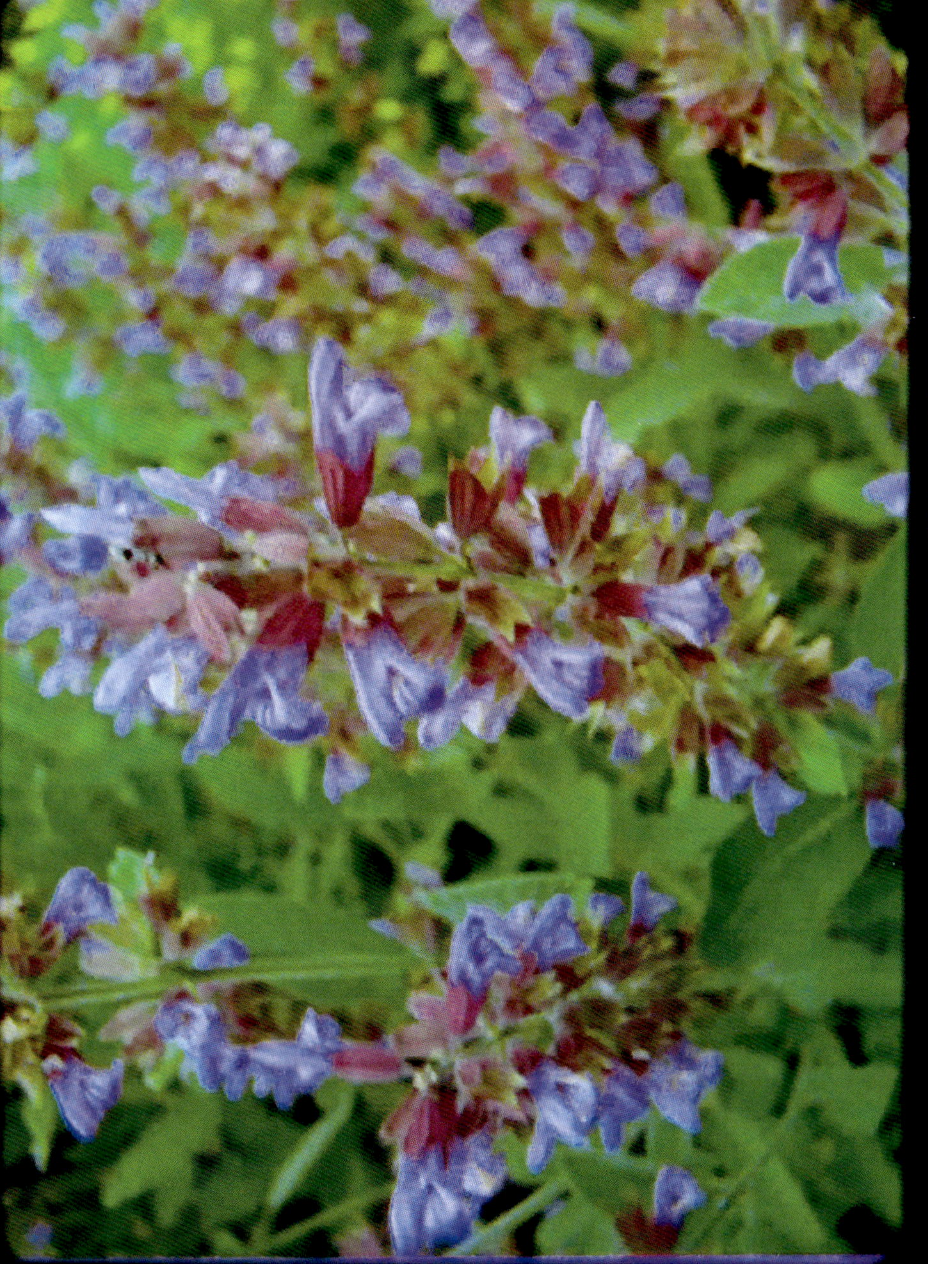

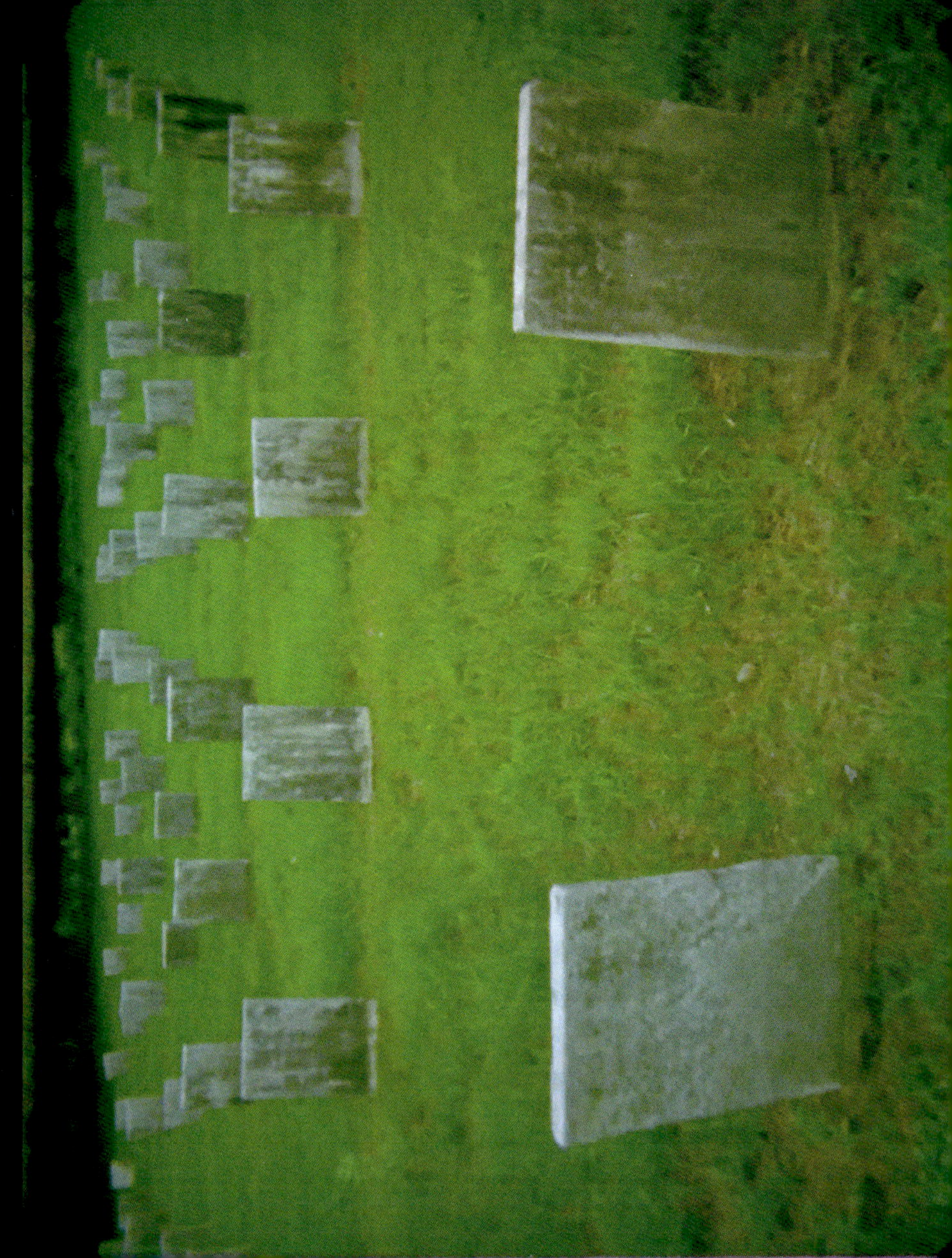

***Pilgrim*, 2017**
Digital video, color, sound,
7:41 minutes

Rhea Anastas in Conversation with Cauleen Smith

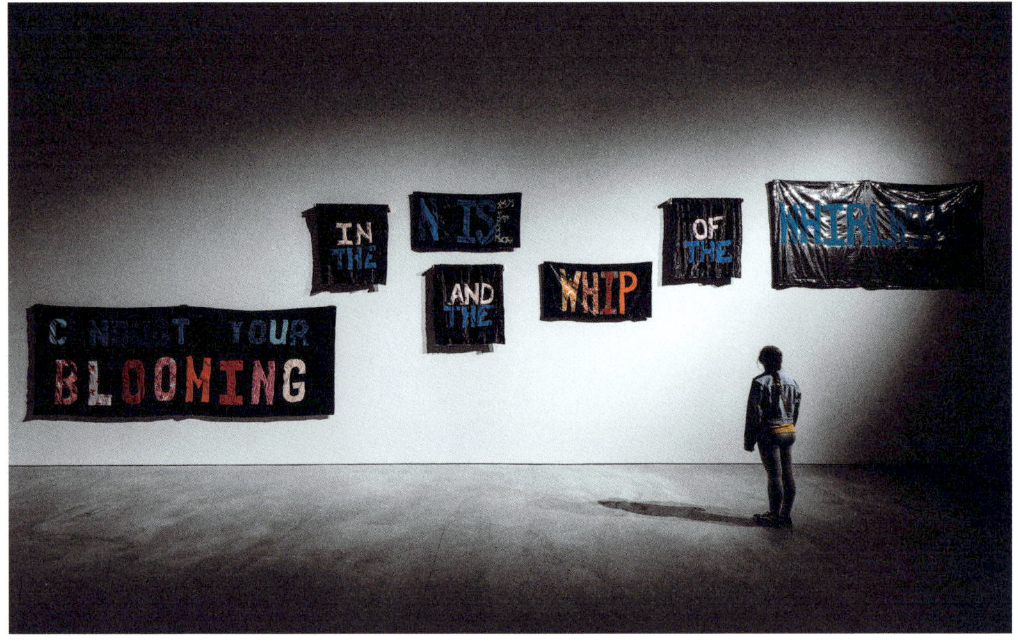

***Conduct Your Blooming*, 2015**
Seven banners. Sequined fabric
with felt, cotton, rayon, letters.
Dimensions vary

On June 12 and 14, 2018, Cauleen Smith and
I met at Smith's studio in Los Angeles to record a dialogue. Compiled and edited from
our second day of talking, this conversation
traverses Smith's most recent films, *Pilgrim*
and *Sojourner*. Originating from a day of filming during December 2015 at Alice Coltrane
Turiyasangitananda's ashram with Smith and
Arthur Jafa both behind cameras, *Pilgrim*
was finished for *The Warplands*, an exhibition
at University Art Galleries, Contemporary
Art Center (cac), University of California, Irvine,
which opened in January 2017, and that I took
as an opportunity to collaborate with Smith.
Early into our work on this show, Smith, Anthony
Elms, and I linked *The Warplands* to *Give It or
Leave It* at ica, aiming to enable Smith to develop
multiple films, as well as other works. In this
conversation—a year and a half after *The
Warplands*, and three months before *Give It or
Leave It*—we view *Sojourner* at a point when
Smith was editing and working on the sound.
To me, the conversation has the quality of
seeing *Sojourner* take on its early shape for the
first time, brought into view within the horizon
of the project.

—————Rhea Anastas, June 14, 2018

Cauleen Smith

After you left on Tuesday, I started listening to a lecture with Fred Moten and Saidiya Hartman, "The Black Outdoors," because of the problem I'm having right now with the new film *Sojourner*.

Rhea Anastas

Can you say a few things about what was really sparking you in the lecture?

Cauleen

Well, I love the way it was about eschewing predetermined answers. Fred Moten and Saidiya Hartman are very feral intellectuals. They are aware of the ground shifting underneath them, whereas other academics only try to cite their way into brilliance. In the lecture, Moten and Hartman were trying to respond to two scholars who wanted to have their theories validated. And Fred just comes correct saying, "We don't all have to do the same thing."

I feel that with art-making, there's this expectation that you resolve what is supposed to be the answer to some question, right? And the problem is, I'm dealing with questions without answers. They only have models or tests or experiments that lead to more models or tests or experiments, which means that the things I'm making look like models or tests or experiments. The questions can't be resolved, which is a problem, because that's what showing in art institutions more or less demands.

As an example, I saw Mike Kelley's work before I knew anything about art or who Kelley was. I was so disturbed by how I could enter the work but also felt very destabilized by it. It is shocking how comfortable I feel reading this work simply because he uses things that I know. But then he's forcing me into conversations about this stuff that are disturbing. Even when pieces are beautifully made, they are horrifying, *and* they don't seem resolved. I

was thinking about this aspect of Kelley's work in relationship to the academics who were trying to get Moten and Hartman to validate their ideas in the lecture—not realizing that they don't need validation. It would be so much better if they just kept asking questions.

Rhea

Right, if it was a flow or exchange. If the conditions are opened up, by which I mean, people conducting themselves with questions—when questions and refining an awareness with questions may produce a new thought.

It's not surprising to me that in the work of a lot of the artists you are interested in, or I am interested in, we see this quality of being destructive towards taste and the decorum of analytical habits.

Cauleen

Decorum is the word, yeah.

Rhea

In your recent work, you study Alice Coltrane Turiyasangitananda's incredible contribution to music and her life, her work. But I don't want to speak about the work as research. It is the techniques—your way of getting very close to Coltrane's work—and it's the specifics of how this happens, which interest me most. I think the word, "research," is impoverished when applied to art-making. What did you actually do? You listened. You read. You spoke with people.

Cauleen

Yeah, I mainly listened.

Rhea

You turned mainly to her musical output?

Cauleen

With Coltrane in particular, there is so much about her life that I chose not to bring into this project. I focused on the music because I was shocked and appalled at the way her music is kind of routinely

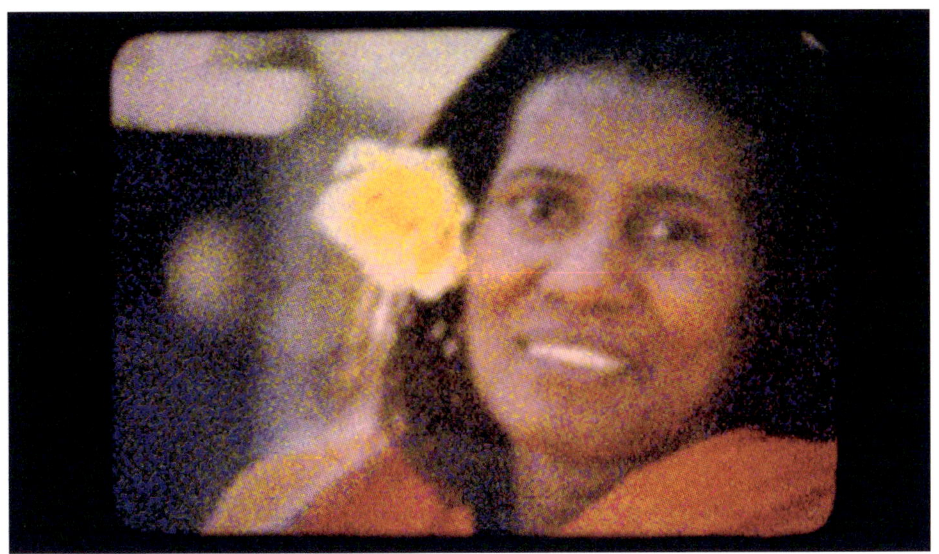

Pilgrim (still), 2017
Digital video and 16mm film,
color, sound, 7:41 minutes

dismissed. Well, not anymore, because in our moment she is one of the most fashionable twentieth-century figures to recuperate. Everyone is suddenly deeply interested in Alice Coltrane.

Rhea
Okay, but that's only, what, four years old or something?

Cauleen
Oh, less than that. It's literally the past two years. When I listened to her music, I couldn't figure out how it was possible that she was dismissed. I just thought, she's like the Yoko Ono of the jazz world, and all these macho heads are resentful of her, her life with John Coltrane, and how he was changing. She's just a stellar musician; she just is. The keyboard and the harp, her voice, the way she uses her voice, which isn't powerful; it's simply a tool. The music is amazing and blew my mind.

Rhea
You're speaking about the early- and mid-'70's music?

Cauleen
That's the stuff I love, after the death of John Coltrane, and then a few years into her move to California. There is this amazing output where she's recording with people like Charlie Haden, and in the same moment she records an album with Carlos Santana.

Rhea
Alice Coltrane was the first figure, and then, within this hypothesis—a comparative one—you take Coltrane, together with Shaker gift drawings?

Cauleen
I had been obsessed with the gift drawings for ten years. Then just three years ago I went to Coltrane's ashram for Sunday services. They had a little book store; I bought everything I could. Most critically,

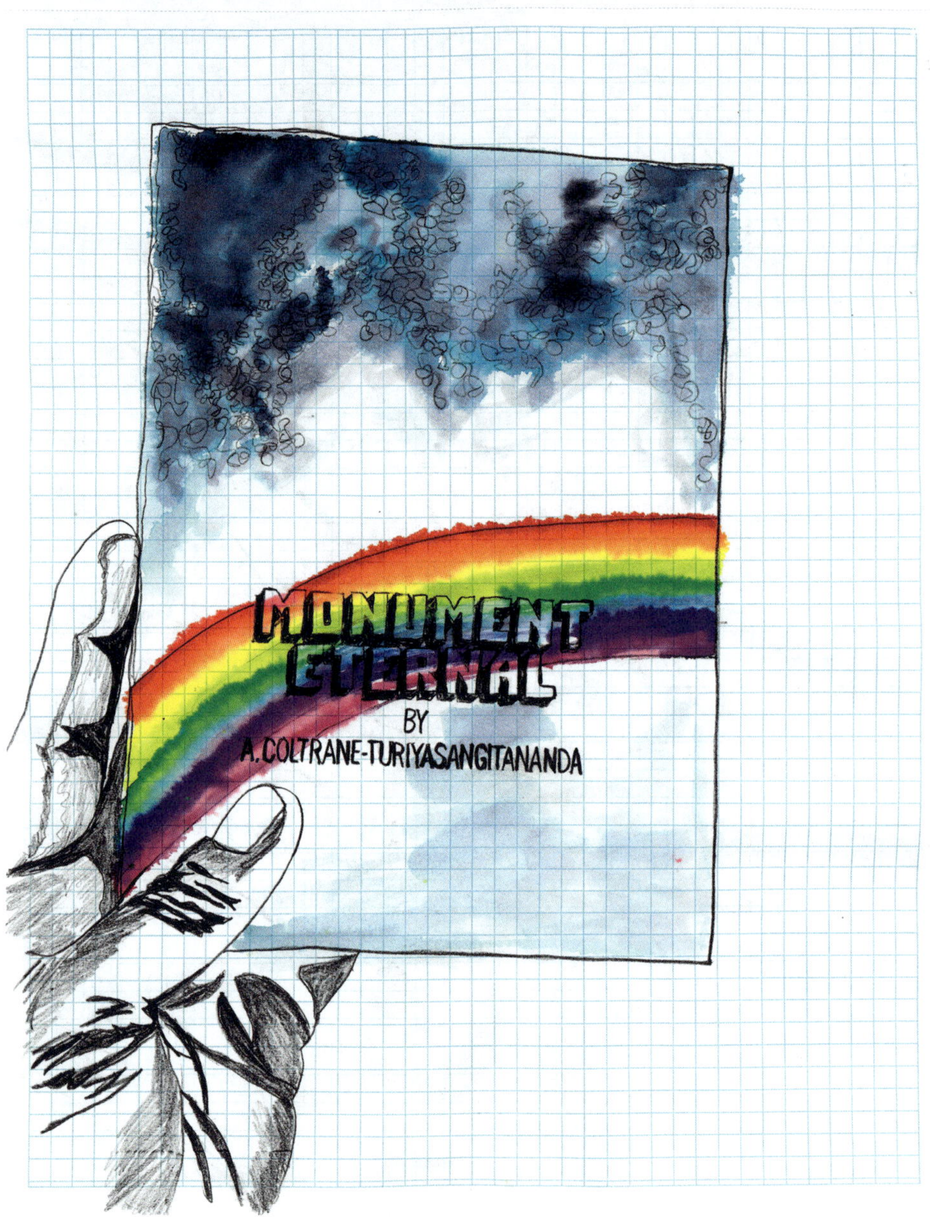

Human 3.0 Reading List,
Monument Eternal, 2017
Graphite, brush and colored inks and
watercolor on graph paper. 9 × 12 in.

I bought her book, *Monument Eternal*. This book describes the series of "austerities" she put herself through on her quest to become a Godhead—like Mother Ann Lee of the Shakers did back in the late 1700s! Turiyasangitananda describes traveling the astral planes and what she encounters— she describes musical instruments that play themselves. And I just got chills because the big aporiae of many Shaker drawings are these little structures that seemingly have no recognizable function, but are labeled "Heavenly Musical Instruments." No one has anything to say about these little drawings of weird little machines that are supposed to be instruments! But here is Alice Coltrane in the late seventies describing traveling astral planes and encountering instruments that play themselves. That was it for me.

The Shaker drawings are compelling and mysterious because visual culture was strictly forbidden, as was playing musical instruments. Only the voice could be used in worship. But after Mother Ann Lee, the charismatic Godhead had been dead for some time, and membership was dwindling—young women started having ecstatic visions, "gifts," and rendering them in ink and paper. In this time of crisis, the Shakers turned to visual culture. This is the reason the Shakers are important to me. After this era of manifestations and the production, mostly by young women, of thousands of mysterious drawings full of all manner of visual references from the Masons to German Fraktur art, [along with] embroidery samplers and quilting, the Shakers carried on for another seventy years or so. Visual culture revived this enterprise.

For Coltrane, visual culture seems less important. She was meticulous about her appearance and that of her folk, and her ashram. But it was all about the Music and the Word. Then I discover Rebecca Cox Jackson, and *this* Shaker Eldress bridges the gap with her incredibly written descriptions of her dreams and visions.

Before Jackson met the Shakers she was already preaching and she was getting into disagreements with the A.M.E. church because she was stepping out doing her own evangelizing. It's very important to emphasize that Rebecca Cox Jackson was never held captive or coerced into slavery. She was born a free woman and died a free woman.

When I learned about Rebecca Cox Jackson and her time with the Shakers, interests that initially seemed disparate suddenly came together. Jackson was an improviser on every level, and spontaneous. Even in her relationship with God. She sometimes tells a story like this: *"I'm working on my sewing, and God informs me that I need to go visit so-and-so. My husband says don't go, but when I go, the woman is dying. It's the middle of the night, it's raining, and there is a thunderstorm. She needs me to sit with her. She wants to know how I knew I should come, and I tell her, God told me to come."*

This woman doesn't use a lot of purple language. She reports. Even when she's talking about conversations with God or visions. Most endearingly, she doesn't like to say negative things about anybody, but she will criticize herself. So when she's criticizing the Shakers it is through posing a question to herself. *"I need to understand how we can be here and how we can live this way when there is so much going on in the world? I need to ask God is this really my purpose?"* It becomes a criticism of herself, but really it is a conflict with these people.

And then I started thinking about women in general turning to visions and projections outside of ourselves just to live, just to be.

Rhea

It's not as simple as just being the head of household, or being a bread winner, or figuring out your own means of a truly independent life and pathway, for [the] living and the work. These worlds of Alice Coltrane, or the Shakers, or Rebecca Cox Jackson, are countering the world around them and what would be socially acceptable. These worlds are asking incredibly challenging questions of the social order.

Cauleen

They are literally in resistance to so many things. In a very elegant, graceful way, Alice Coltrane seems to have been in a kind of profound resistance to the legacy of the very male-dominated jazz world.

Rhea

There is another group on your conceptual map.

Cauleen

Yeah, the Combahee River Collective. . . . What a relief to find this group. I still struggle with the fact that it was so recent that I encountered their work. Through the efforts of Black Lives Matter activists, the *Combahee River Collective Statement* came to me. These particular visionary women, many of whom are still alive, are Marxists; they don't talk about God. So I can sit with them more at ease.

I think what they're asking for through the 1977 statement is to just try and imagine what it would look like if black women really did function cooperatively to further our own interests and stop serving all these interests that are actually *trying to kill us*, as Fred Moten says.

Rhea

Within Coltrane's world, or Jackson's world of other-worldly projections and visions, there is a real contrast with the materialist, unsparingly negative, anti-capitalist attitude of the Combahee River Collective.

Cauleen

There is something about the Combahee River Collective—Barbara Smith and her cohort—that makes me feel like there is room for all of this ecstatic spiritualism in their Marxist world. There is a way, in which, through writing this document, they are praising each other. Reifying each other. This is very important. I wish even more could be known about their interpersonal struggles, because I have a feeling things ain't changed much. . . .

Rhea

That is astonishing; to think of it as praising each other. For that to be what the writing, the statement, does. I love that way of receiving it.

Cauleen

Yes! Instead of assigning roles and labor to individuals, they speak of themselves as a "We." It's like that 1970s/1980s feminist book you gave me—*Sexual Difference: A Theory of Social-Symbolic Practice* by the Milan Women's Bookstore Collective. I'd never read a document that was so insistent of the chorus as voice instead of a single narrator/historicizer. The Combahee River Collective does this as well, and it is so powerful, and, for me, it's celebratory. I imagine a real joy in doing work that permits a ceding of the "I" to the "We." You know, it's funny to think about that in relation to the way I came upon the text. Black Lives Matter founders are very determined to remind us who started that hashtag and that movement. We are living in such different times. I imagine that when Smith and her cohorts were writing this document, the notion of "branding" the self would have been both unthinkable and undesirable!

Rhea

How did you decide you wanted Arthur Jafa to film *Pilgrim*? You were telling him about your idea to film at the ashram?

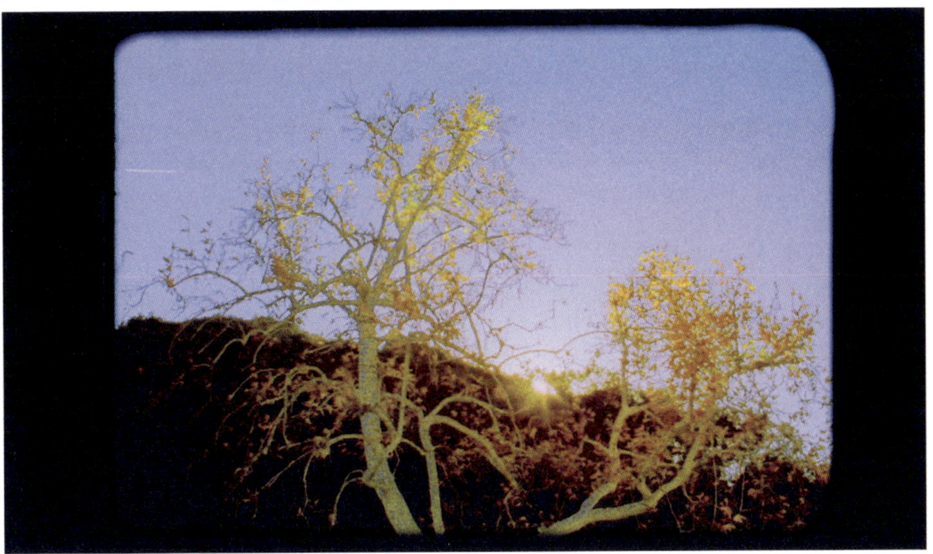

Sojourner (still), 2018
Digital video and 16mm film,
color, sound, 22:03 minutes

Cauleen

One, he's just a good friend and he was willing to do it. I was surely opining about my own lousy camera skills. He probably said, "Why don't you ask me to shoot for you?" That was really part of it, and then realizing that I was curious how he would see it. I didn't give him a lot of direction. A couple notes: "Make sure you film John Coltrane's tree." And so on.

Rhea

And places to film, you cleared them?

Cauleen

Yeah. Shooting all in one day. There are some things they asked us not to film. Radha, who is a disciple, was with us. Quite comically, she and AJ had this very strange tension between them, I mean, she was really hard on AJ. I don't know why.

Rhea

Was she feeling protective about locations and the camera?

Cauleen

Probably. It's their home. It's very private. He was up before sunrise filming. That's how she met him. Maybe that wasn't the best start to the day! (laughter)

Rhea

You said you also needed to look through the camera, to do your own observing there, so obviously you're looking in another way. One thing you're doing is looking for traces of Coltrane. Looking for objects that she arranged, looking for places where she sat, looking for where she sat at the keyboard. I feel that the camera is doing that.

Cauleen

Right, her presence. Yeah, and literally her—that organ. Or the way that they have enshrined her. I think that was AJ's first time there and so it really was a pilgrimage. When we found the paper with Turiya's writing, it felt like a sacred scroll to us, you know?

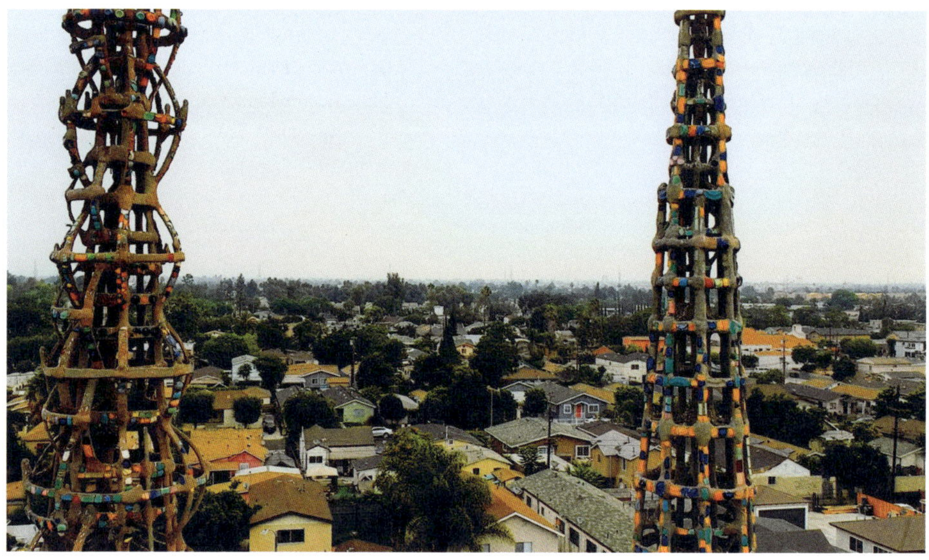

Sojourner (still), 2018
Digital video and 16mm film,
color, sound, 22:03 minutes

Rhea

Maybe that's part of what is so incredible about his filming. When he's looking through the camera, something about his own encounter is [also] happening.

Cauleen

I think so. Especially because we're in the presence of this woman who is still in mourning over Alice. That's why it's difficult, too.

Rhea

It's very palpable. It creates a tone that is really different than *Sojourner*.

Cauleen

The tone in *Sojourner* is actually. . . . It's funny, because Noah Purifoy hasn't been dead very long, but he's very clearly left that site. His work is there. His legacy is there. His ideas and thoughts are there. But it doesn't feel tender or precious. It just feels like the Parthenon or something; it feels long ago. You're imagining him making

these things, and it feels like it was the distant past, but it was just a few years ago that some of those pieces were finished. You can feel that this is work with a long memory—that it grew out of the Watts Tower Community Art Center and migrated into the desert. *Sojourner* is able to play with the sites more because they belong to us; they have been gifted to us.

Rhea

When you edited what you had filmed, not only from Coltrane's ashram but also the Shaker sites, the rigidity of the Shakers and Coltrane's spiritual and musical spaces are coexisting. They're combined in *Pilgrim*.

Cauleen

They are. *Pilgrim* begins and ends with tombs as far as I'm concerned. There is Mother Ann Lee's tombstone at the end of the film and [in] the beginning of the film is Alice Coltrane's organ enshrined in Plexiglas. These women were both

Godheads, and to me, it's about that bridge; these women who had to go elsewhere, across the Atlantic, across North America, to build worlds that they could live in.

Sojourner makes more pilgrimages to sites in Philadelphia. I tried to find the house where Rebecca Cox Jackson might have lived. A municipal building is now on that site. Also, Fletcher Street Riding Club Horses, John Coltrane's residence, Sun Ra's house! Philly is just so rich.

Sometimes the music is doing everything. I thought, if you can just listen to the way this woman plays keyboard and literally takes us through this insane trip. . . . I actually can use her music as a way to talk about these different speculations. If I'm thinking about her music as scores, because her songs are about a kind of travel outward and inward, and I make images to speak to that, then I might be doing something.

The song I'm using for *Sojourner* is, "Om Supreme." It's about California. The song has three minutes with no lyrics, and then they start singing, and the voice says, "When I told you to come to California." That's the very first line. I had listened to that song over and over, and I didn't realize that she's transcribing a conversation with God.

Rhea
And then the word, "California," becomes a mantra of the song.

Cauleen
Uh-huh. To me that song marks not the beginning of her time here, but it's very important in the sense of her explicitly saying, I came here with a vision. I already had a plan. I already knew that I was going to build this ashram, and that California was a place where it was possible.

I don't think anybody cites this song or *Eternity*, the album it's on, as one of her masterpieces. To me, it's a moment where

there's a total mix of the gospel and blues tradition, and that influence on jazz, with the Hindu tradition of spiritual music. Those four strands of repetition—they're happening at the same time, almost coequal. Whereas later she moves all the way into the traditional Hindu form. These songs are wonderfully uncomfortable. It's my favorite moment in her oeuvre.

Rhea
Is it the tension that you like?

Cauleen
It's also a collapse of time. How old is this Hindu tradition in these songs? It sounds ancient. How old is this gospel sound, as you hear it in West Africa? Ancient. From another place. And then somehow through her they are together and they're compatible, wonderfully compatible—in this way that you just don't expect to hear. No one has done it since or again. It's very legible.

I was talking to my friend, Courtney Bryan, a composer, and she didn't hear it the same. She was like, "Oh, that's so interesting that you hear that." She didn't hear the incompatibility of the things. What I'm hearing is what I heard growing up in church, smashed up against what I heard as a kid in the airport with the Hare Krishnas . . . and I just think, that's weird. That's wonderful. That's so California.

And so this song is sort of like this perfect mash-up of two things that I wouldn't have known how to get into the same space, but in California I guess that happens all the time. That's why I chose that song. Now that I'm editing to it—I can love a song, and then when I start editing to it, I have to hear it in such a different way. The second I put that song with images, the voice became so much more prominent.

Rhea
Yes, but that also seems to be the really crucial bridge that we can only see it through

California. We have to understand that it's through this lens of Coltrane going west.

Cauleen
Wow.

Rhea
Back to *Pilgrim*, I think of this film as having little or no narrative structure. Does this film actually have connective shots, things that [have to] do with narrative? The film's evacuated of it— actually being event-driven or something happening realistically that cameras [could] capture and retell.

Cauleen
It has to do with editing. It's not narrative; it's editing. Well, okay, that's the tricky thing about editing. Editing is the narration. Editing is the story and the content. Editing is actually the final re-write of any narrative film. But for me and the way I work, editing is all the writing. It is where the content gets made. I'm aware that people enjoy interpreting pictures of people and things. But when I am putting one image next to another image, it's the juxtaposition that makes the deepest meaning for me, and I hope, for the viewer. The relation creates a temporal coherence/cohesion. This temporal coherence is what I would call narrative. It's haptic. It's totally about a feeling.

Rhea
And it's very spatialized somehow. That's what I take from the word, "haptic."
It's very much about the eye and space.

Cauleen
Uh-huh, a relationship between all these things and the sound, because the sound is really the trick. That's the secret weapon. Most of what you feel in these films is coming from just paying attention to what Alice Coltrane is making happen in the music. In *Pilgrim*, I'm very often editing off the main beat. I'm editing on her breaths in between.

With musicians, something about the way they play versus how they breathe is really interesting to me. I always feel like I can hear the phrasing, and so I was just trying to edit on her inhales and her exhales, where I thought they were happening. That seemed like a much better way.

Rhea
I guess that's why I have a very rough, untaught, inchoate sense in watching how the film is helping me think about that recording as a performance—I mean, her as the performer inside that recording.

Cauleen
Because it's not about the music. It's about, when does she lift her hands off the keyboard, and when do they go down? That space in between. In the editing I could follow her hand. I could make a cut at a point that was about her body or her breath instead of the beats, or the notes.

Inside, her music seems very free and very sensual and very tactile in a way that the actual form of the religion does not. The ritual of religion is just so tight, and her music is so very open. I'm sitting there in her ashram during the morning service. They play a recording of her teaching. I'm listening to her voice, and then they get up and start singing. And they don't use her organ, they bring in their own keyboard.

Rhea
Because her organ is not to be played by anybody else?

Cauleen
It seems not. No. That was the great thing about going there and seeing them play her music. They even argued about how Alice would have done it and stuff like that. That was really helpful in terms of demystifying how that music works because they sing, play her songs, play her music, and then argue about it, about doing it correctly. I thought that was fantastic.

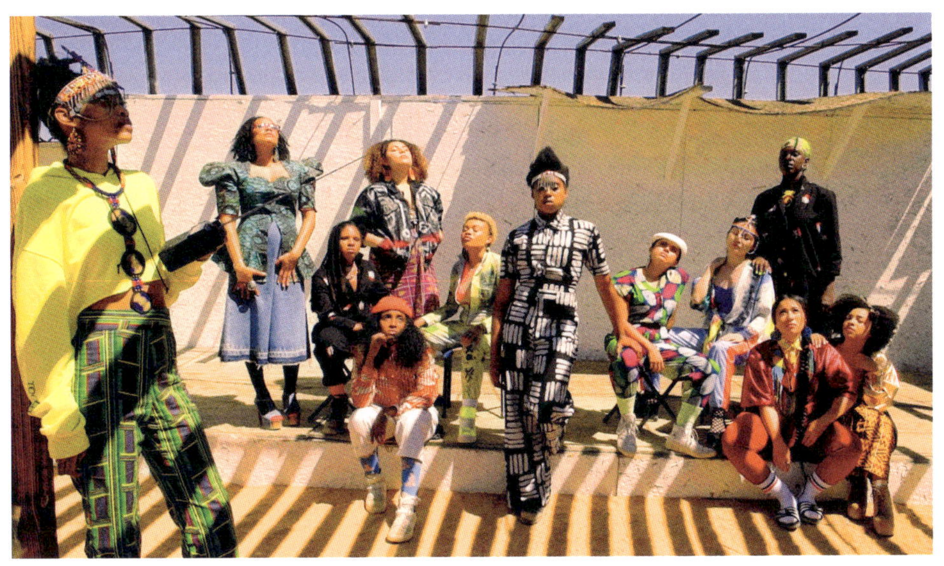

Sojourner **(still), 2018**
Digital video and 16mm film,
color, sound, 22:03 minutes

Rhea
What role does structure play?

Cauleen
In the simplicity of the form in which she works I hear such freedom. I don't even know. That might be the kind of comment that would trouble the musician. That's probably not her intention. It's all about devotion for her. But to me, even in the later stuff, she goes to this place where I'm like, what did you do? The music feels like a narcotic in a weird way. I guess a wiser person would recognize that as the divine.

Rhea
What did you feel while filming *Sojourner* when you were looking through the camera at this group of twelve black women? What did you think about this image that you were making—how you felt about it, and how others were going to feel about it?

Cauleen
Actually it's a pretty mixed group of women—black, Asian, Latinx. I enjoy the way the blackness can absorb and mark everything in proximity to it. Without altering the identity of the women in the film, they become practitioners and not just consumers of black culture! I'm getting this idea from Hortense Spillers, of course. But back to your question—I thought that I was having the same kind of ambivalence about the image I was making as I had when I looked at Bill Ray's original image. I thought there was a part of me that wanted to remake his image, not just by recasting it, but remake it into something more ambitious in terms of its representation of a range of [the] human. It's very strange to me that in Bill Ray's set of photographs, he's really only photographing young black men or children.

There are maybe one or two pictures that have adult black women in them. The images featured in the magazine are of

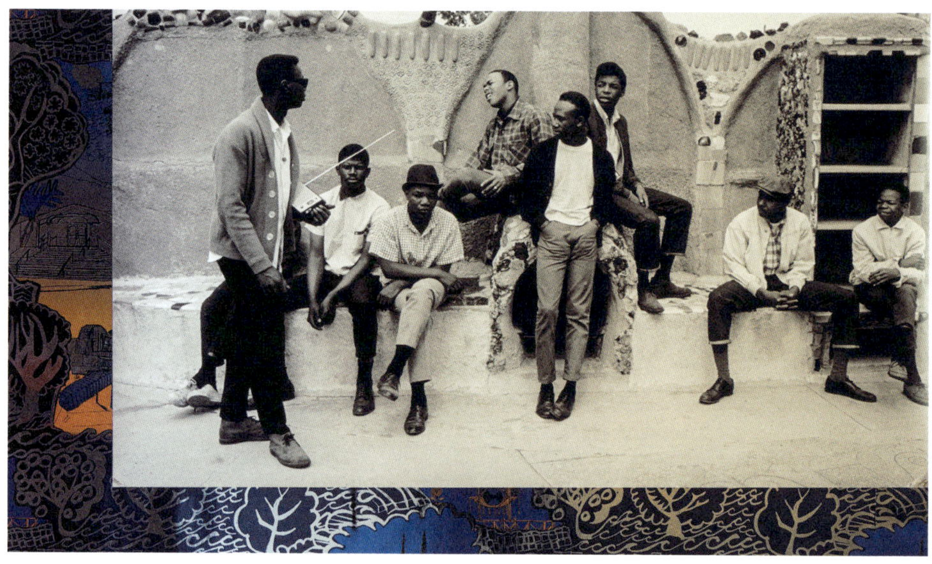

Give It or Leave It
(installation view), 2018

women activists in the community. Cropped close-up shots of serious black women. In the street photography, the women are captured from a distance; they're not a subject, they're part of a landscape or something. I was really troubled by that. Then I was troubled by the glamour and the beauty of that one particular shot that I'm reenacting. . . . The fashion level. I was very ambivalent about it because I wanted it to be a document of history. But it just felt like a lie, and it still does.

Rhea

Does that speak to the socially typed, narrow racial visibility that the bodies of people who are called black are subjected to, this way that the visibility that's projected—though it may be an imagery that's glamorous and powerful—its underside is rabidly abject and violent?

Cauleen

Yeah, I think what Bill Ray was succumbing to was an attraction to a particular kind of sexy, rogue, feral, black male youth who went around burning down the city. Counter to that, the people themselves [were] these sort of elegant, thoughtful, languid people who wanted to sit around the Watts Towers and get their picture taken. He has to deal with that problem and then there is the problem of what *LIFE* magazine does with it, which is put all these really crazy captions under things that are racially charged and totally stereotypical and would embarrass that magazine if they looked back on the captions.

All of that is one big troubling image that I'm then remaking, so just think about that. What am I really remaking? It's kind of crazy that I felt that I didn't have to think about all those problems until it's all right there in front of me, and I'm spending thousands of dollars to make it happen.

There were a lot of interpersonal relationships among the women I filmed [of which]

I was not aware, very much in the same way that Billy Ray probably had no clue about how those young men did or didn't know each other. And then that power dynamic—that I could just summon this. I could get them dressed. And there is this huge gulf between me and the image I'm making, and what is happening with them, and why they're even there. They're there to be a part of the film shoot. They're also there for each other. They're there to watch an artist work. They're there because it's a free trip to the desert.

Rhea

Yeah, or they're identifying with it, and then using it, and going along with it.

Cauleen

And I thought that, well, though the image is successful to me because it has all the same problems that the original image has, it's also a failure because it has all those same problems as the original image has. To me this speaks to the problem of representation and image-making. I'm hoping that I can edit the film in such a way that I move past that image into something that feels less like a construction, and even less like an attempt to represent, and more like a kind of looking.

When I was reading the script to them and they're holding hands and stuff. Those were their decisions. They knew they were being filmed, they knew they were being watched, they were performing, but all of those decisions were their decisions. When they decided to stand up and move to make a new composition, they were making that composition. Not me.

Rhea

But it sounds like in both taking apart and embodying this photograph—it doesn't seem a coincidence that this is a photograph—you're actually kind of at war with the whole idea of art that's reliant on representation, that believes in representation as a language with all of the meaning models, or visual singularity.

Cauleen

Yeah, don't you think maybe representation is somehow linked to this idea of the subject or personhood, and all the problems around it?

Rhea

Absolutely. That's why you had to take up Ray's subject at the time, this particular group of people who he created to look this way in his photograph. Perhaps you had to take up that type of surface and really face it forthrightly.

Cauleen

I think it actually dissolves somehow or it needs to dissolve somehow. This is the burden of designing a whole shoot around figures and space. I prefer the anonymity of a group, as opposed to a portrait, which amplifies individual subjecthood. This is evident in past works, like the *Solar Flare Arkestral Marching Band* and *Crow Requiem*, or *H-E-L-L-O*. Here, I tried to turn these women into props by making them carry those banners. Then they become like tools, which is an incredibly violent thing to do to them, and it was violent to film it.

Rhea

Right.

Cauleen

But then the moment that I have them holding the banner, obviously, whatever the banner says is supposed to take precedence over them, and they're just serving the message. I took these women [and] I took great pains to turn them into these glorious subjects, and then I just reduced them. . . .

Rhea

Yeah, they're just holding a pole.

Cauleen

I'm constantly at war with this idea of representation. It doesn't get resolved.

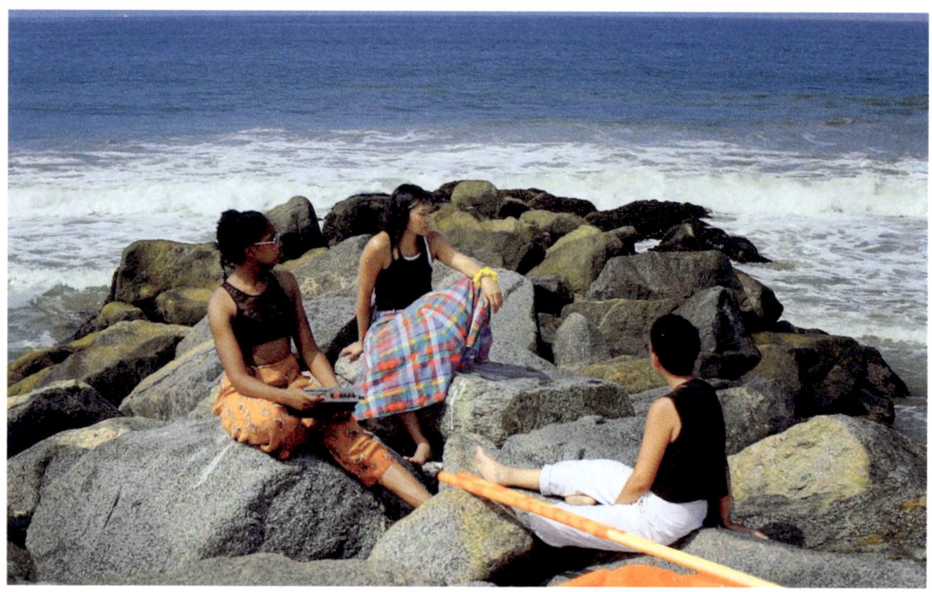

***Sojourner* (still), 2018**
Digital video and 16mm film,
color, sound, 22:03 minutes

Rhea

Given your struggle with stereotypes in film, it doesn't surprise me that this kind of image of women came back into this project and had to be dealt with, even though the project also has these Godhead figures, who are scarcely in their bodies. You're dealing with this huge spectrum.

Cauleen

The body needs to come back, and it's a very vulnerable body. It's a very, very vulnerable body. Yeah, it seems like it really has to come back. I've been trying to figure that out while being attracted to intellectuals who abandon their bodies for deep thought and transcendence. Ha!

Rhea

I absolutely understand through watching *Sojourner* that the sun and the dryness and heat of the desert put their bodies in a very different, destabilized place.

Cauleen

I wish there was a way to show it: getting ready to be filmed, they're just shivering. Shivering. Then I say, "Action!," and suddenly they're floating across the desert as best they can. I think I would have preferred it if they had been shivering.

Rhea

That's so human though. We try to project ourselves. We believe in all these images and reason our way through; we try to propel ourselves, to give ourselves these purposes.

Cauleen

But, inevitably, because I am just a total heathen and more like a Marxist than a visionary, I'm stuck here in this material world, you know what I mean? I'm just making work for people like me who are stuck here on this planet.

I've always thought of myself as really resistant to Afro-Pessimism, but I'm realizing now that maybe I think that the horror and surrender is more beautiful than anything that could occur in a resistance. Everything we already have in black life and black culture, to use black culture after Hortense Spillers's thinking, is already so amazing.

What is it that we already have? The struggle of black people in the diasporas has been one of equity. Did I ever show you the prototype see-saw that I was thinking of building for the ICA show? I couldn't think of a more literal symbol for equity than a see-saw! Ha!

We have been trying to make ourselves "equal" to those who would render us sub-human. We do this by performing the values of the powerful better then they perform them themselves. By acquiring wealth the way they acquire it. By gaining celebrity and social status in the way that serves the systems of the powerful. Once we attain success by the measurements of those who would oppress us, we ridicule or condescend to those who have not attained equity with the oppressor. But we are in a system that DEPENDS on people being poor, DEPENDS on an underclass. The ones who have achieved attainment and success need the underclass, because what are they if there is no one over whom to exert power?

So what do we need? We need to recognize that our relationships with each other and with our environment, our cities, our homes, the land on which we live.... We need to recognize that caring for this is everything. Everything. EVERYTHING. In the same way that you don't have to give birth to a child to love a child, you don't have to own a place or thing to care for a place or thing. The fear of losing, or being taken advantage of, is a legitimate fear. It is inevitable. Capitalism demands robbery, pillaging, and rape. No matter what we do, we will be abused by the system.

Our power lies in the ways in which we produce culture from thin air—from trauma, pain, irony, laughter, and love. We make a culture that literally influences the entire planet. Our horror is our power.

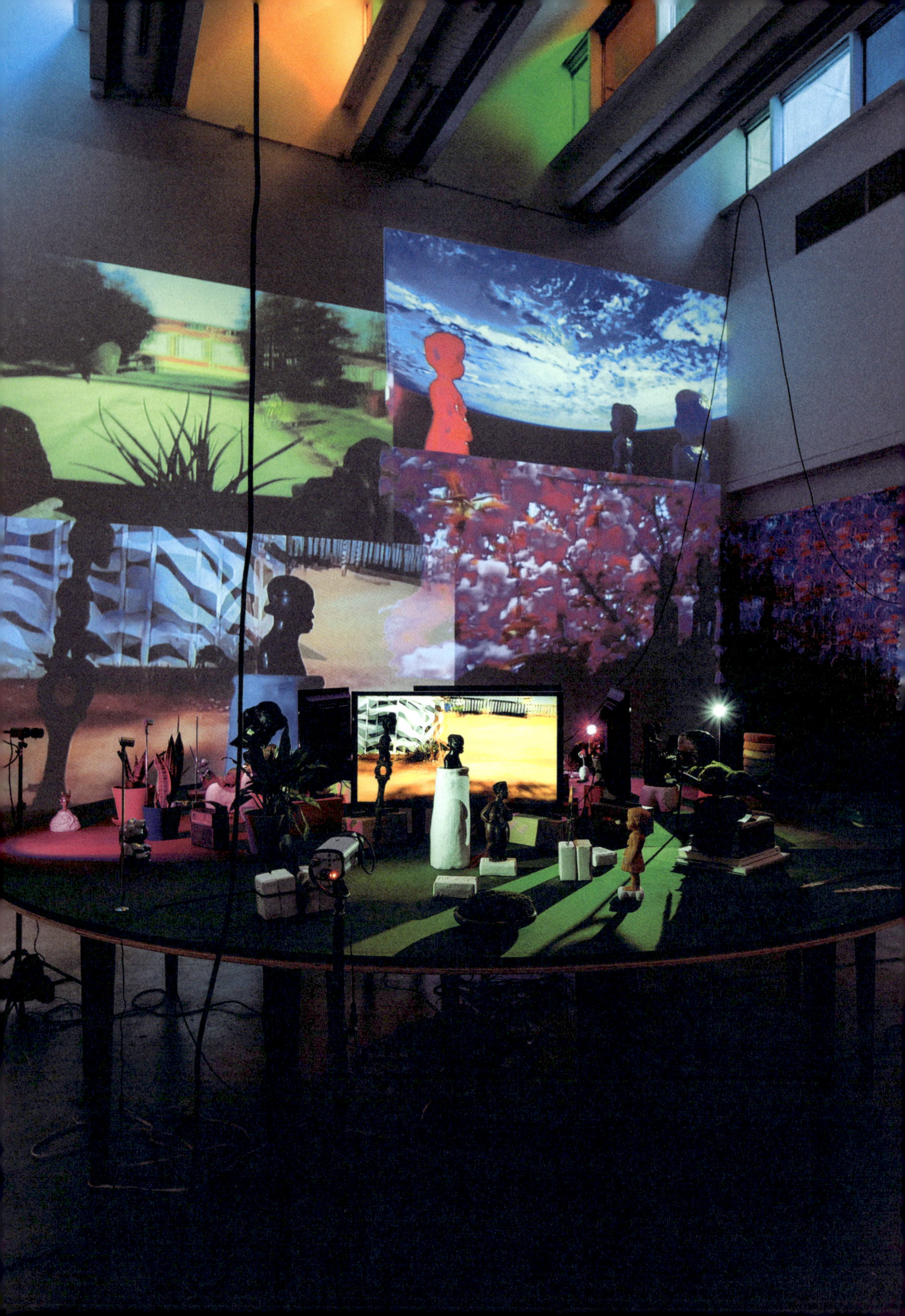

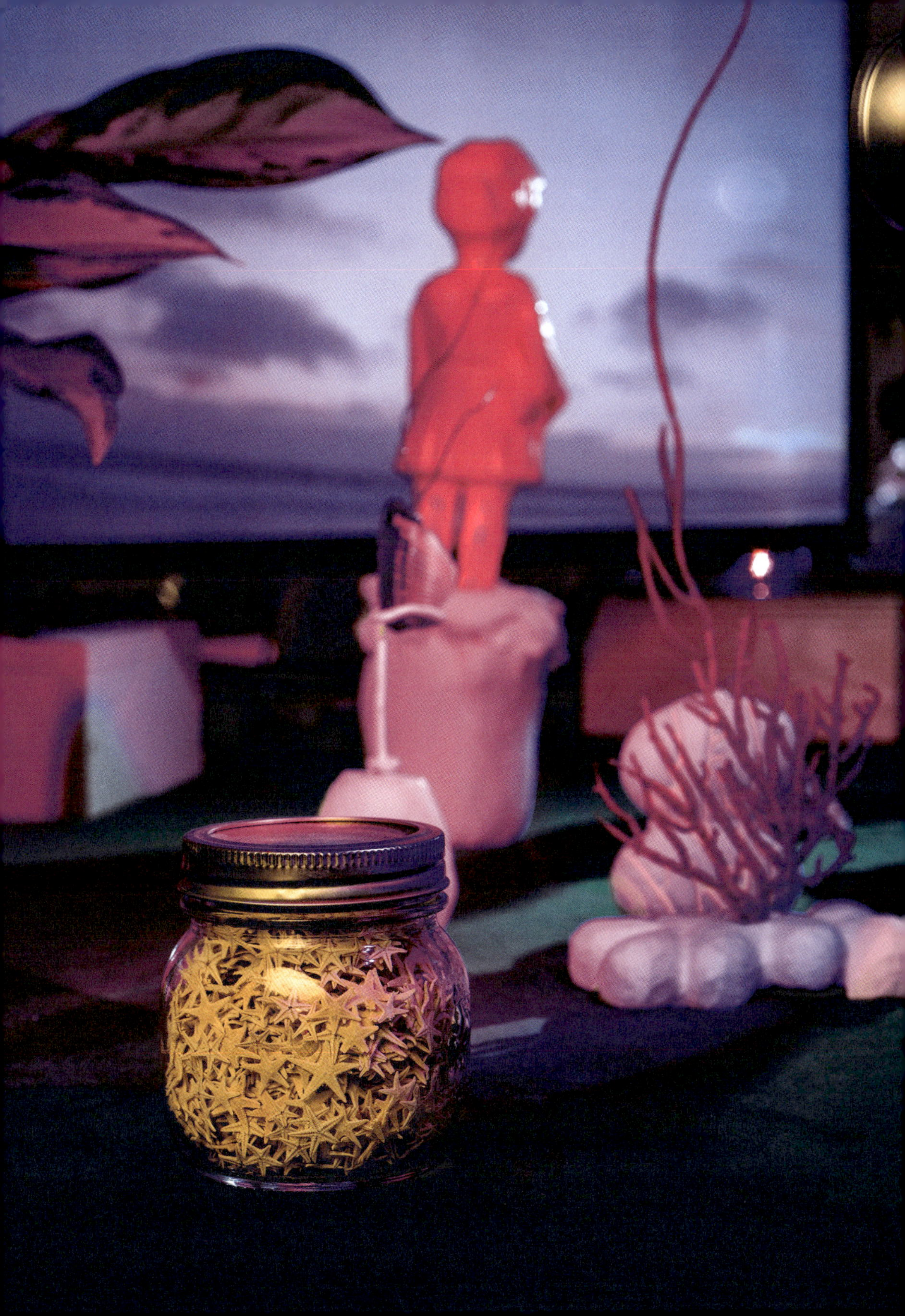

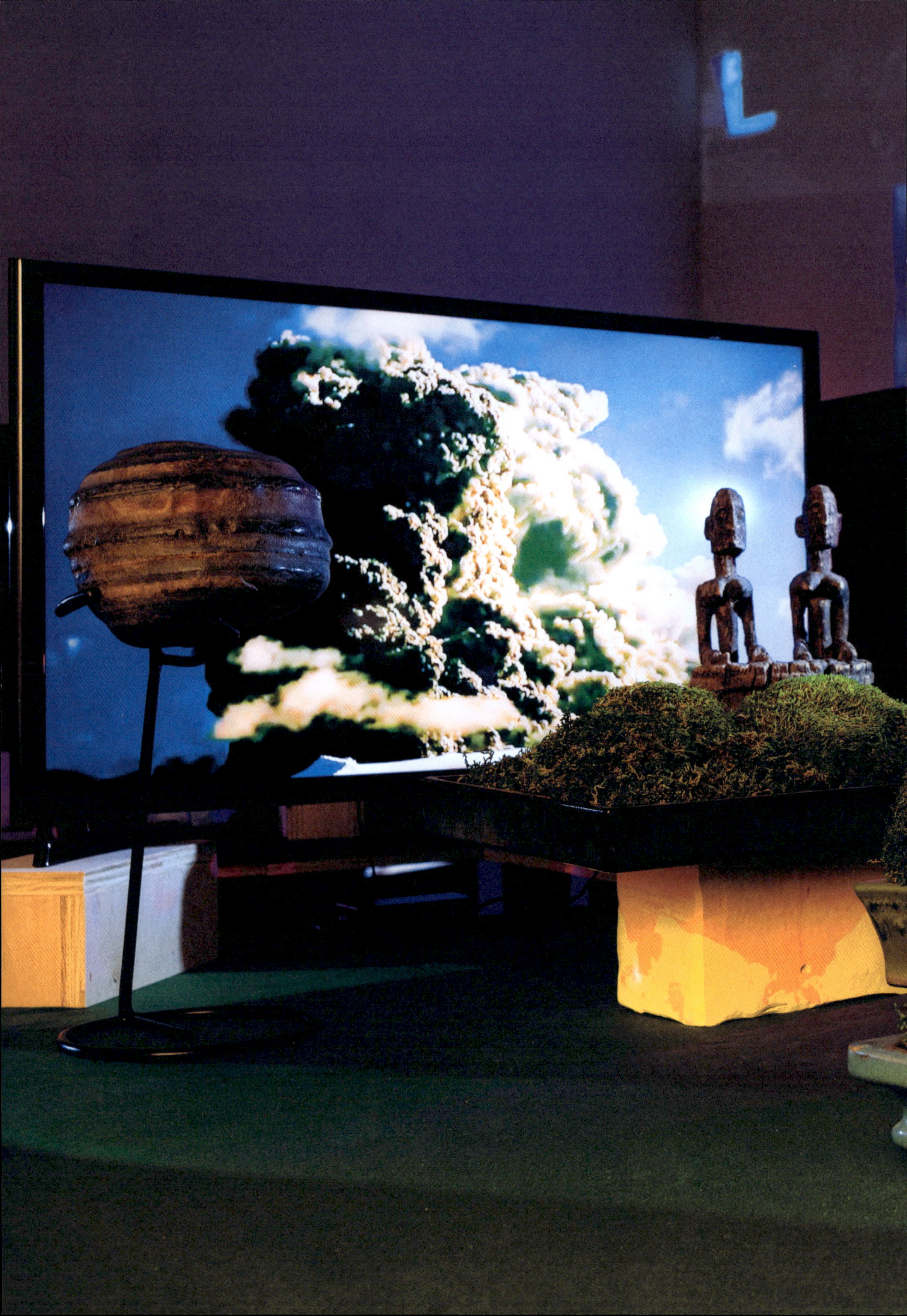

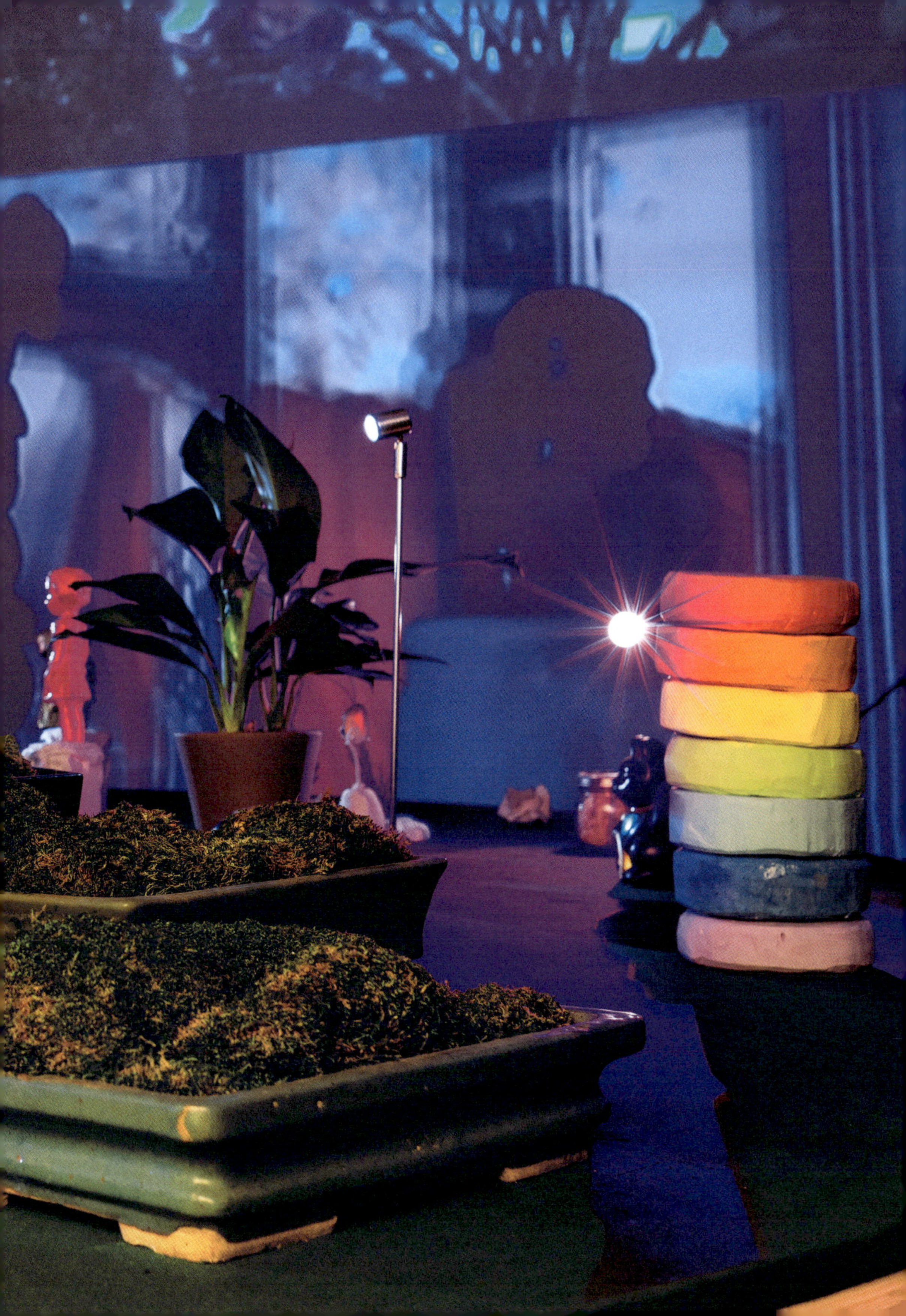

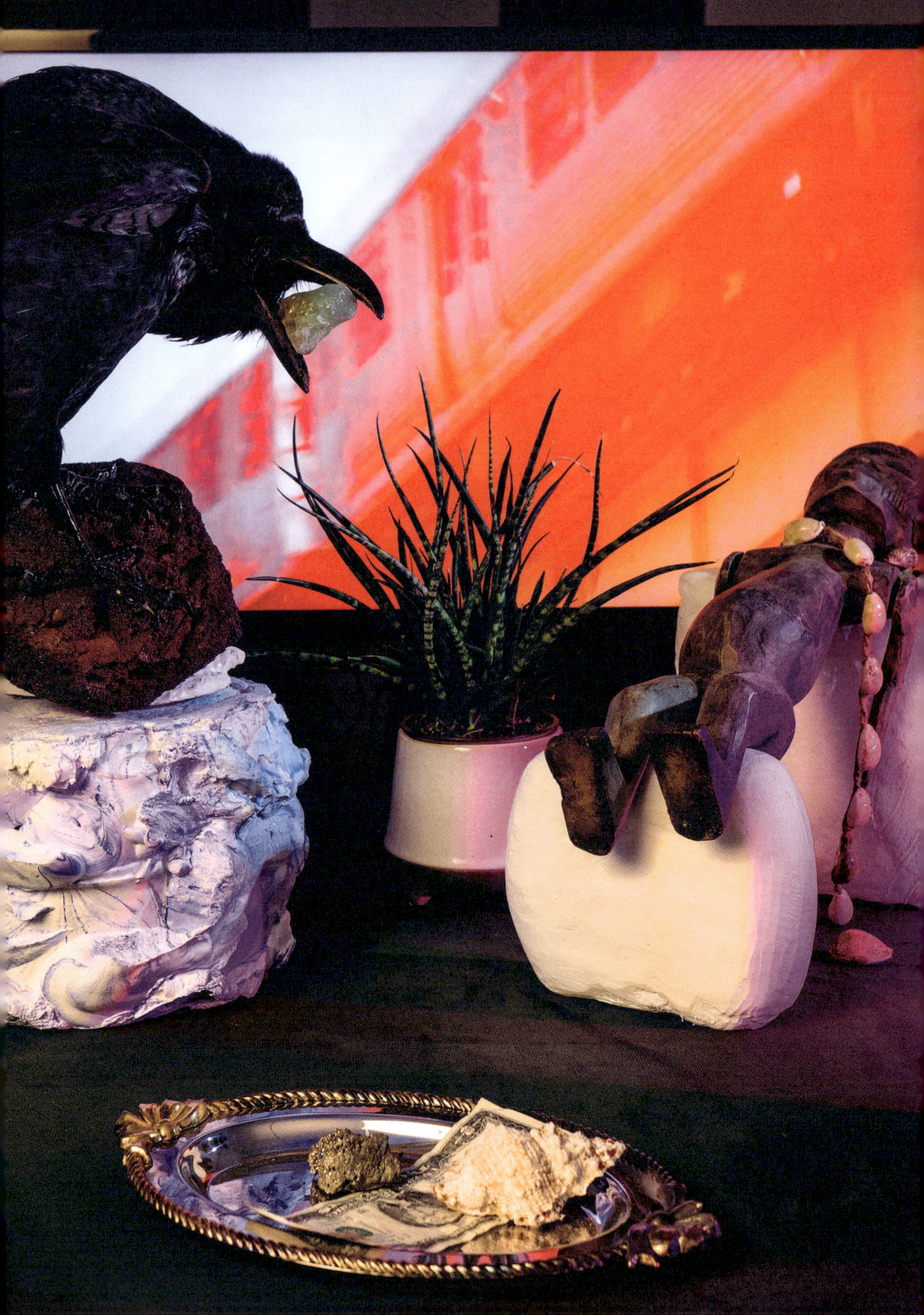

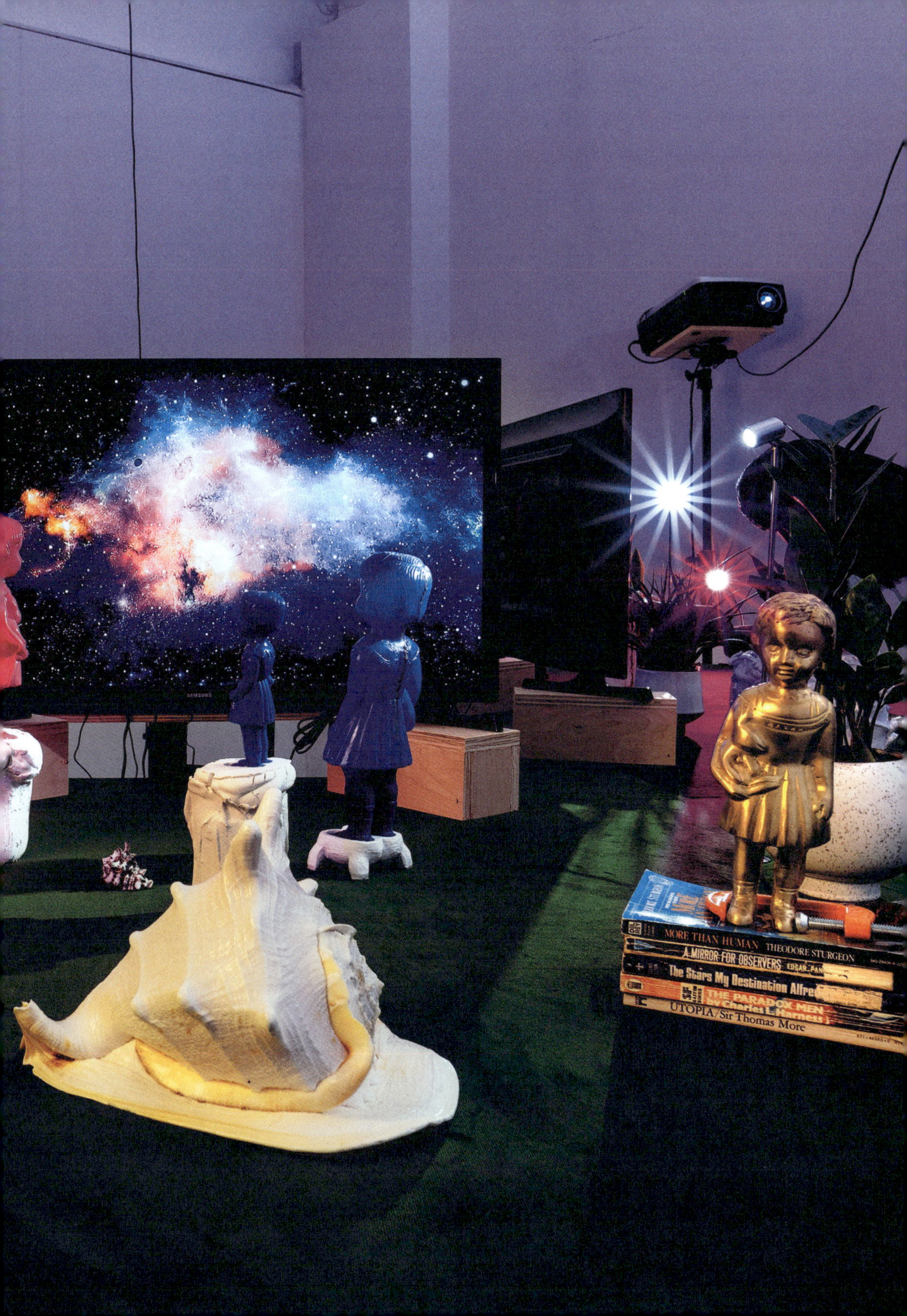
MORE THAN HUMAN   THEODORE STURGEON
A MIRROR FOR OBSERVERS   EDGAR PAN
The Stars My Destination   Alfre
THE PARADOX MEN   Charles L. Harness
UTOPIA / Sir Thomas More
SAMSUNG

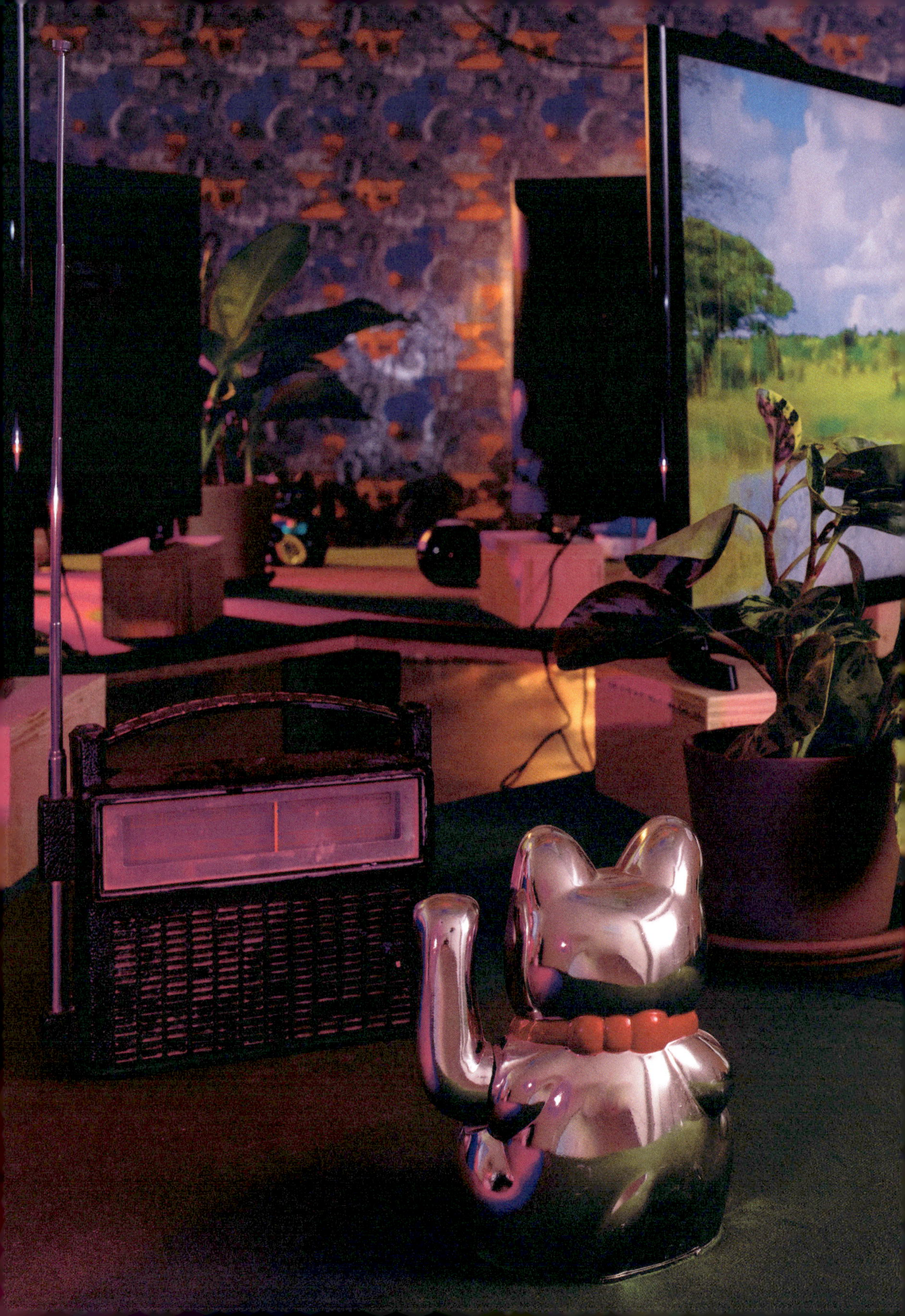

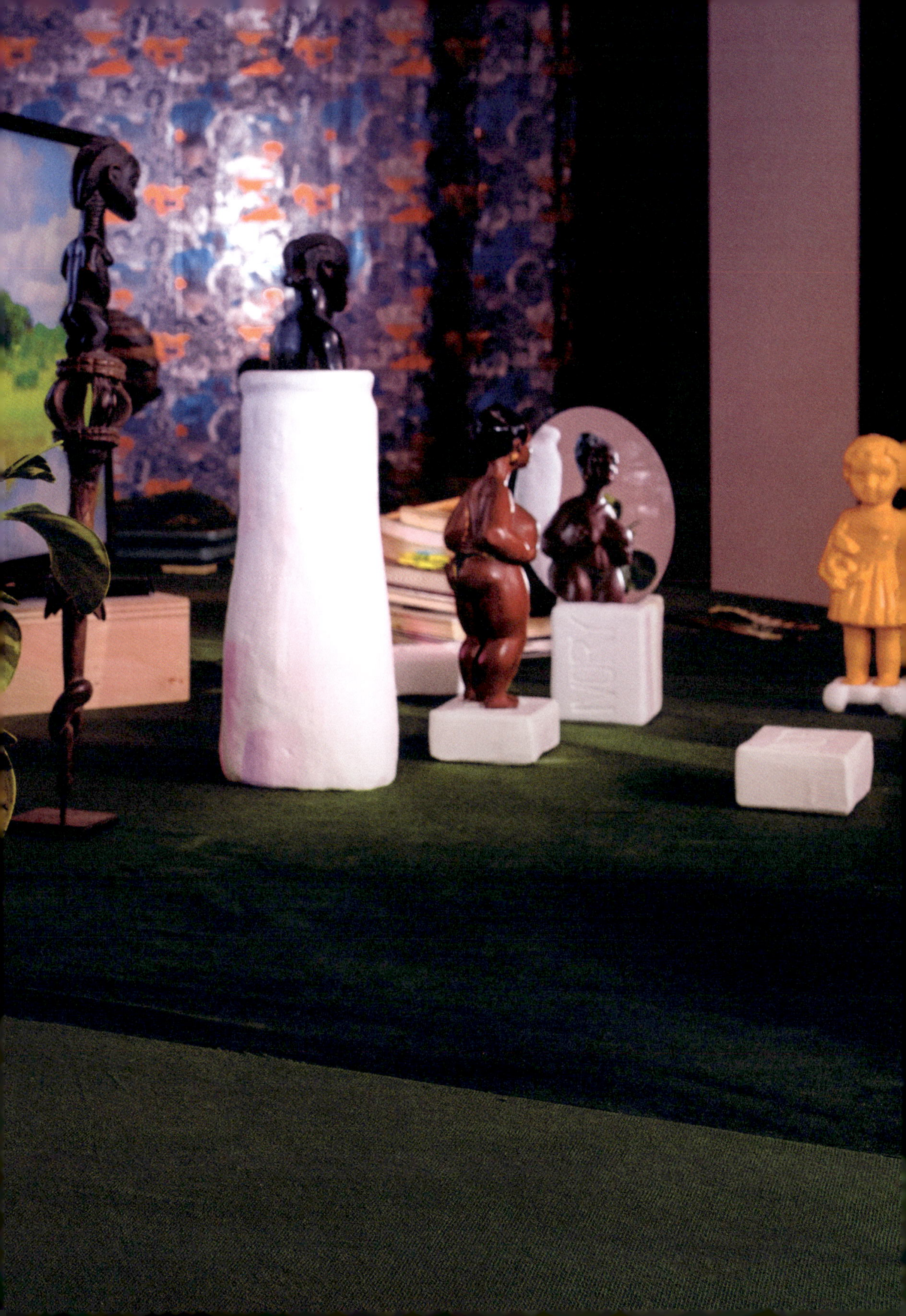

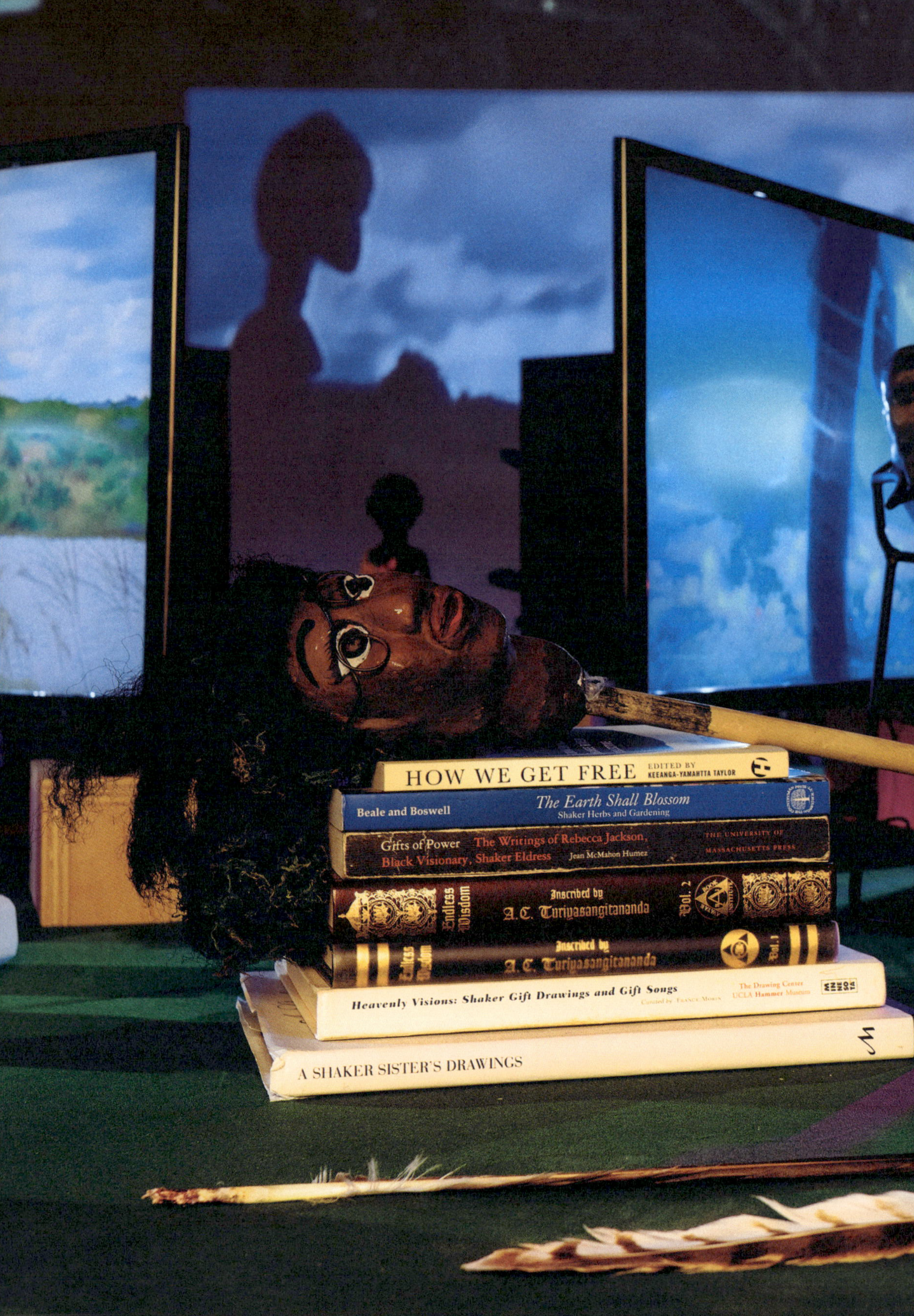

HOW WE GET FREE   EDITED BY KEEANGA-YAMAHTTA TAYLOR
Beale and Boswell   The Earth Shall Blossom   Shaker Herbs and Gardening
Gifts of Power   The Writings of Rebecca Jackson, Black Visionary, Shaker Eldress   Jean McMahon Humez   THE UNIVERSITY OF MASSACHUSETTS PRESS
Endless Wisdom   Inscribed by A. C. Turiyasangitananda   Vol. 2
Endless Wisdom   Inscribed by A. C. Turiyasangitananda   Vol. 1
Heavenly Visions: Shaker Gift Drawings and Gift Songs   Curated by France Morin   The Drawing Center UCLA Hammer Museum
A SHAKER SISTER'S DRAWINGS

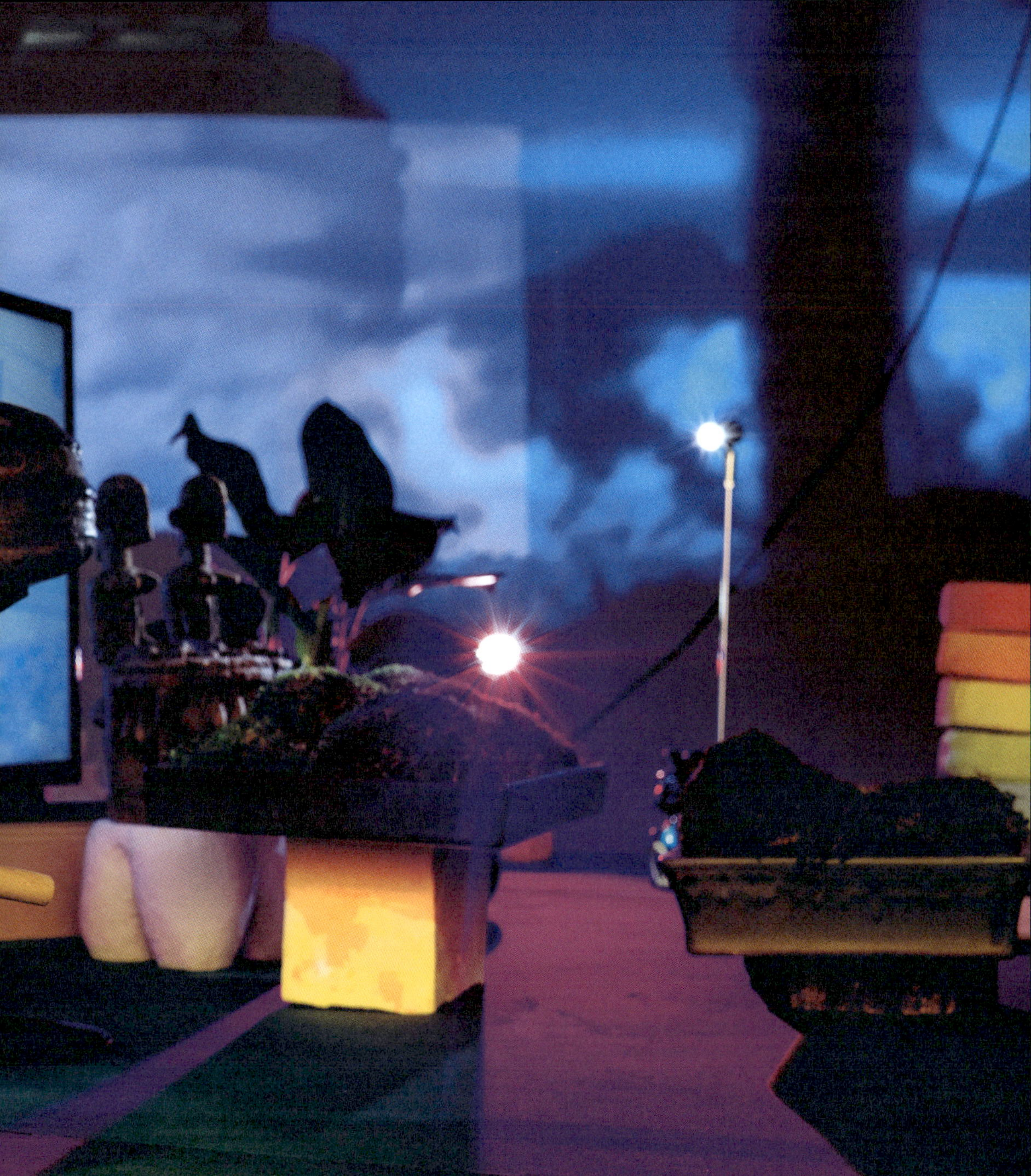

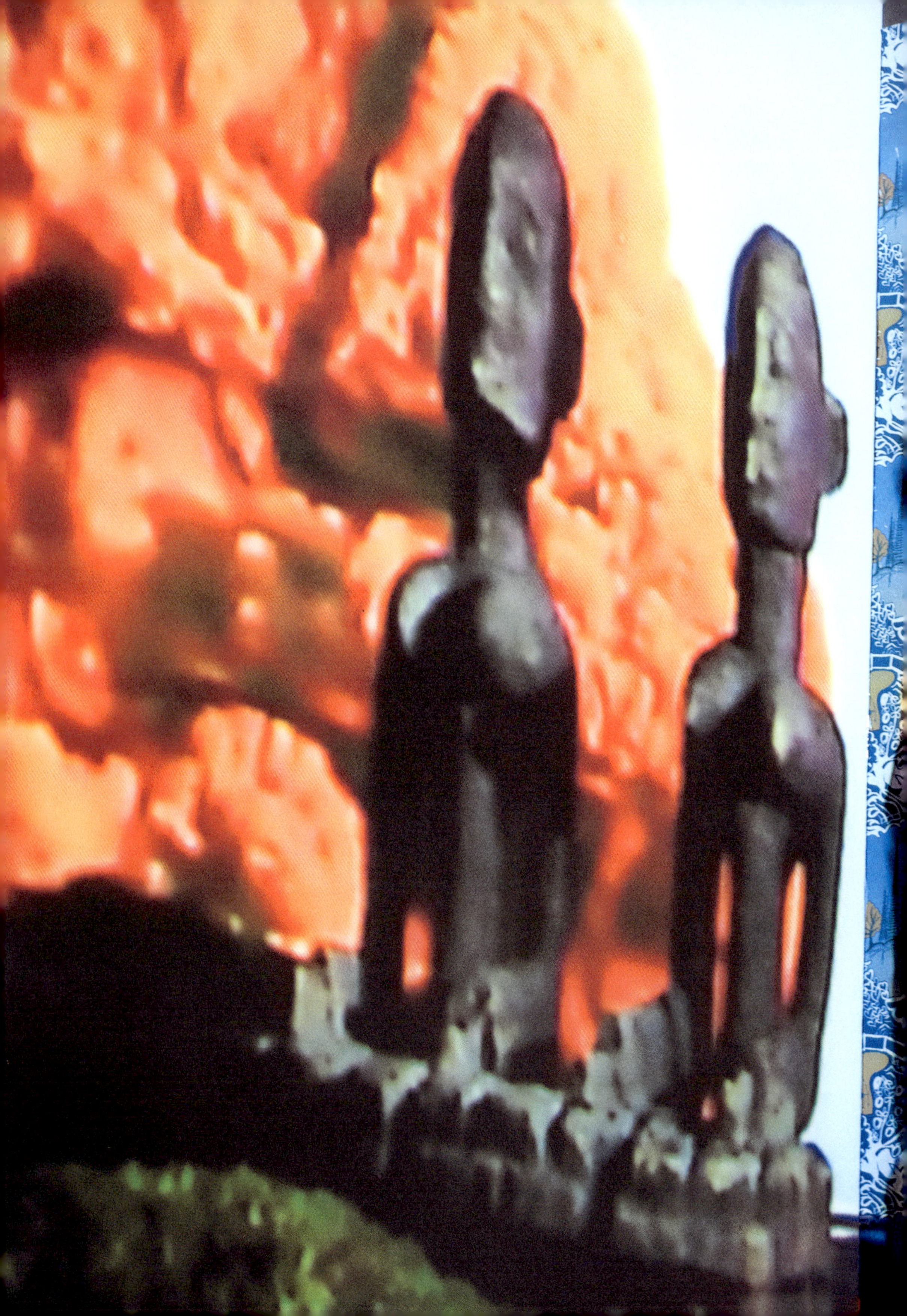

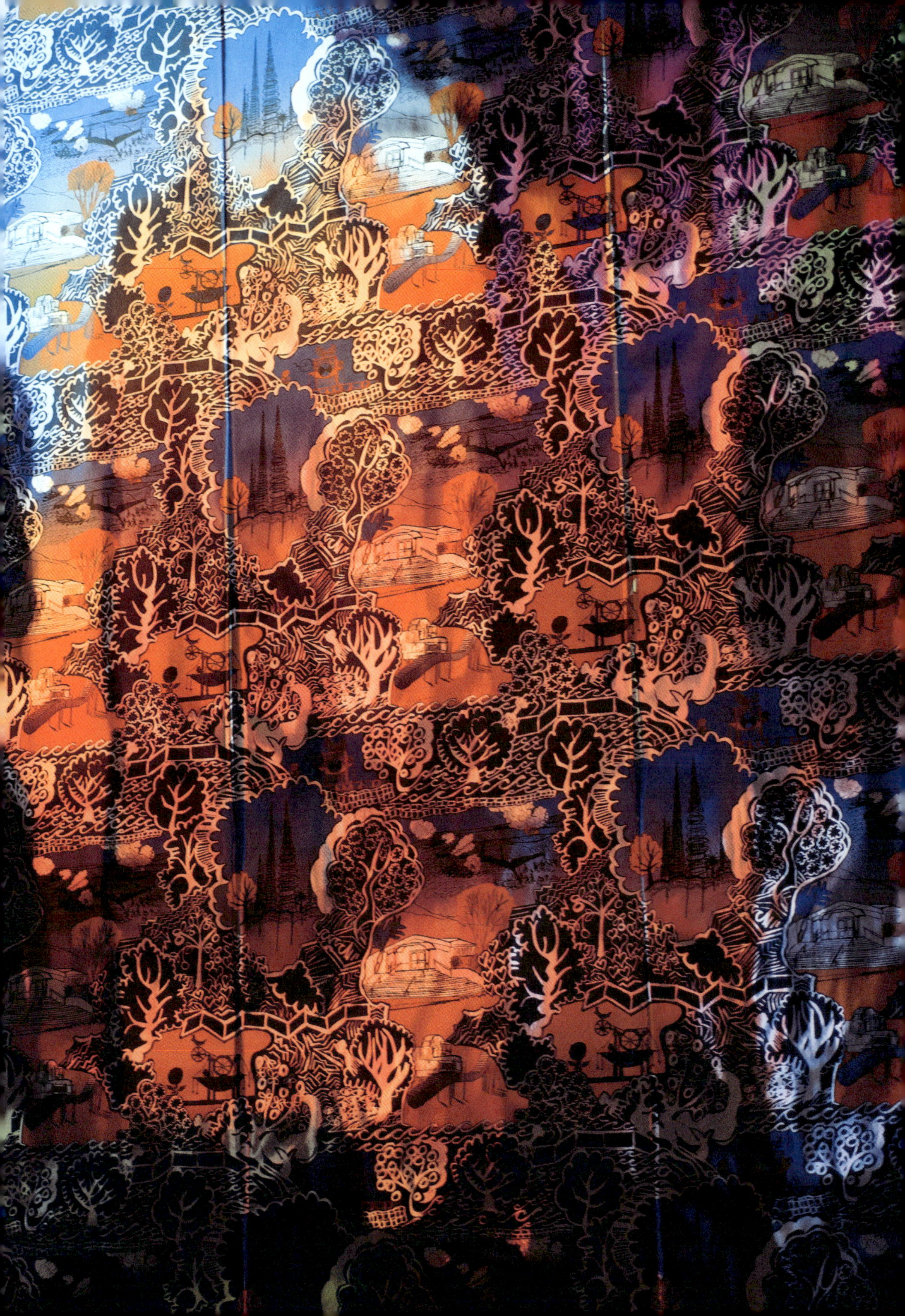

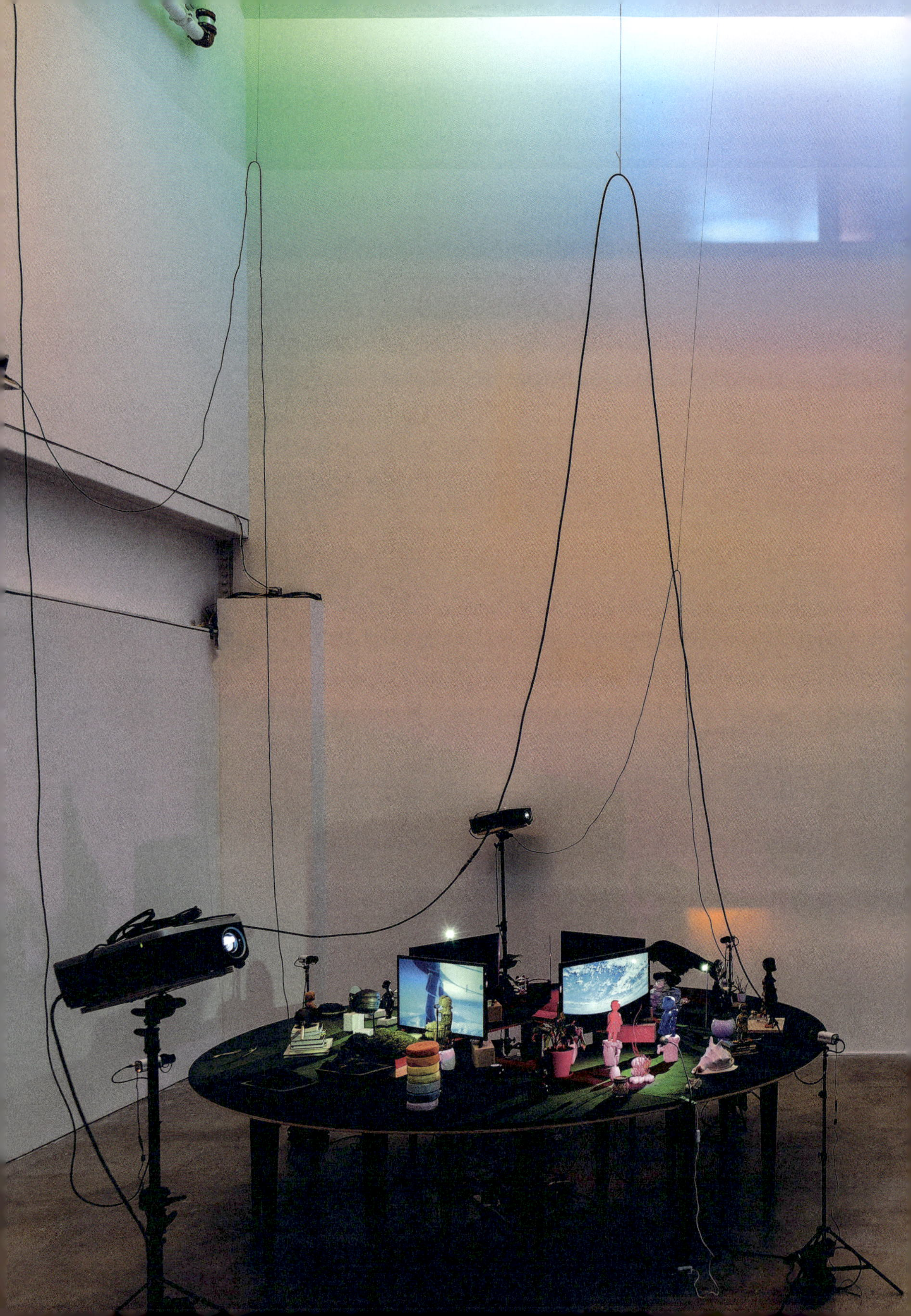

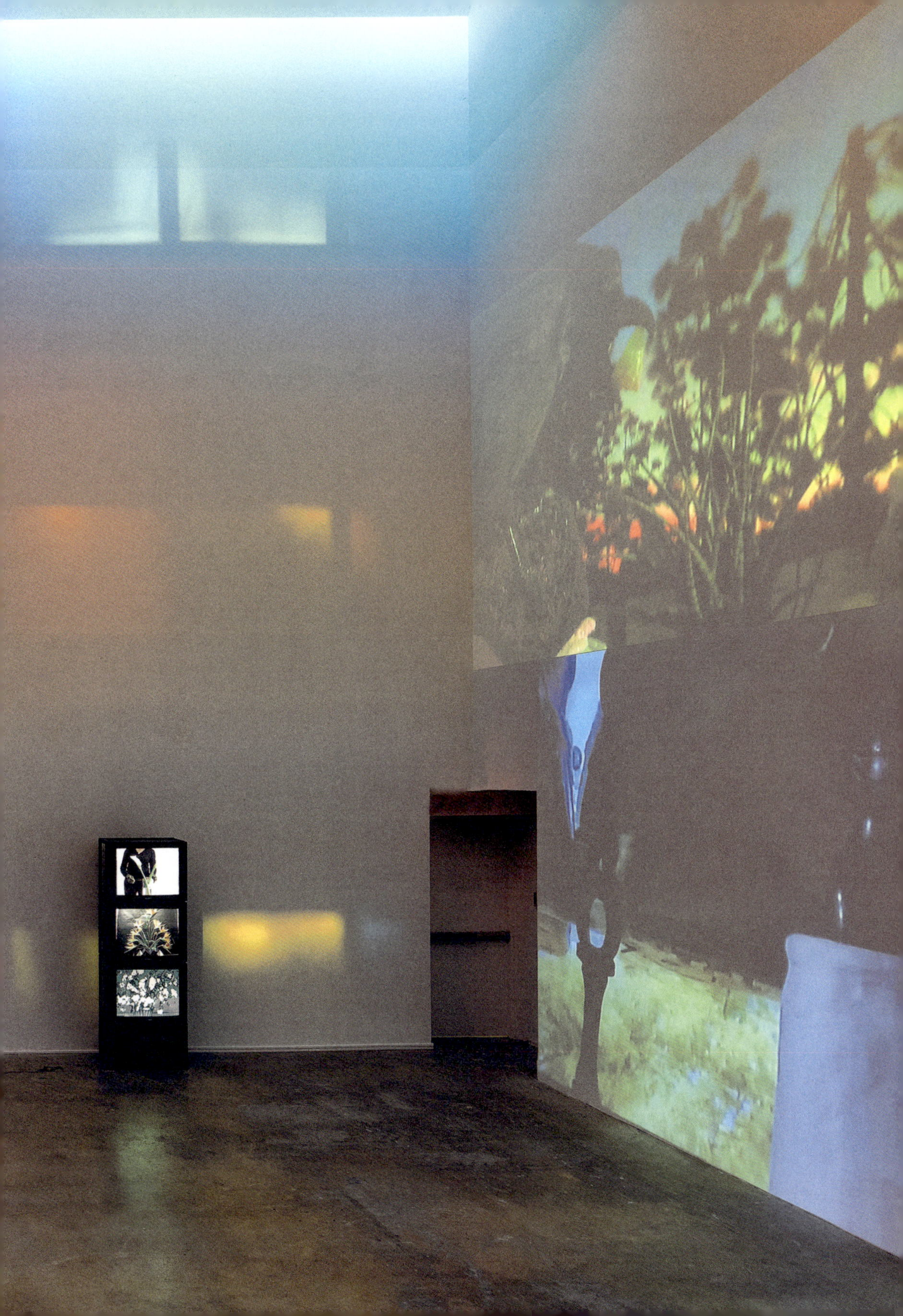

*Black and Blue Over You, 2010 /
Strelitzia Satellite Meditation, 2012 / Cotton Plant 187?, 2018*

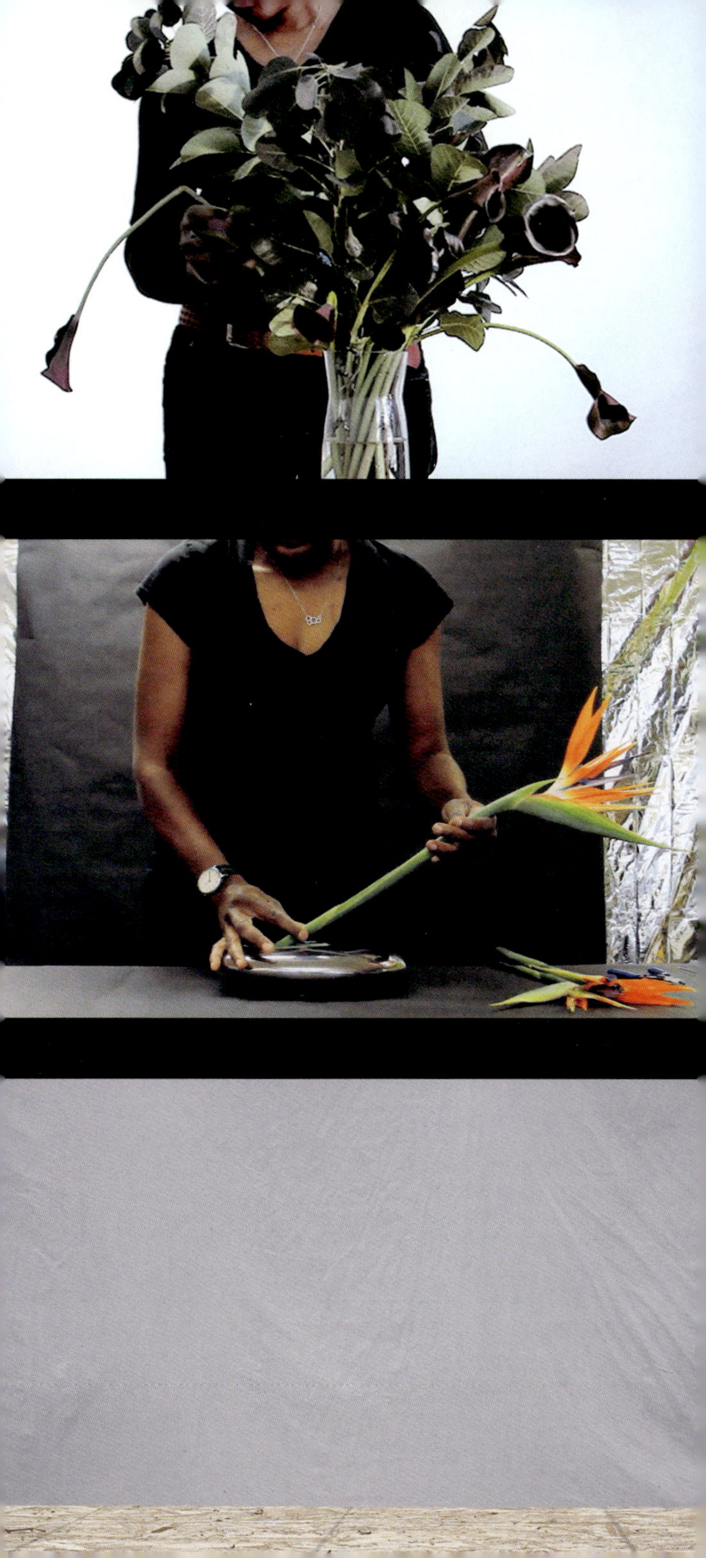

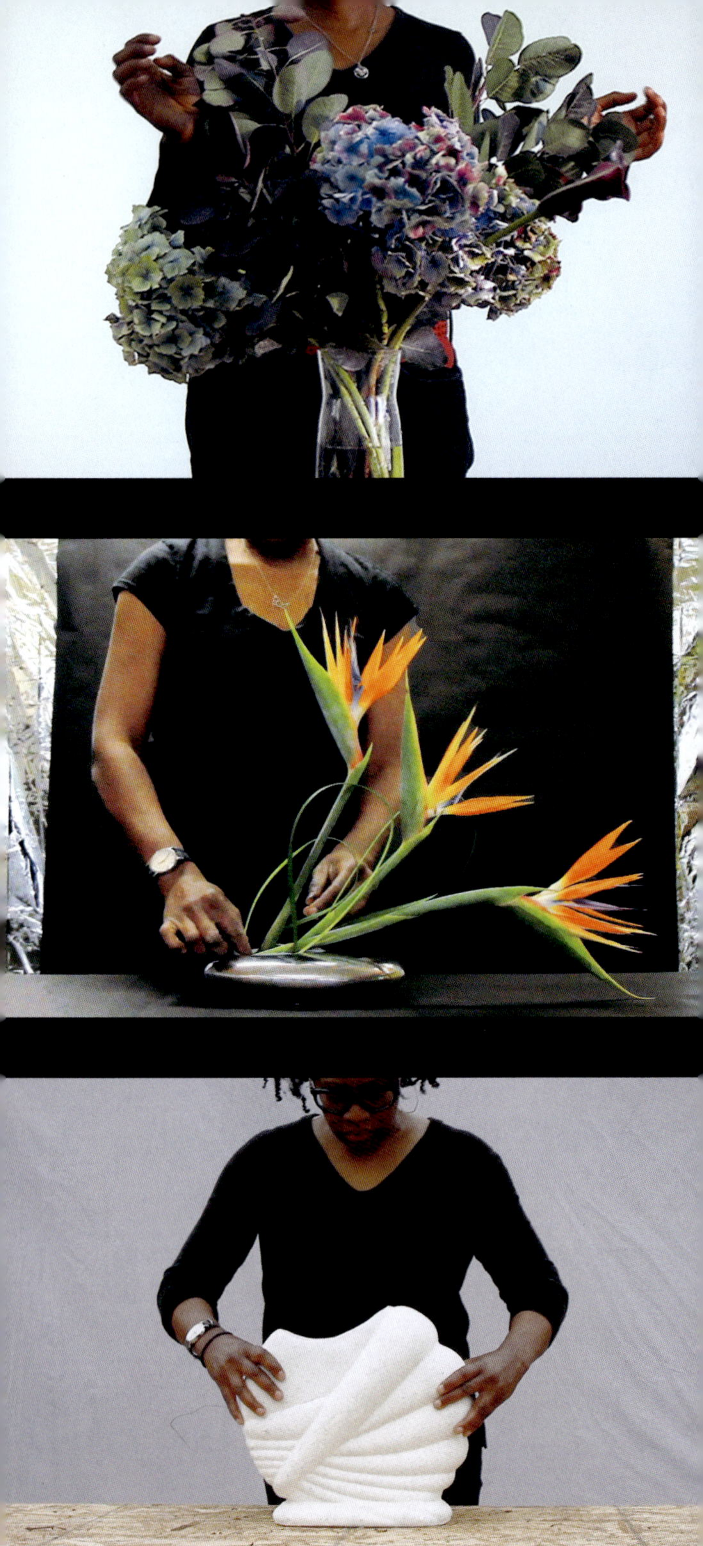

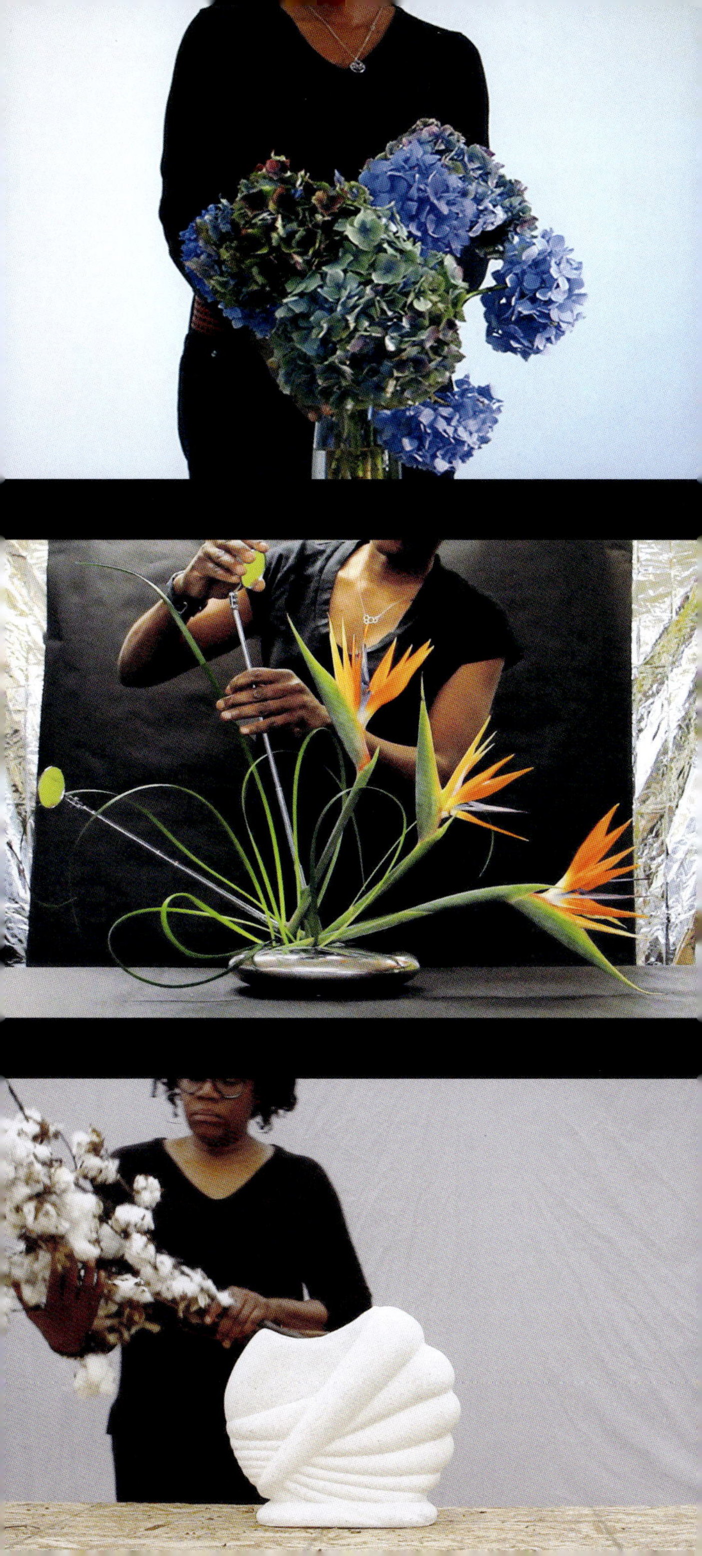

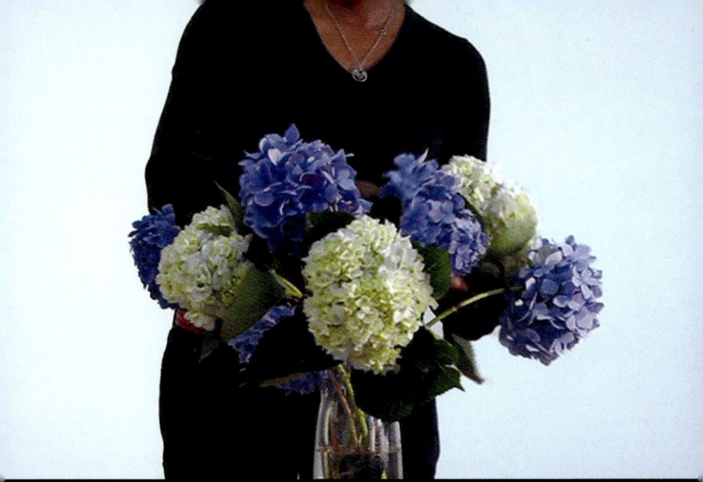

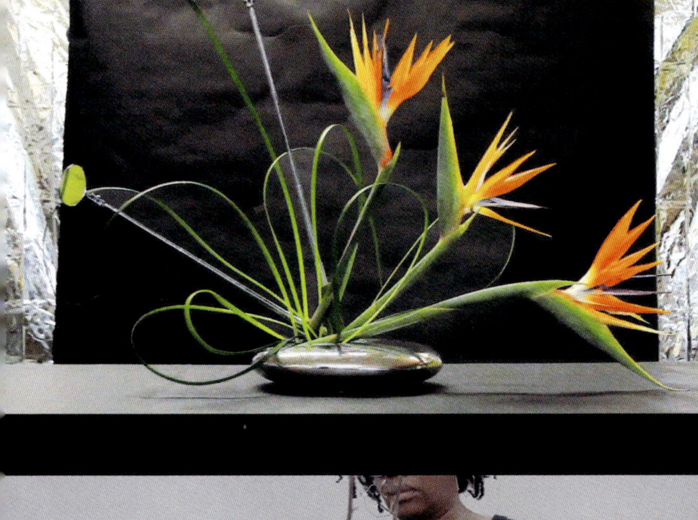
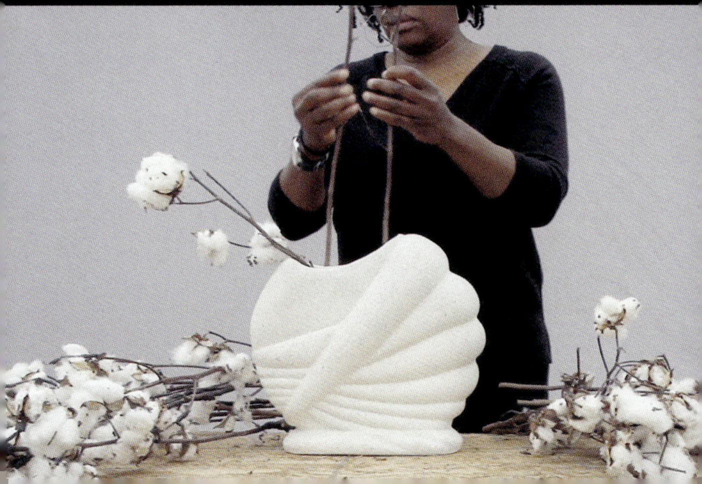

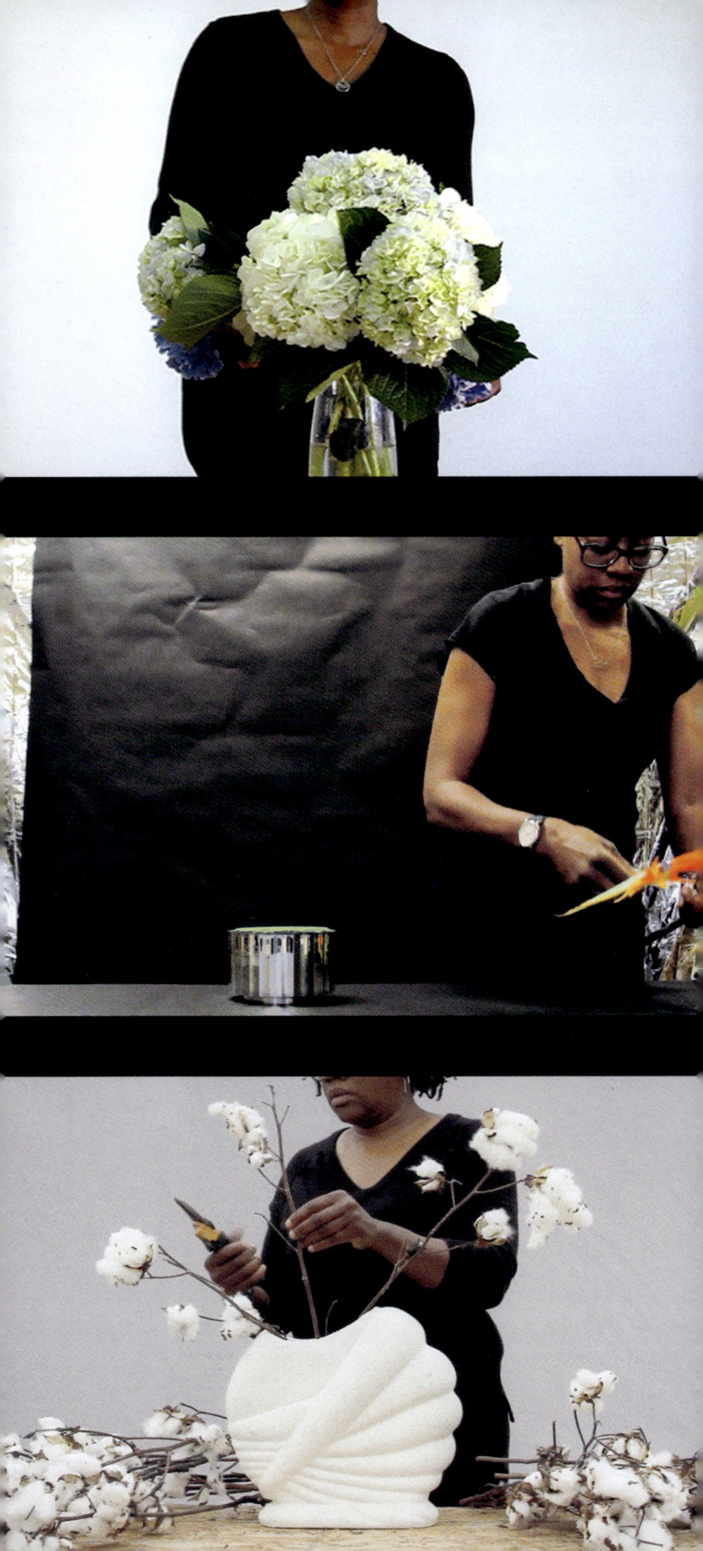

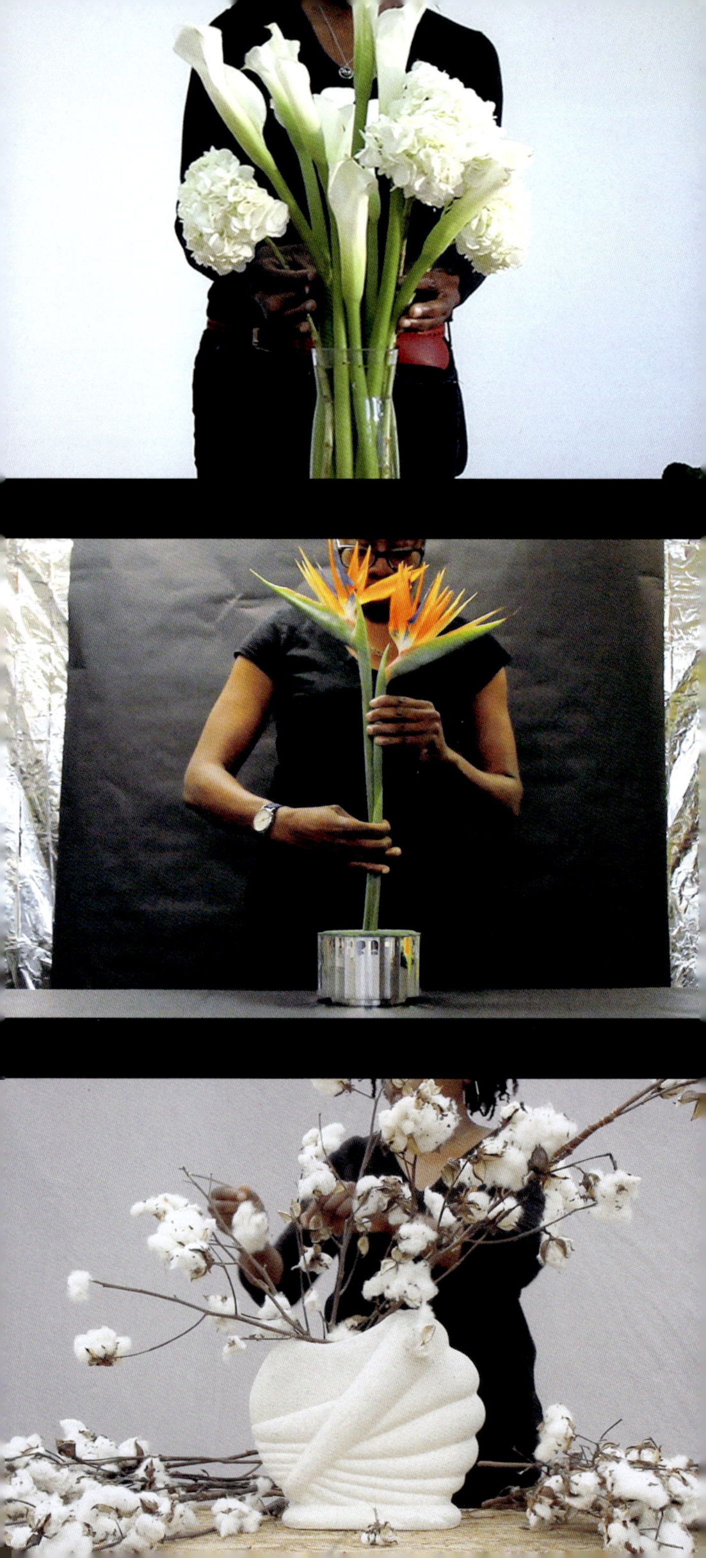

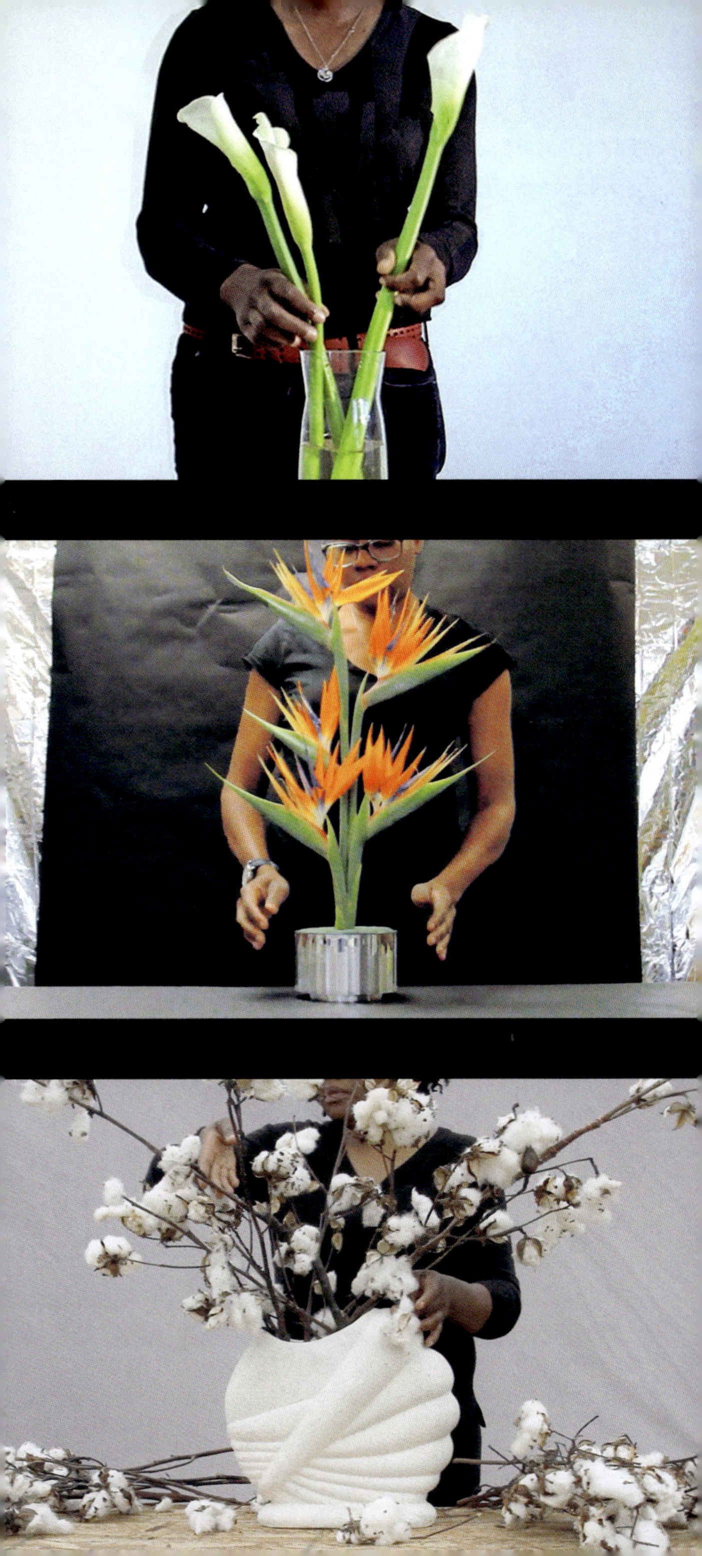

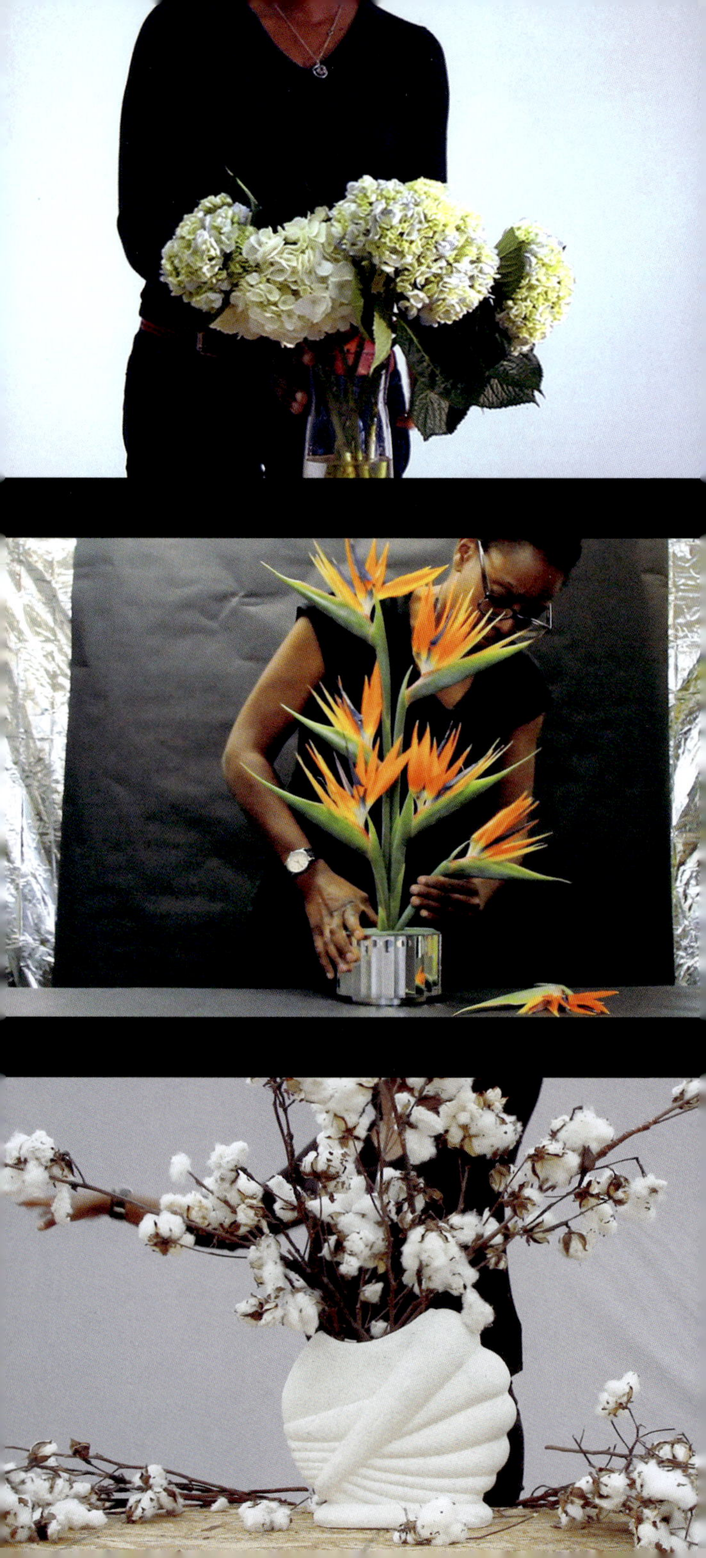

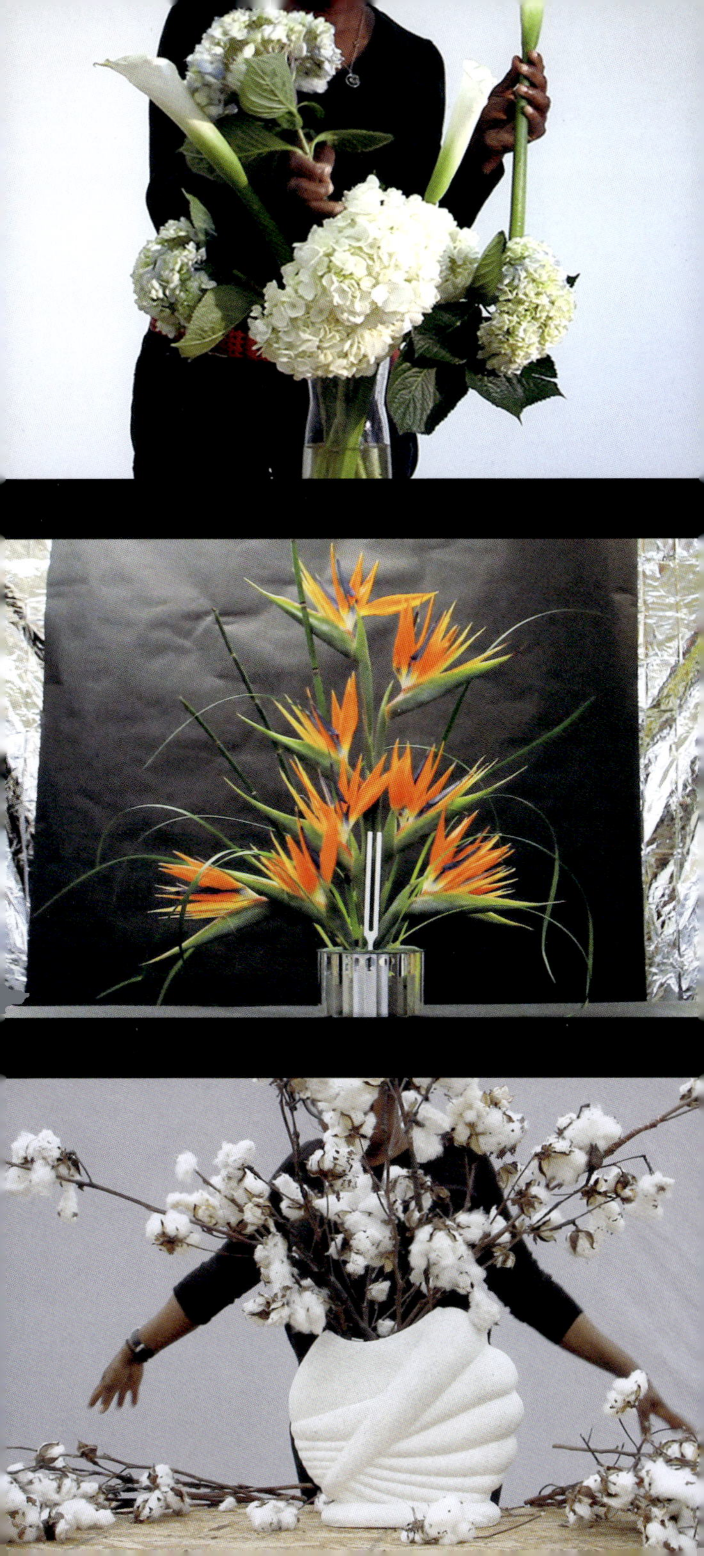

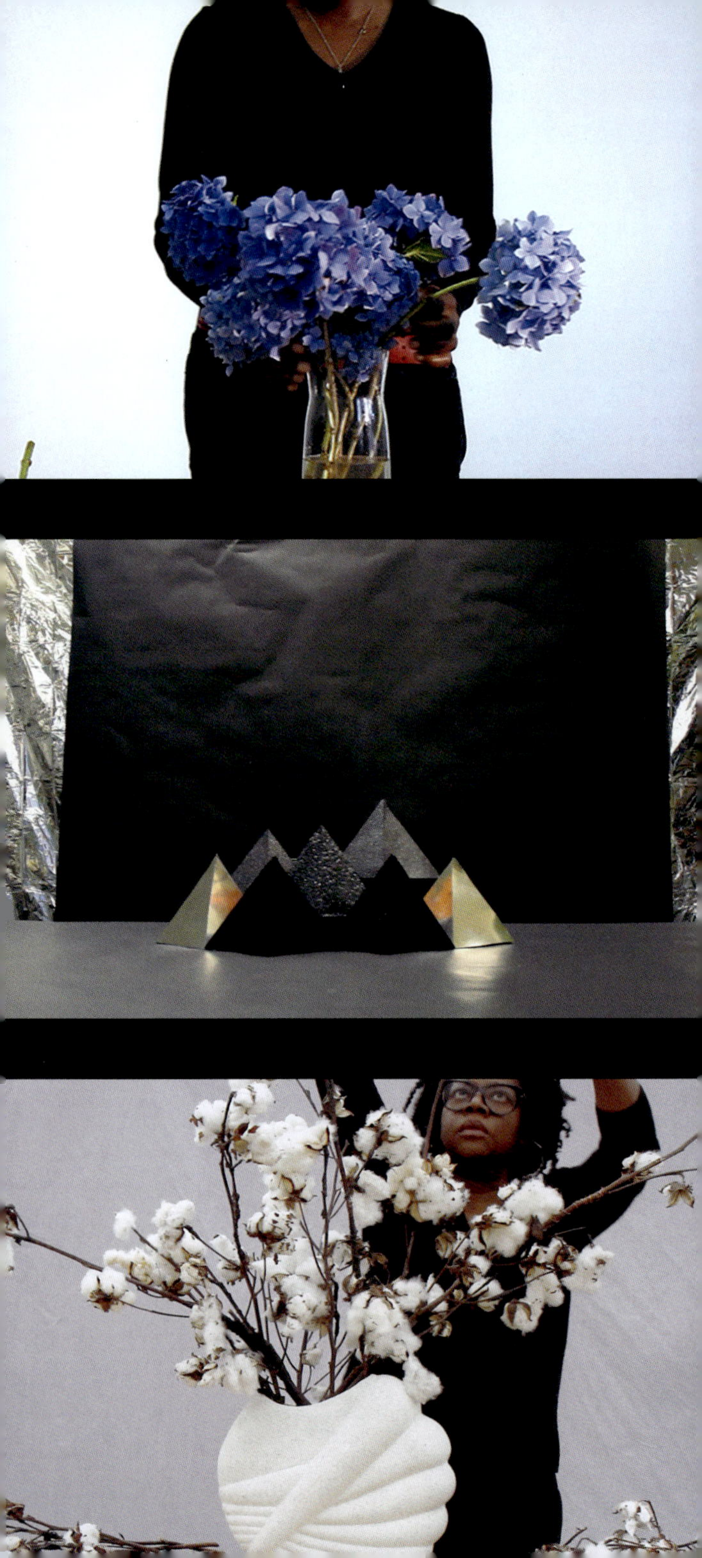

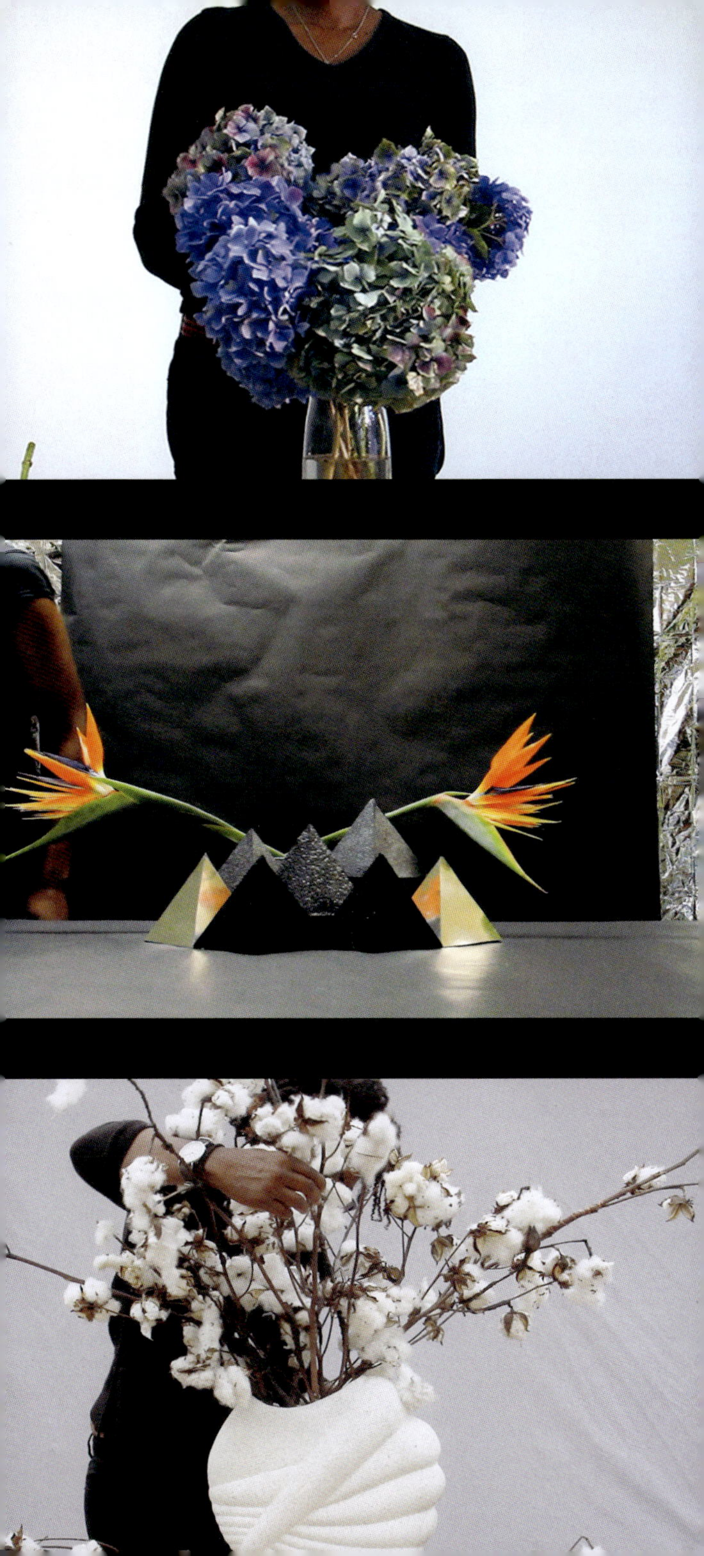

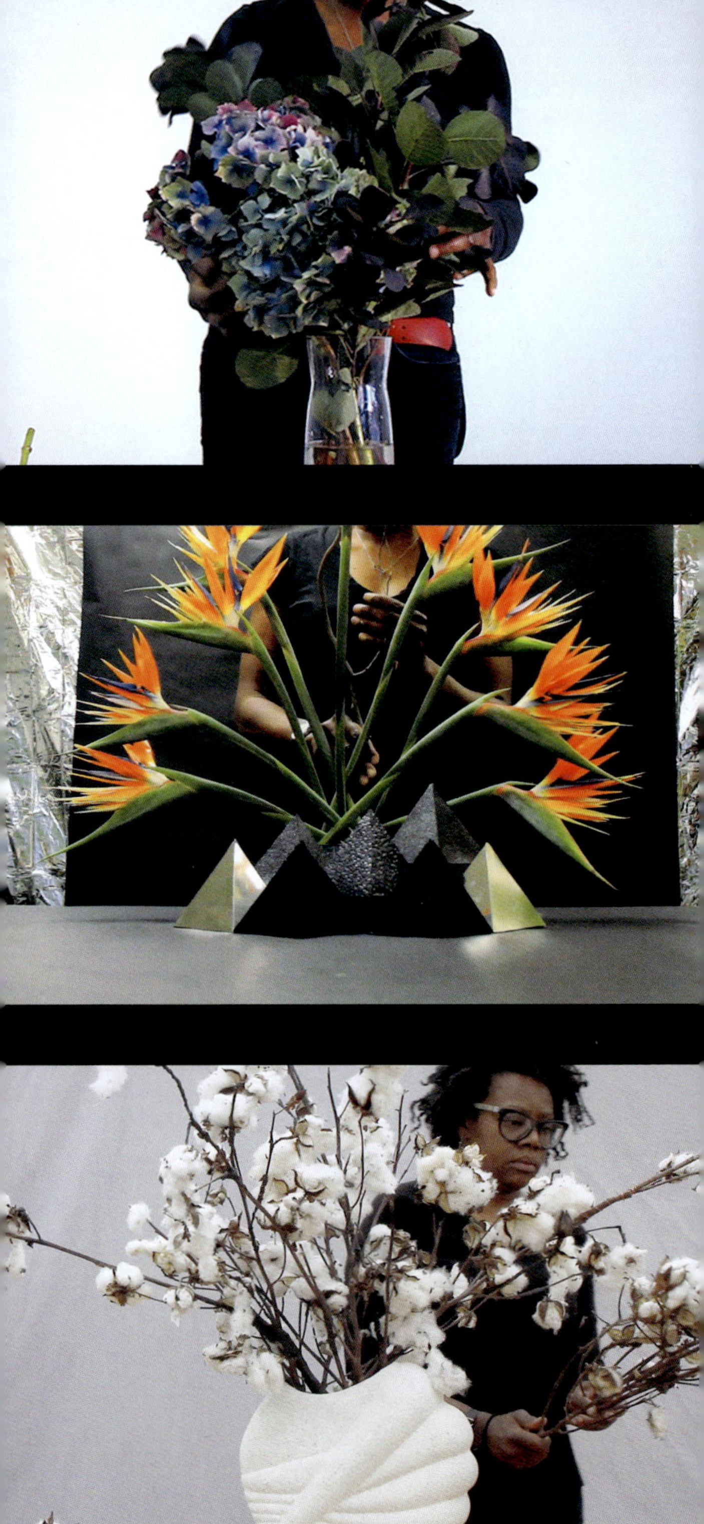

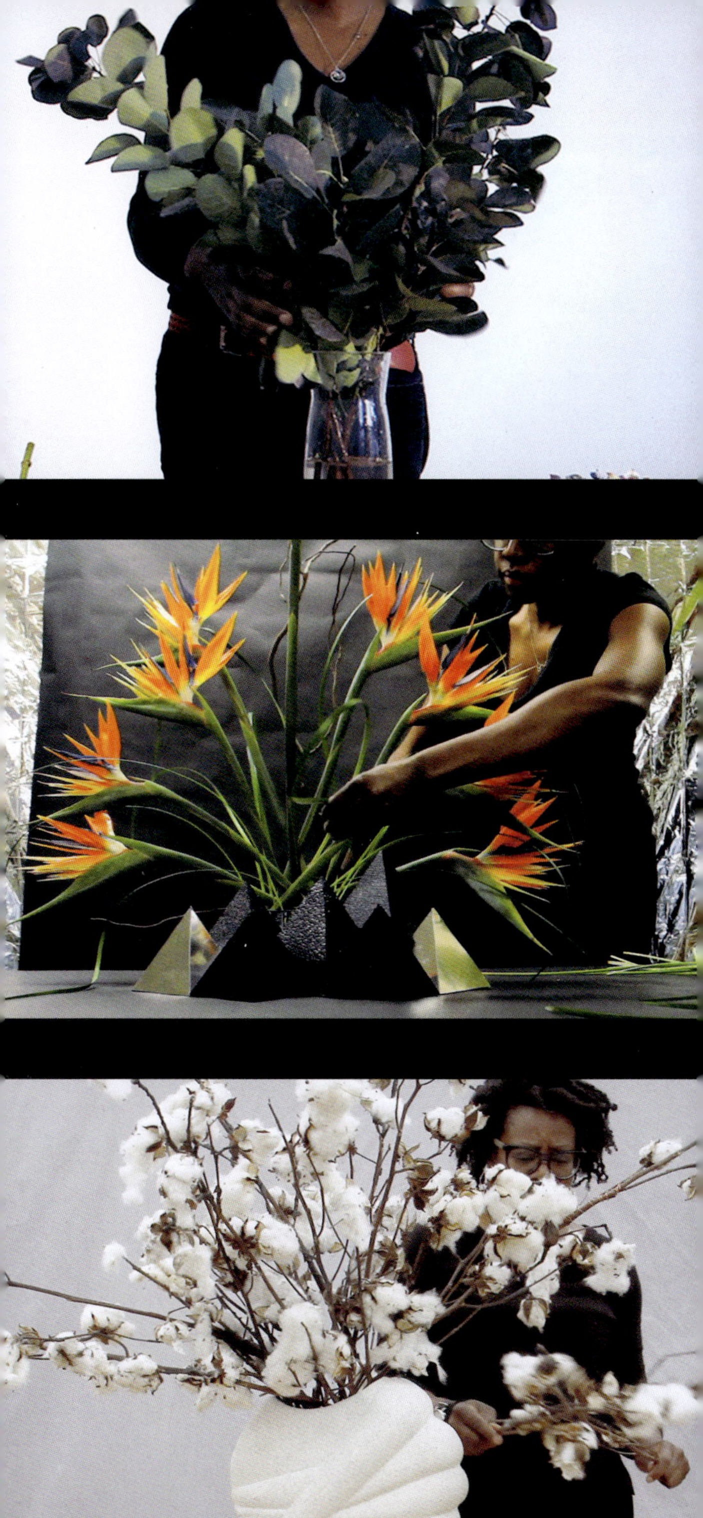

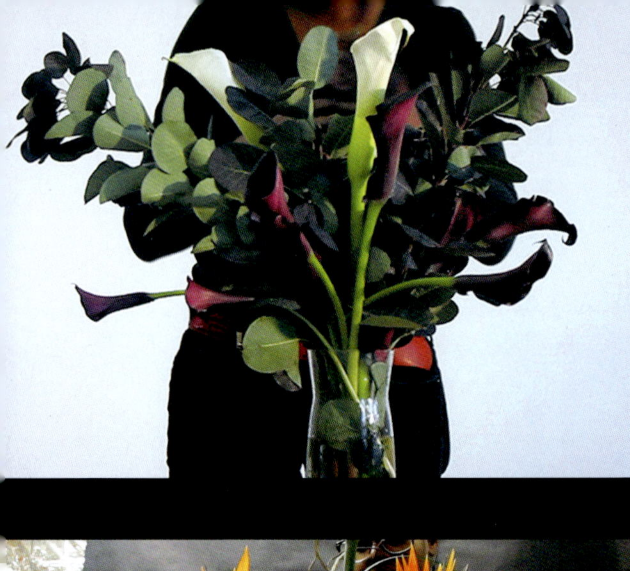

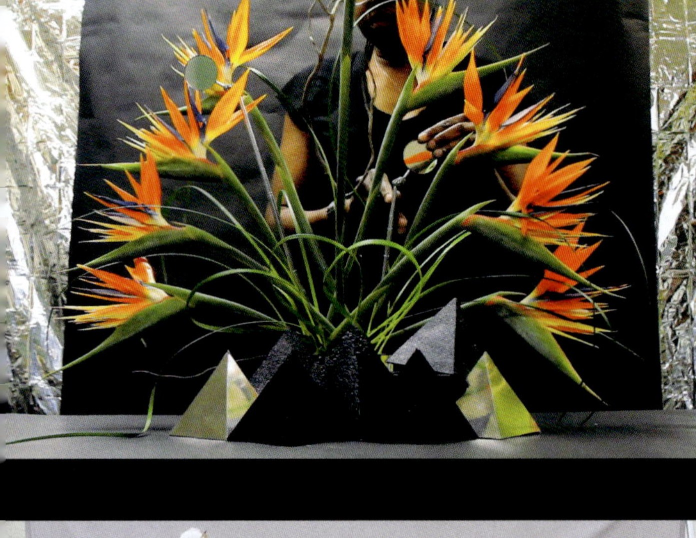

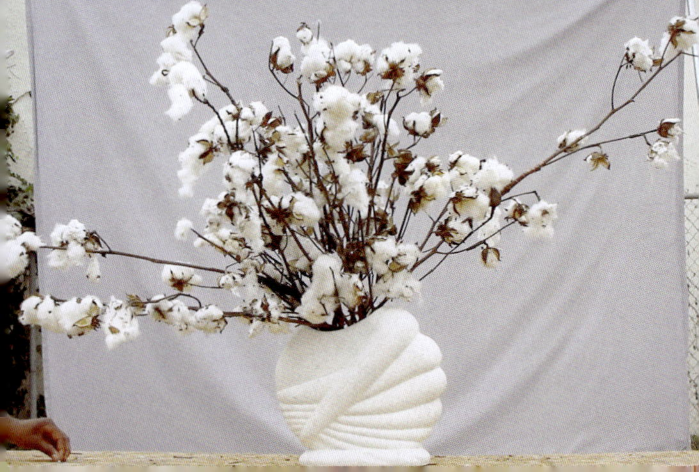

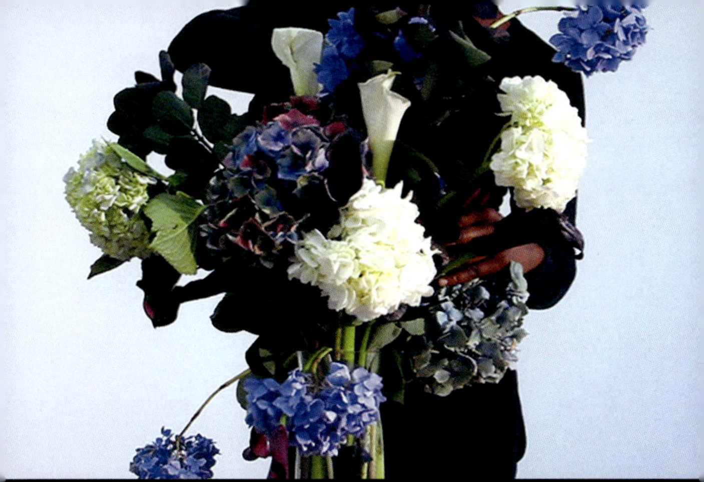

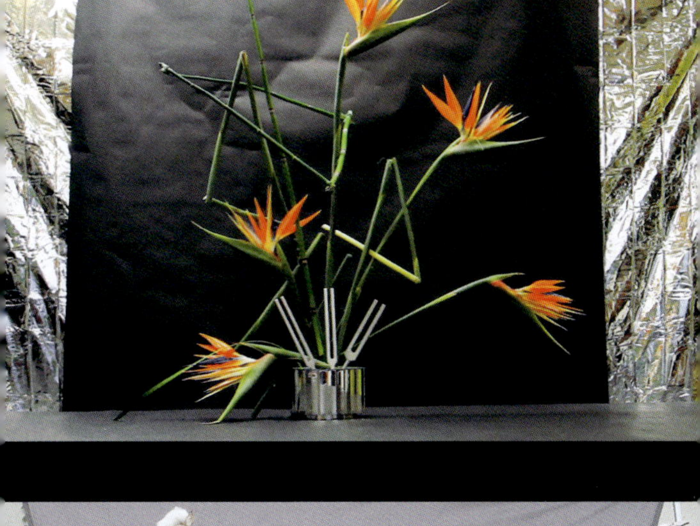
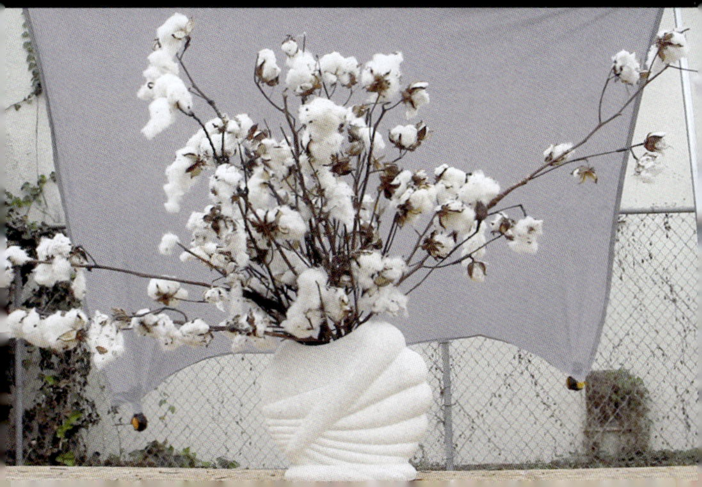

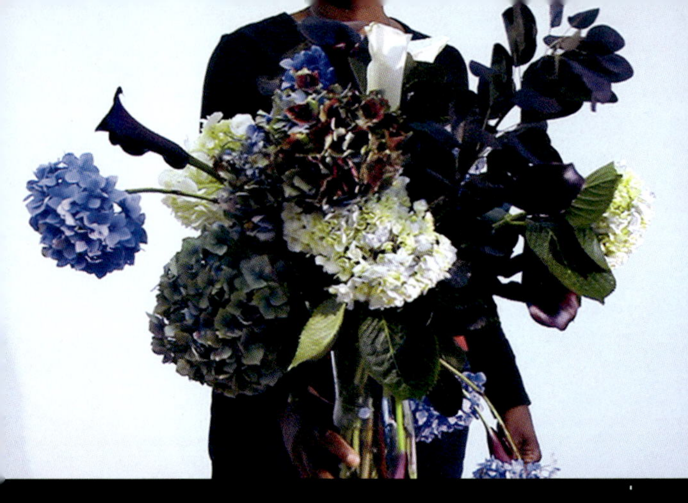

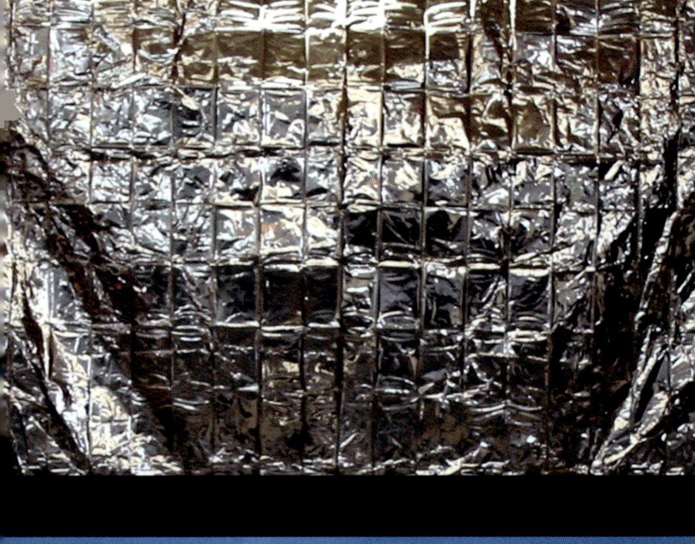

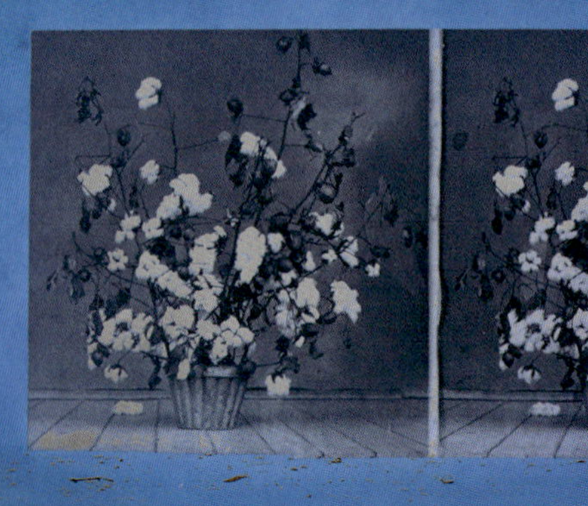
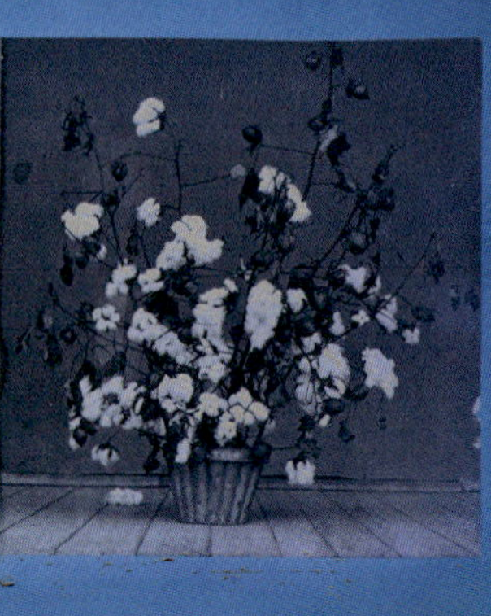

Cotton Plant 187?, **2018**
Digital video, color, sound.
6:43 minutes

Strelitzia Satellite
Meditation, **2012**
Digital video, color, sound.
4:44 minutes

Black and Blue Over You
(After Bas Jan Ader), **2010**
Digital video, color, sound.
9:40 minutes

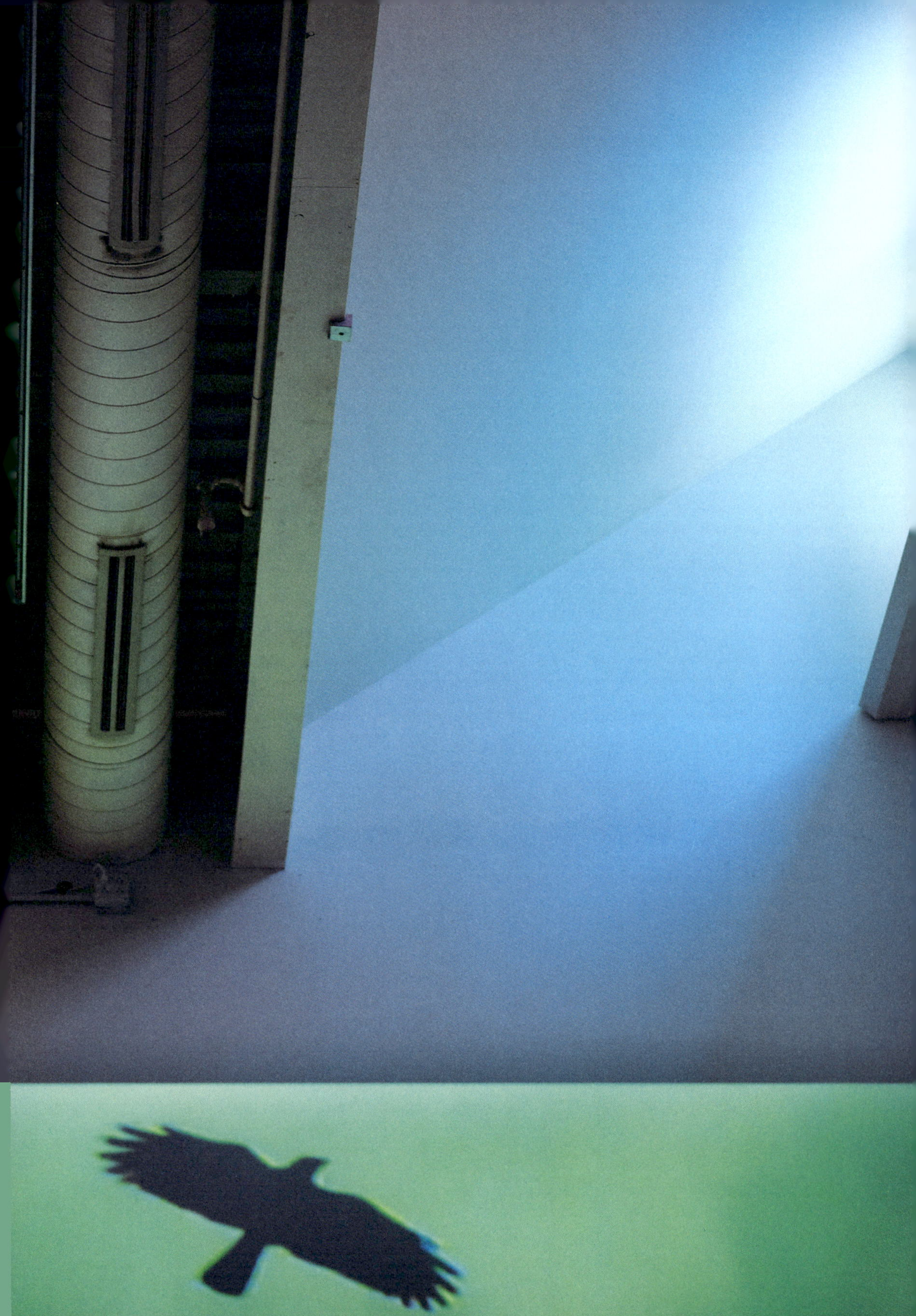

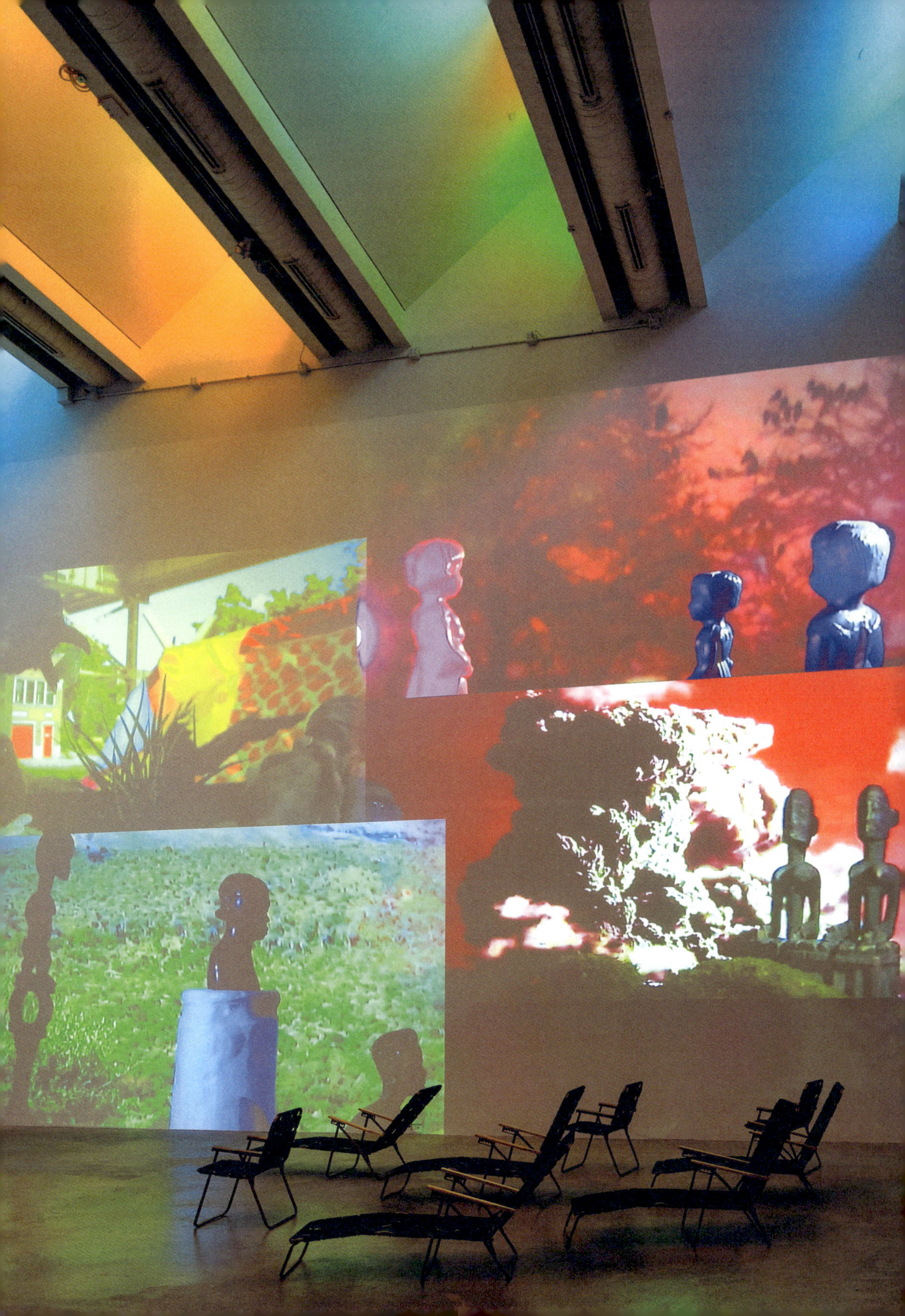

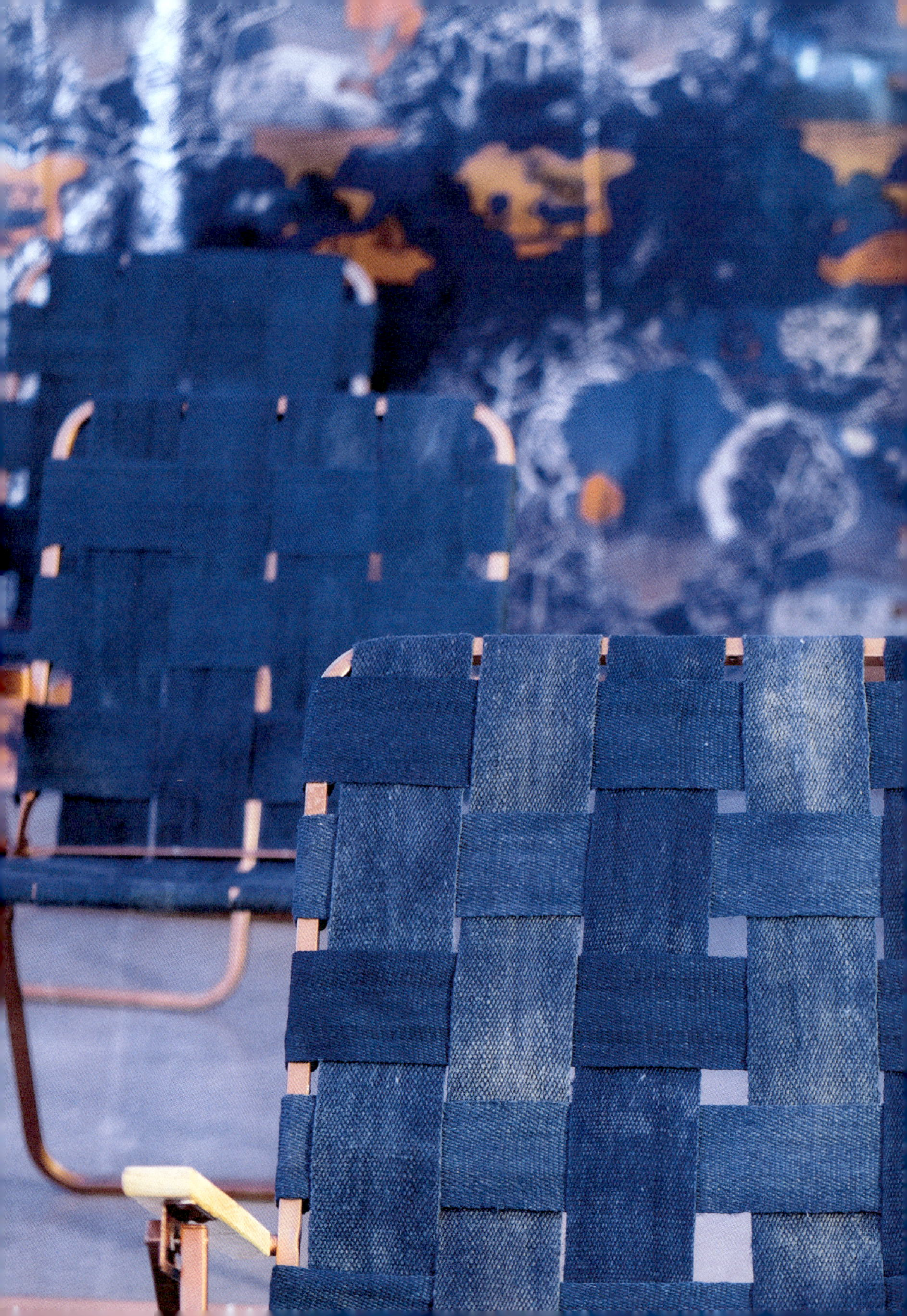

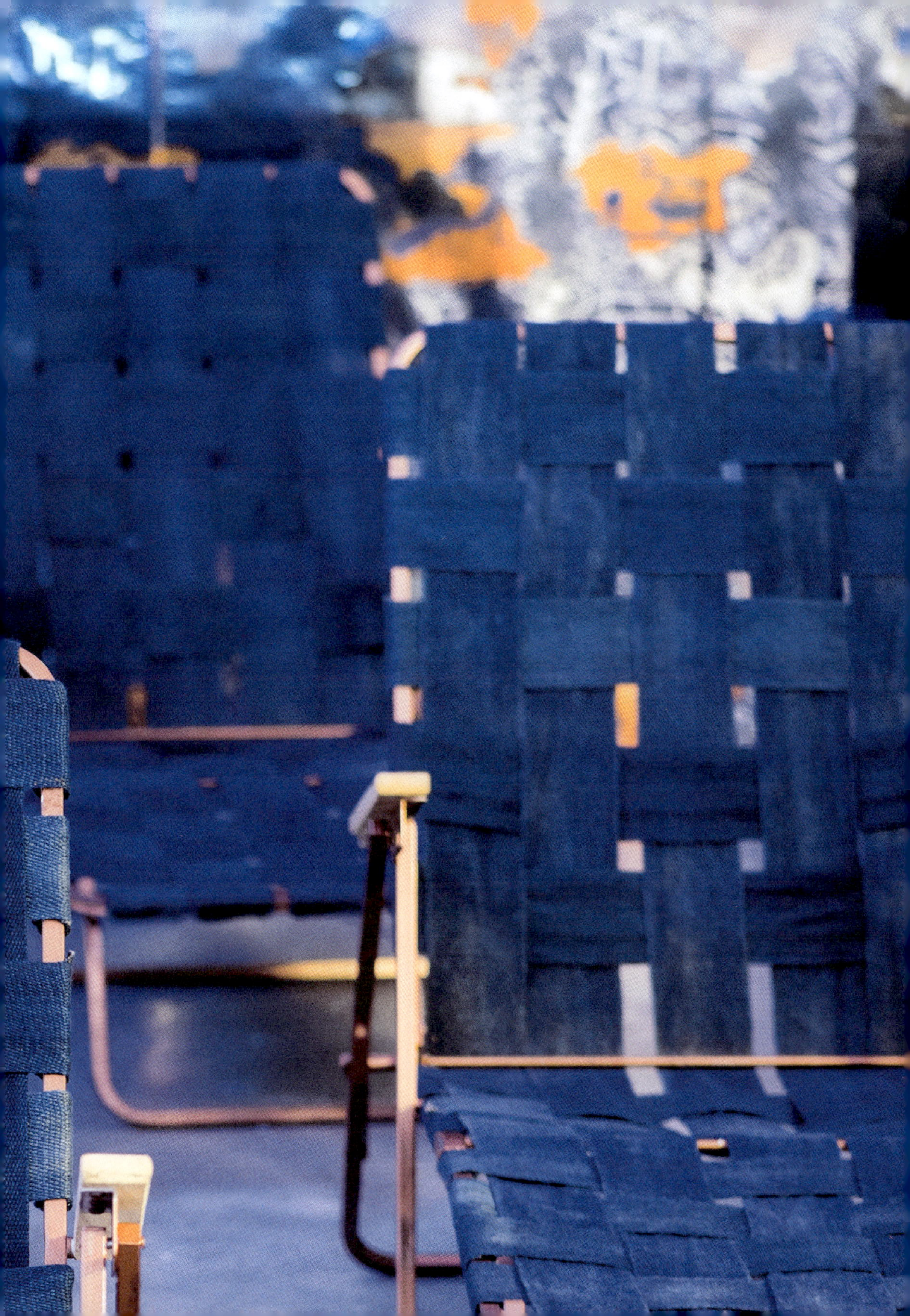

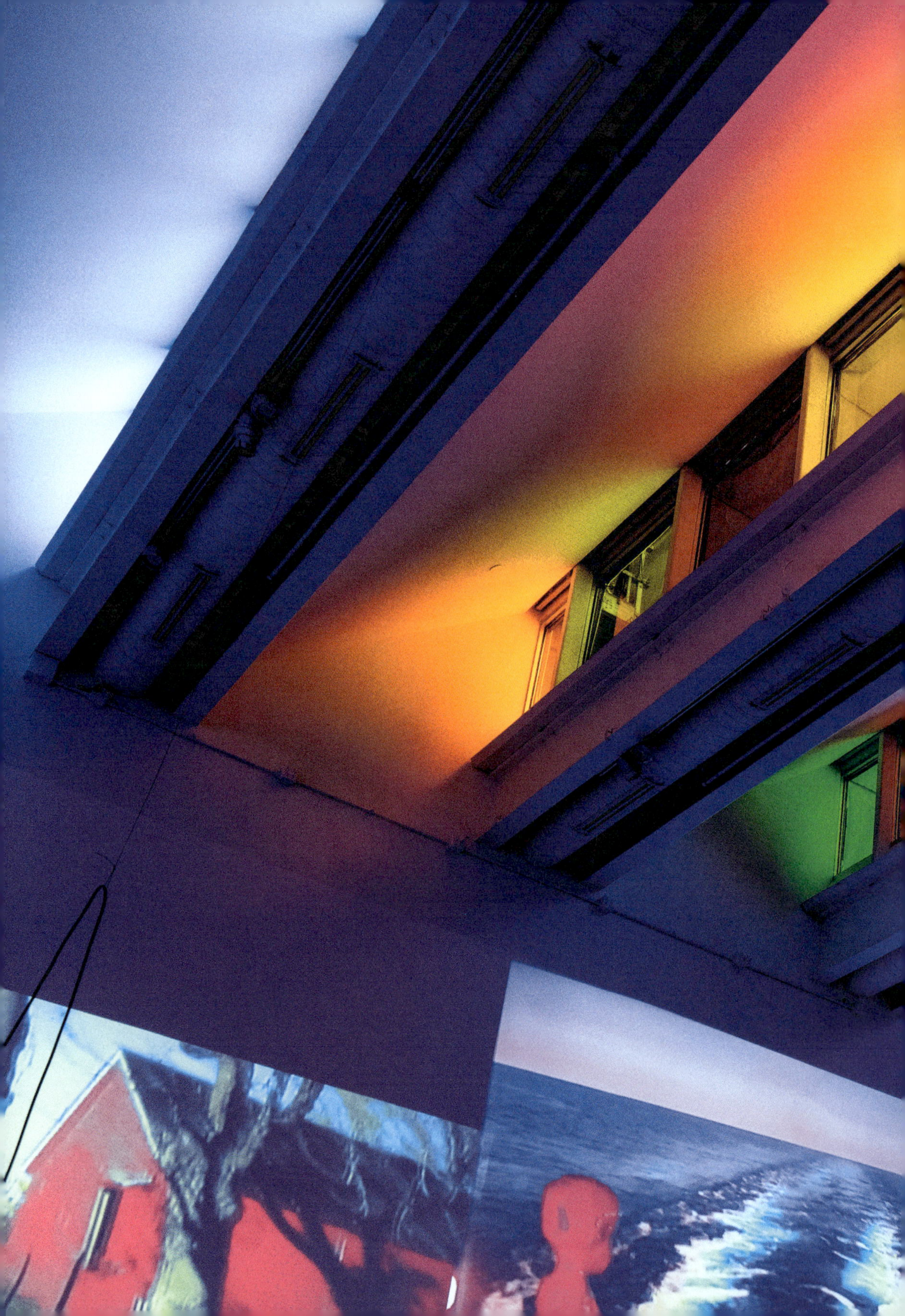

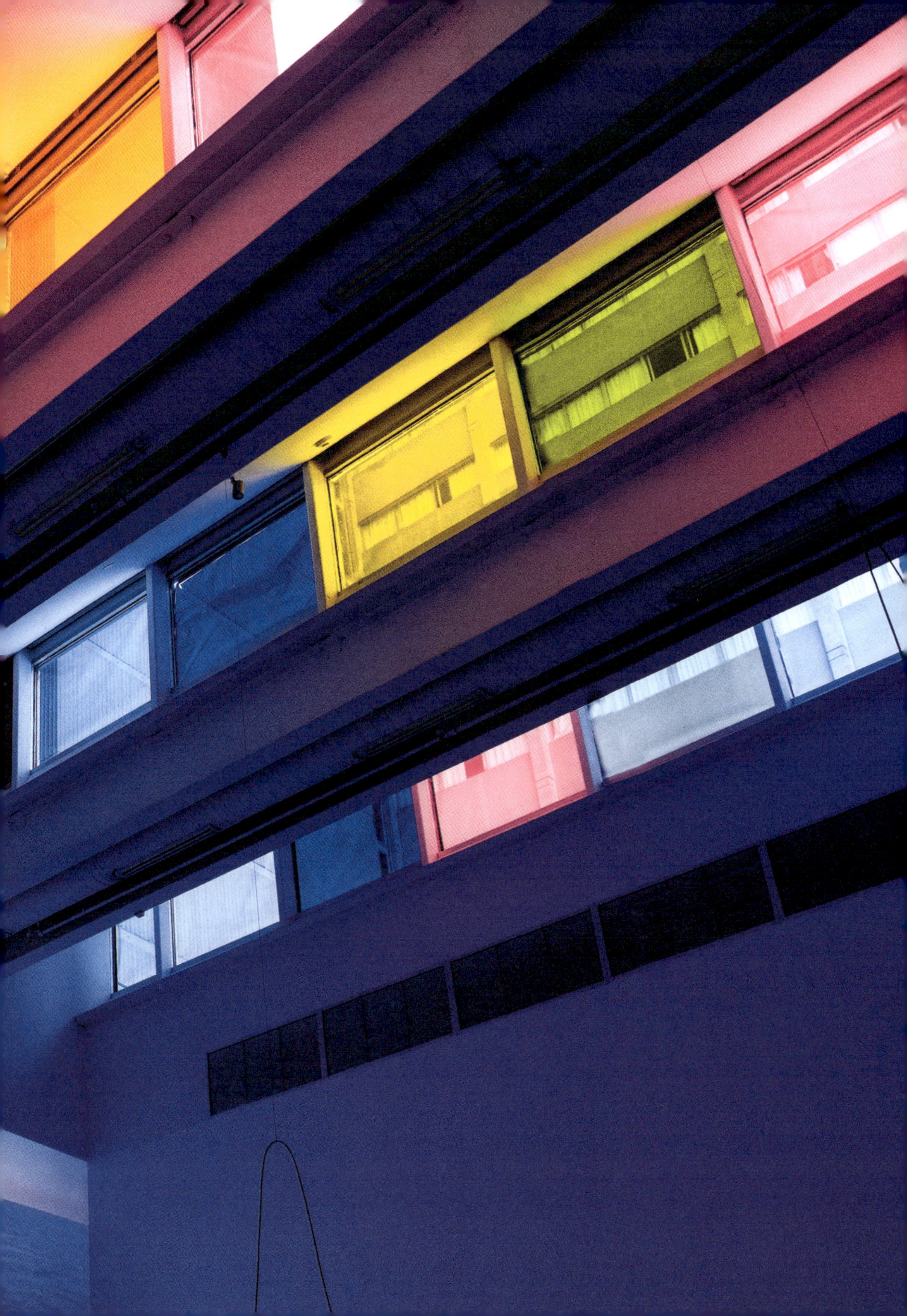

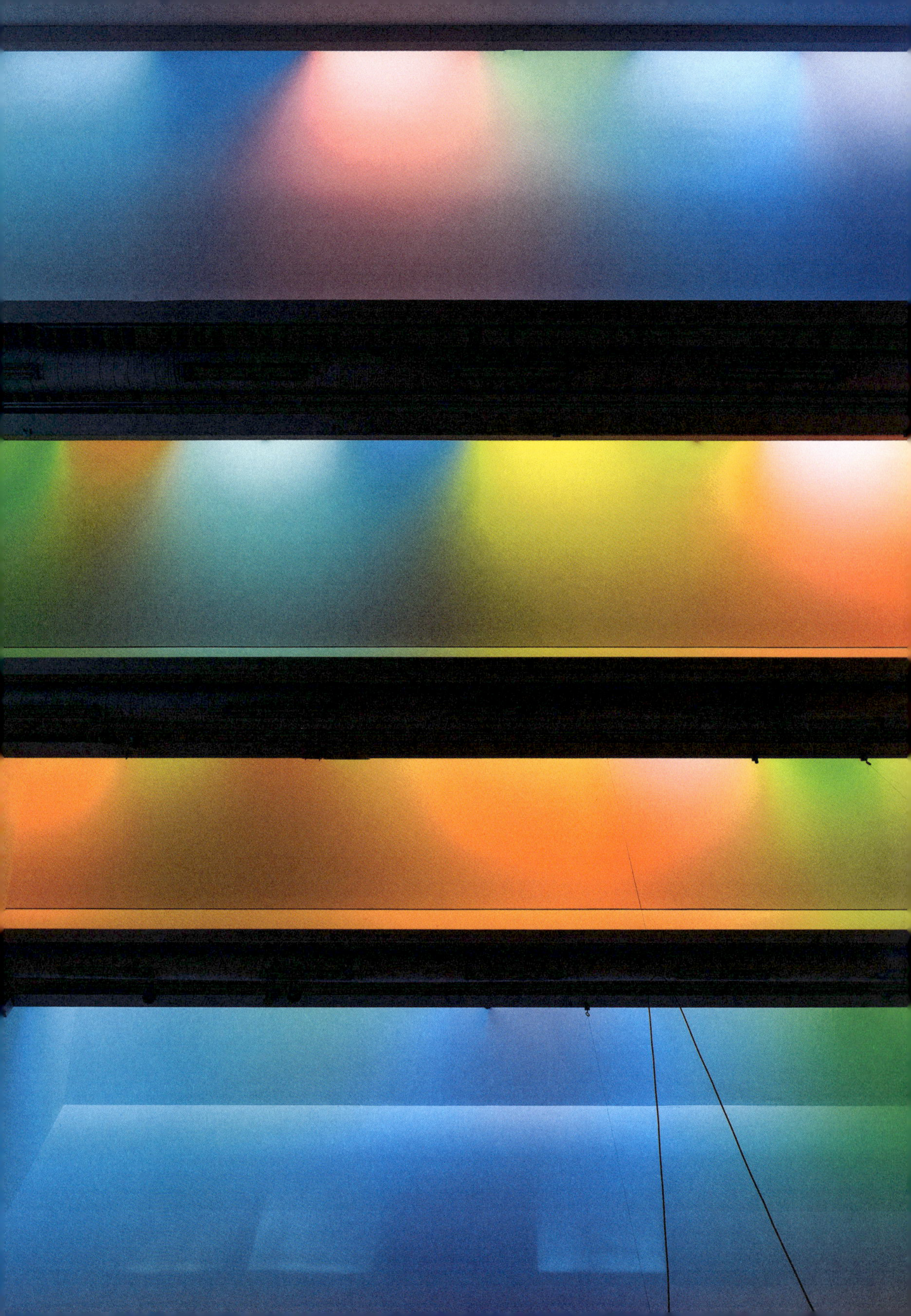

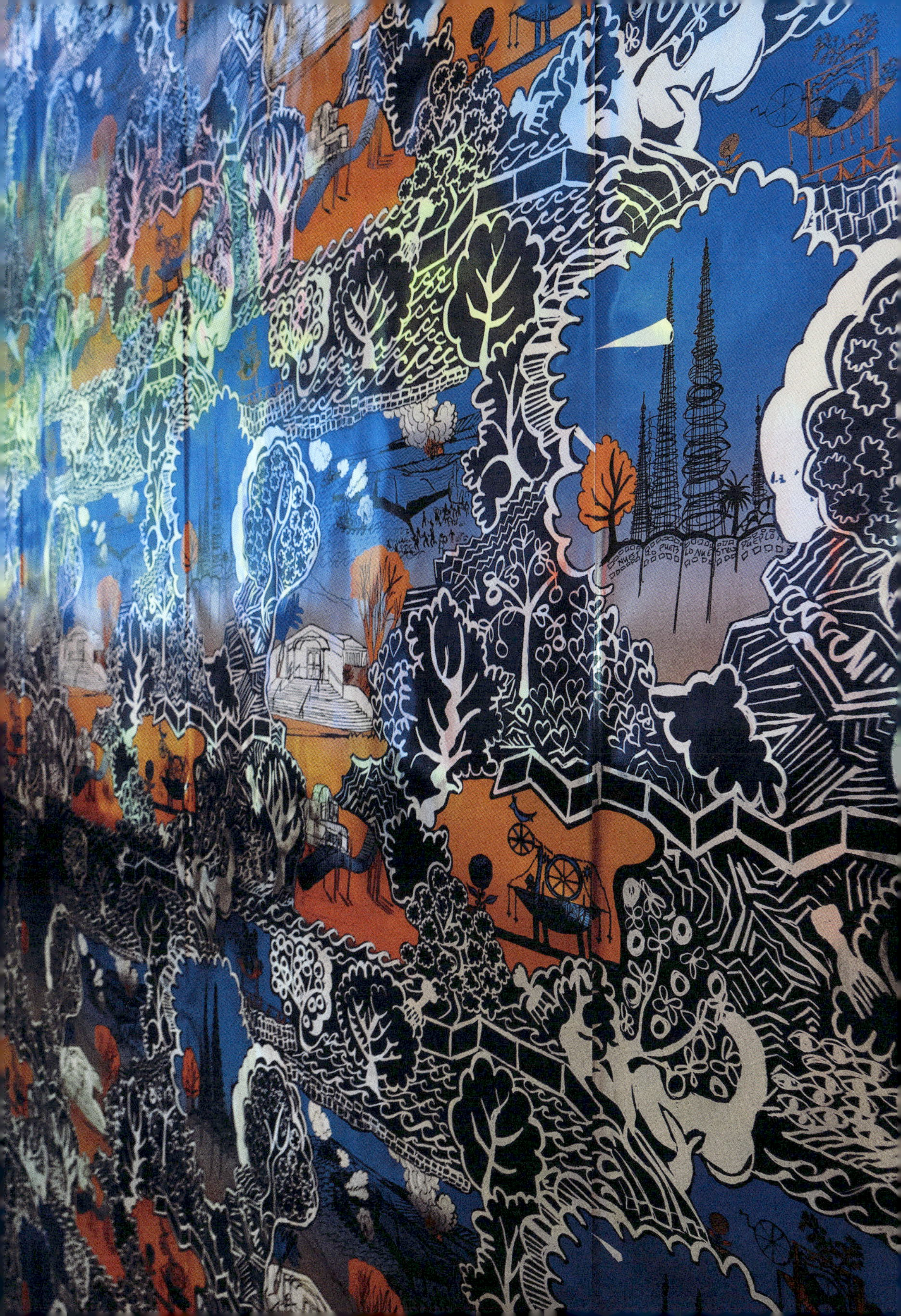

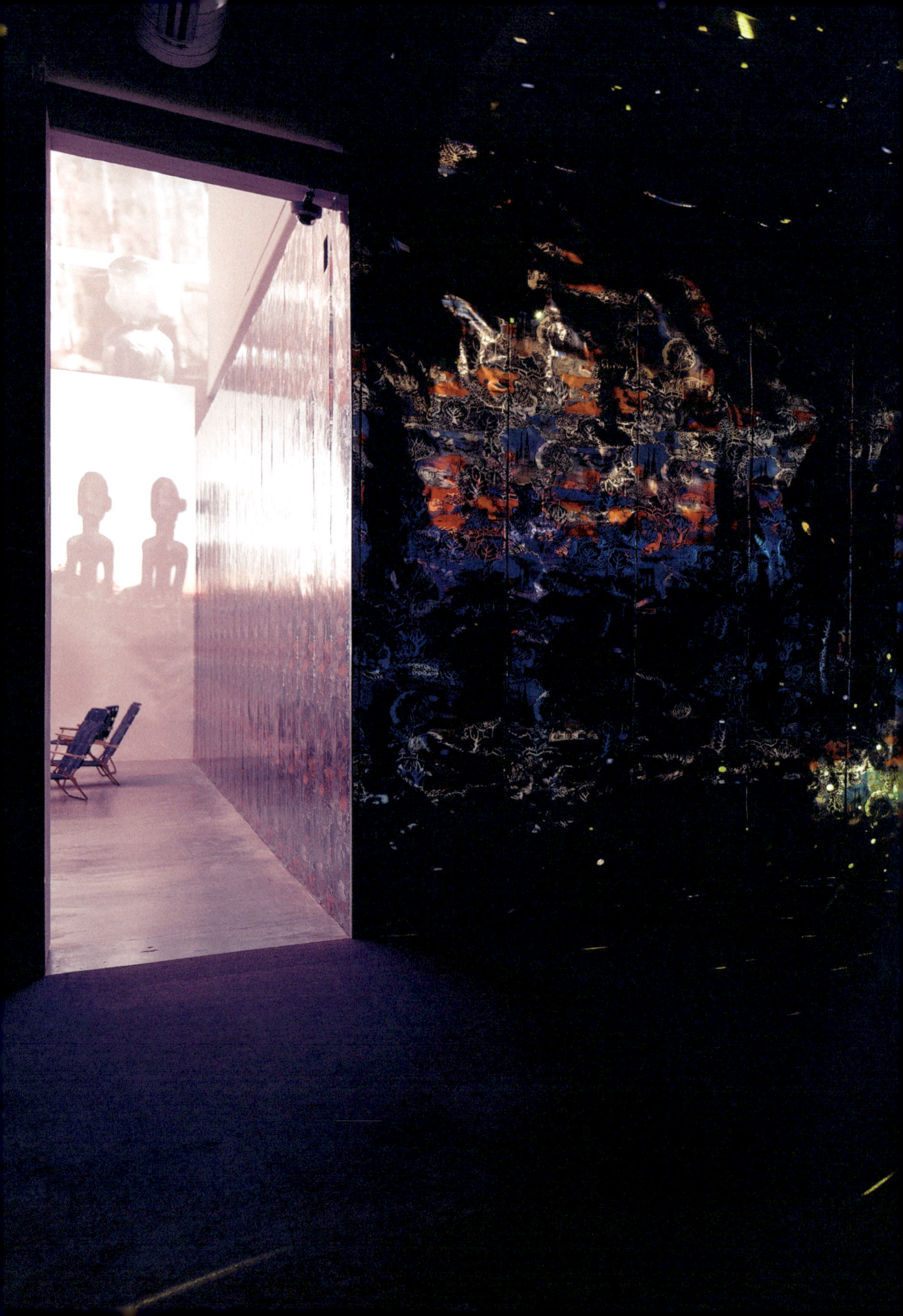

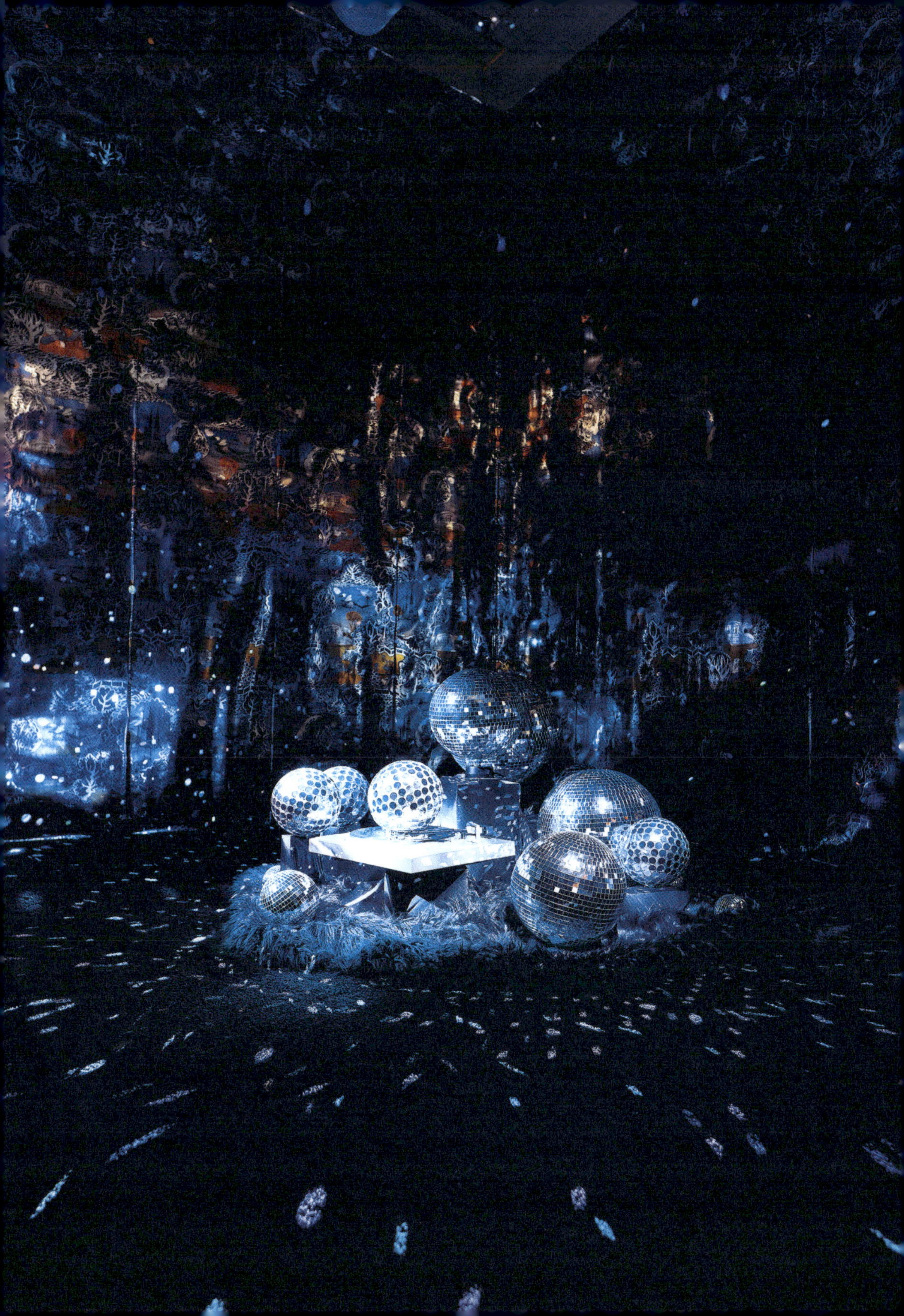

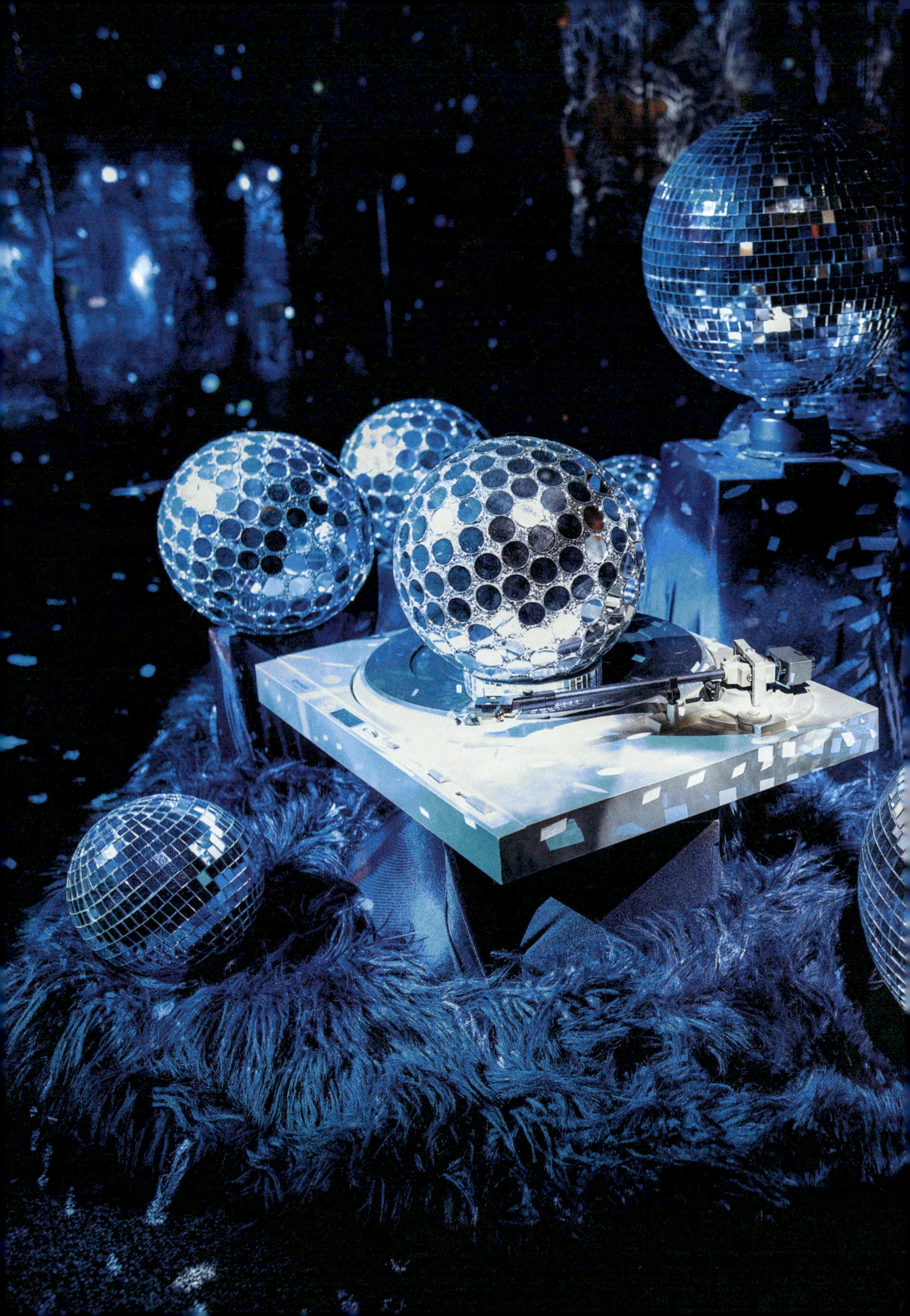

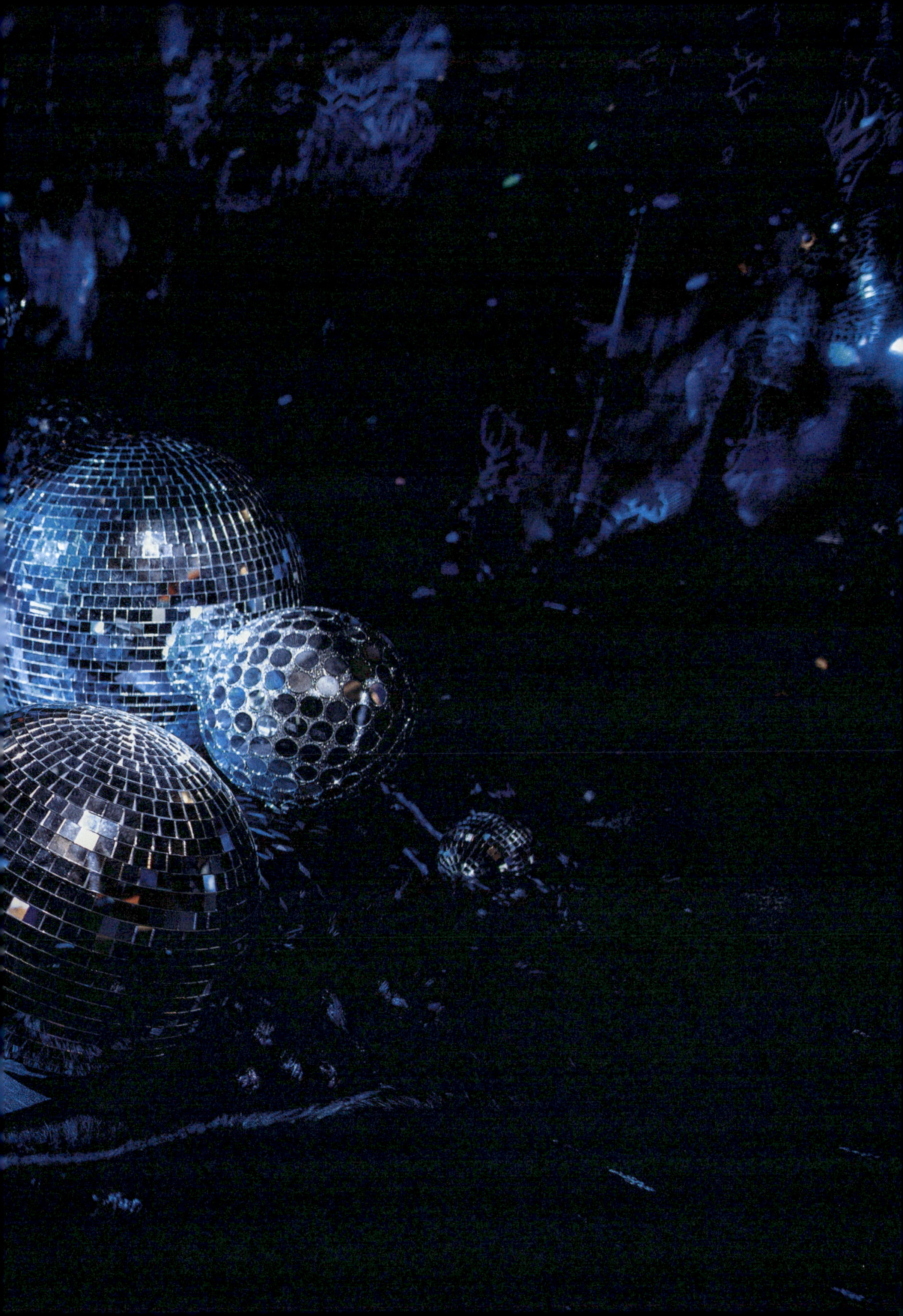

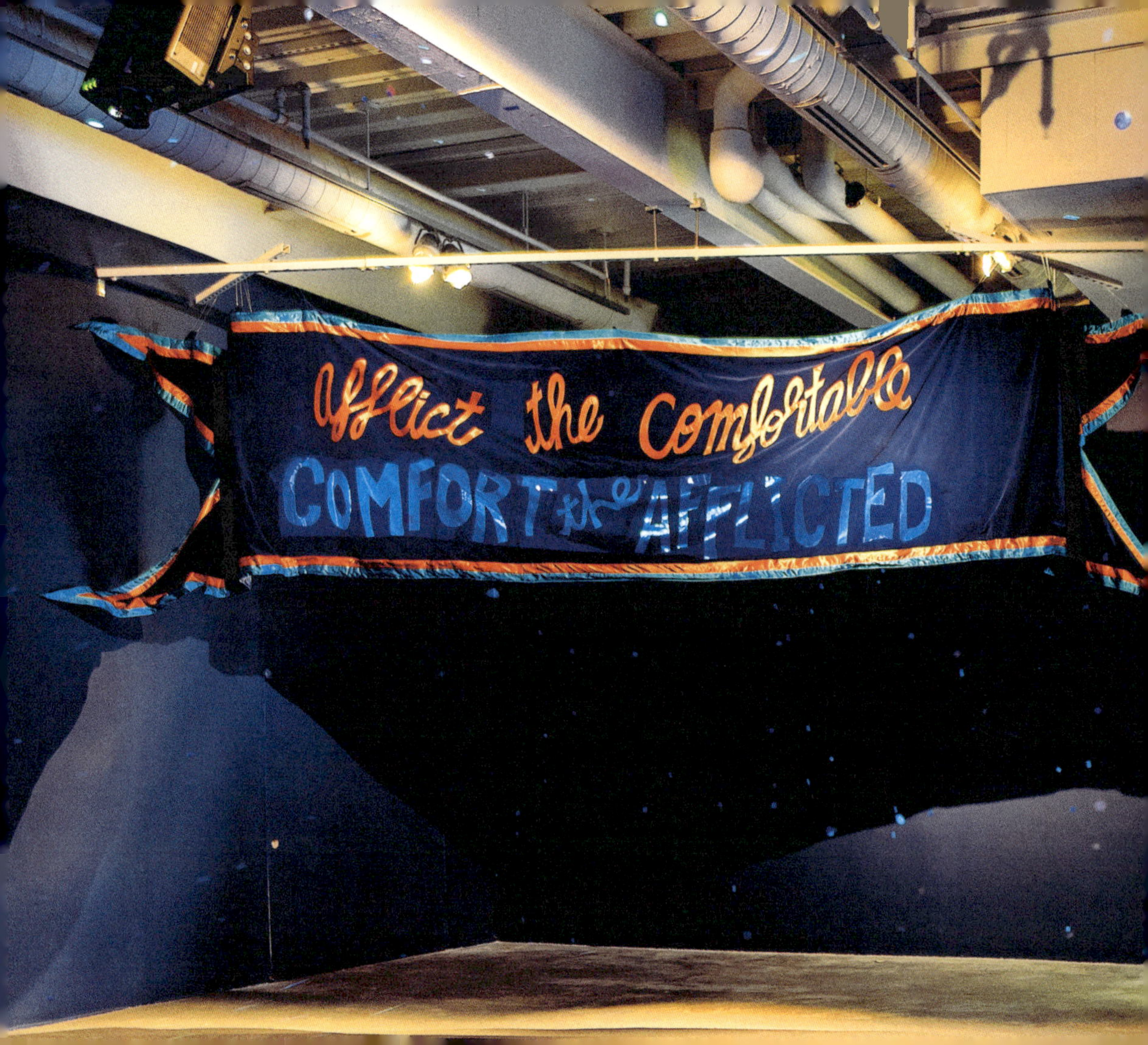

Afflict the Comfortable
COMFORT the AFFLICTED

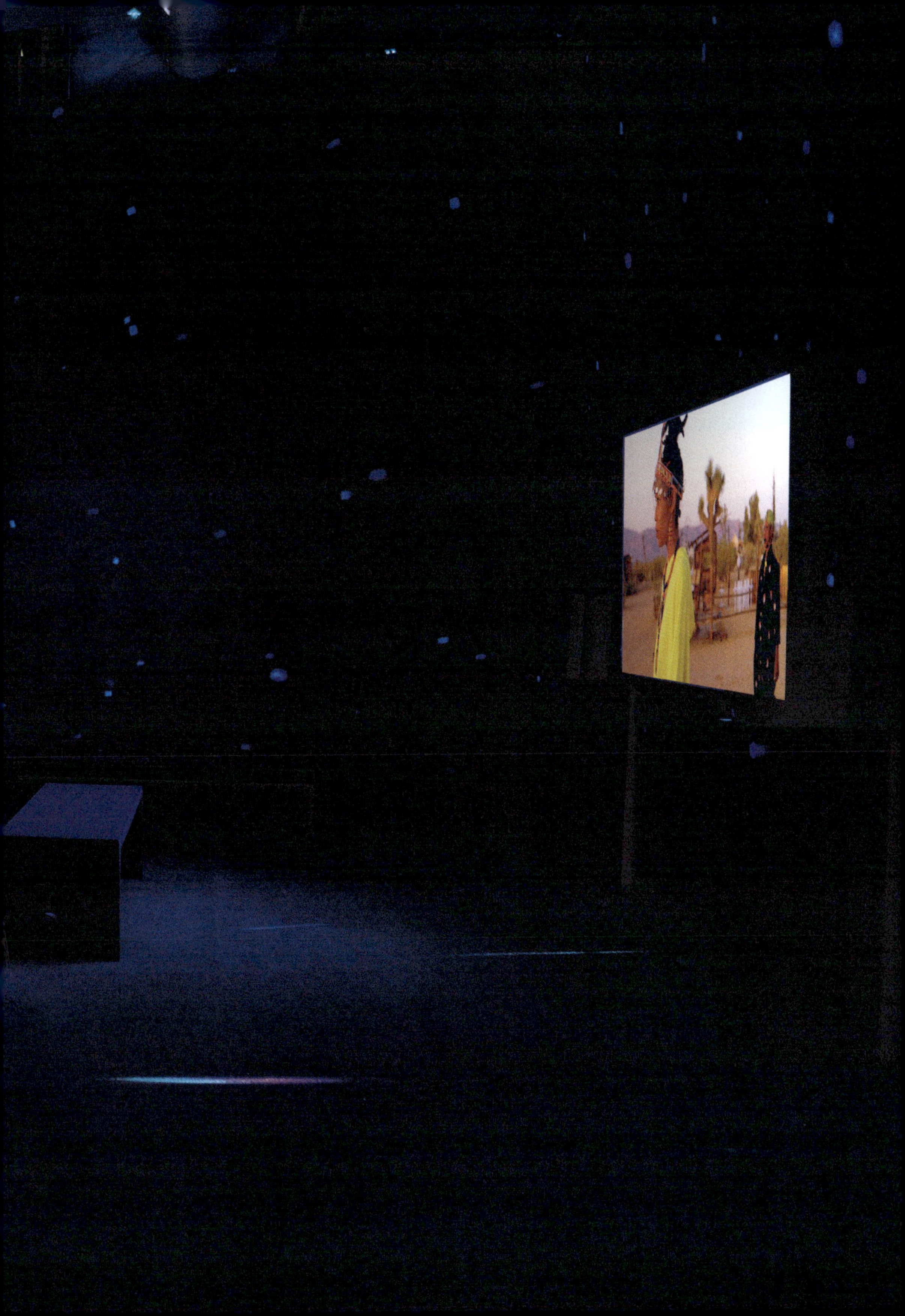

Don't listen to *me*. I'm supposed to be accompanying *you*!

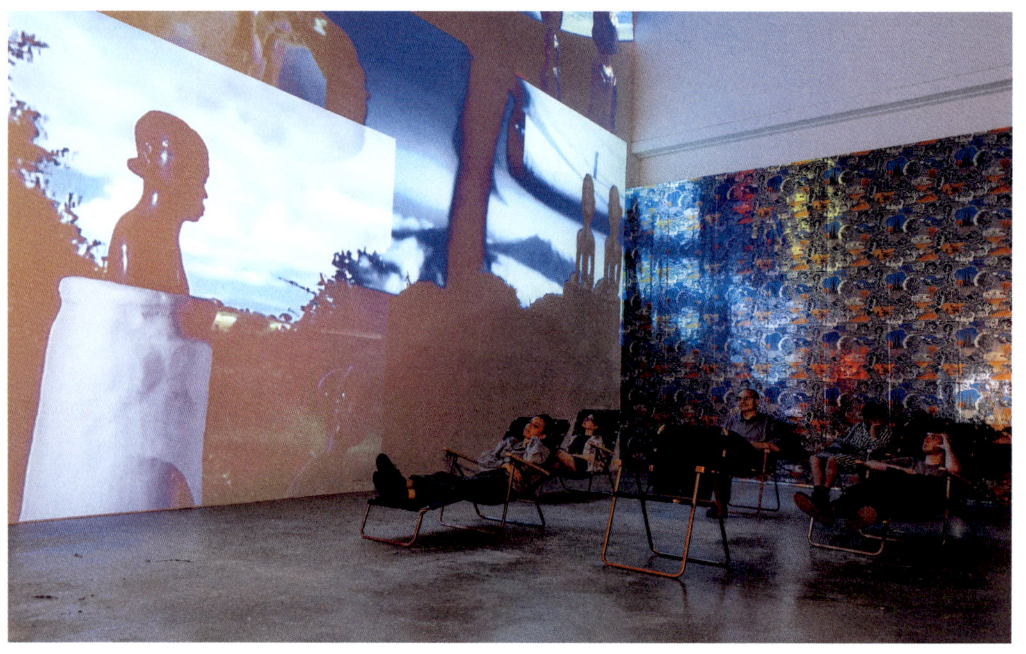

Give It or Leave It
(installation view), 2018

"'Would you rather love or write a love song?' she asked right off. "Play free jazz or be free?" There didn't seem to be much question or much choice. I laughed, hoping she would as well, but she only stared at me, the nothing-ever-was-anyway look now indisputable."[1] This she is not Cauleen Smith; still, the questions remain. How I "love or write a love song," or, "play free jazz or be free," speaks volumes to my attentiveness relative to Smith's films and videos, objects and spaces. The answers appear easy. Yet even if this were the case, I shouldn't. Too male too white too heathen too oblivious. Too implicated in traditions that would rather purchase the free and define a noun than live a verb. And yet I have to.

Pause to note: Cauleen Smith is a filmmaker, unabashedly. In her methods and source materials, Smith can be said to look to the past for present-tense repairs to the future. These repairs manifest as films and videos—yes—but also drawings and banners and processions and manifestos and reading lists and intermedia assemblages and transformed spaces. Her desire to repair leads her to uncover primary sources in libraries, potent places, and fellow travelers. She looks to tune into those who form their own solutions—those who move beyond taking measure of our reality to gift us with unknown worlds unto this world. Composer/keyboardist/intellectual Sun Ra, poet Gwendolyn Brooks, activist Harriet Tubman, ersatz sculptor Simon Rodia, spiritualist Rebecca Cox Jackson, Shaker Godhead Mother Ann Lee, composer/keyboardist/Godhead Alice Coltrane Turiyasangitananda, sculptor Noah Purifoy, the activist Combahee River Collective, sculptor Paul Thek, music organization the Association for the Advancement of Creative Musicians—this list grows unabated. Sometimes the artistic results of Smith's attention toward these traditions, in form and content, become as simple as slowing time and embracing the spectrum of the world's visual and aural rhythms.

Before worrying about individual works here, or which facts or histories are most pertinent to *Give It or Leave It*, it's valuable to

1. Nathaniel Mackey, *Late Arcade* (New York: New Directions, 2017), 56-7. Essay title taken from a list of advice by composer Thelonious Monk, copied down in a notebook by saxophonist Steve Lacy. Accessed: <http://www.openculture.com/2017/12/thelonious-monks-25-tips-for-musicians-1960.html>.

simply spend time—to start at the middle of the exhibition and in the middle encountering. From a lawn chair, seated at slight recline under the multicolored gel skylights of *Sky Learns Sky*, amidst the tabletop social landscape and CCTV projection of *Epistrophe*, facing a series of three flower arranging videos. Drift or float or project. Blending aural cues calm the quicker-paced visual stimulation. The laid-bare nature of production is made visible, edges apparent, edits distinct, coiled cables and power strips fed, sandbags and camera stands steady, monitors and sculptures front and set. It doesn't take more than six minutes to get a feel for the ebbing-flowing tide of the observable mingling rhythms. Stay longer—much longer—and here's a gilding in and gliding out of feeling, location, discovery, and detailing. Peaceful in movement—to the right, liquid rippling and brittle crackling, then above, atmosphere manifesting among an airy rustle and assembled crows cawing. Tone proliferates. From another room muffled audience clapping. From farther on broadcast voices are teaching, declaiming, declaring. Overlapping from another direction, the lyrically curling piano pushes forward. Interrupting at another angle the obdurately clustering organ. Agile windy tinkling permeates from nearly every curve. Speculative didgeridoo waves apace. Attentiveness stills you in growing awareness of even more distant spaces than this blending landscape can directly impart.

> Monday evening, February 18, 1850. I was instructed concerning the atmosphere and its bounds. I saw it in its form—it is like the sea, which has her bounds—"Thus far shalt thou come, and no further." It covered land and sea, so far above all moving things and yet so far beneath the starry heavens. Its face is like the face of the sea, smooth and gentle when undisturbed by the wind. So is the atmosphere, when undisturbed by the power of the sun and moon. When agitated by these, it rages like the sea and sends forth its storms upon the earth. Nothing can live above it. A bird could no more live or fly above its face, than a fish can live or swim out of water.[2]

This distant experience is remarkably similar to that of the lawn chair's slight recline. So the questions: Who halts and also guides? Higher power? Equal partner? Within *Give It or Leave It*, you are a point within patterns of musical and geographical and historical and spiritual and physical caress. Each from elsewhere, even as it offers up seemingly intimate glimpses of new expanses. Maybe I am obliquely delaying direct discussion of Smith's efforts. Indeed. To

2. Rebecca Cox Jackson, in Jean McMahon Humez, ed., *Gifts of Power: The Writings of Rebecca Jackson, Black Visionary, Shaker Eldress* (Amherst: University of Massachusetts Press, 1987), p. 220.

understand *Give It or Leave It*, or even much of Smith's past efforts, it is important to acclimate and attend, even, for a time, to be a good ride in prismatic splendor.

In delay is space—space for qualities and states rather than quantities. Every little thing rather alive. These intervals as you grow to accept them set everything in mixture: sound, sculpture, video, wallpaper, projection. A tuning fork chimes from the corner and breathing becomes a way to quickening orchestration. Cauleen's expanded sense of cinema—films made for a broad landscape and setting, not for the standard architecture of theaters—builds similarly to artist/filmmaker Elaine Summers's definition of intermedia, as, "when you enter the image and get wrapped up in it."[3] Smith's intermedia assemblage is incessantly visual, no matter how she might appeal to musical or literary or geographical models, as one is foremost placed amidst her images. Her structures are groundwork for getting wrapped up in haunting and vulnerability and tactility and chromaticism and—.

> *An Aspect of Love, Alive in the Ice and Fire*
> LaBohem Brown
>
> It is the morning of our love.
>
> In a package of minutes there is this We.
> How beautiful.
> Merry foreigners in our morning,
> we laugh, we touch each other,
> are responsible props and posts.
>
> A physical light is in the room.
>
> Because the world is at the window
> we cannot wonder very long.[4]

It's all there: here. Let's not wonder. To declaratively list the positional pivots embedded in *Give It or Leave It*: Alice Coltrane Turiyasangitananda's Vedantic center, the Sai Anantam Ashram; a 1966 photo shoot by photojournalist Bill Ray at Simon Rodia's Watts Towers; Noah Purifoy's desert assemblages; Rebecca Cox Jackson's visions and her primarily African American Philadelphia Shaker community; and finally, the politics of the black feminist Combahee River Collective.

Each broadcast along CCTV cameras and Triton monitors; all projection video and astral, along the Earth's rotation, a social gathering. *Italicize attentions to this.*

This is not only *Epistrophe* unfolding to a landscape responsible for props and posts to histories of black creativity, spiritual generosity,

3. This definition was quoted in the wall text for the 2018-19 exhibition *Judson Dance Theater: The Work Is Never Done* at the Museum of Modern Art, New York.

4. Gwendolyn Brooks, *Riot* (Detroit: Broadside Press, 1969), p. 21–22.

and communal building in this package of minutes. It is time to think with the striking women who hoist banners for spirit throughout Smith's latest film, *Sojourner*. More so even, the languid nearly visible presence of *Sky Learns Sky*, which rotates in polychromed packages of minutes trying to teach us, we, how beautiful. Can we get to the world at our window with wonder? Yes, by navigating Smith's work as a subjectivity within subjectivities—as Smith guides us through what it is and how it is to be a receiver of spirits broadcasting from above heads and behind hearts and between eras in feeling. The signs, rules, and methods are not always apparent. Think how the handheld transistor radio plays a prominent part on both the tabletop of *Epistrophe* and in the narrative flow of *Sojourner*. Turning the dial on a transistor radio to catch a signal is an experience equal parts frustration and magic. Is the signal strong enough? Is it wracked by interferences and other signals? Is it there? Did you catch it?

> Spiritual Perception. When looking through the spiritual eye, or the third eye encased within the human mind, one can see vividly beyond the ken of human eyesight, beyond the material atom, and into the future, thereby transcending the limitations of time and space.[5]

The many-colored searching geometries by Smith change to sharpen soul and drift attention and soften mind past the leaden anchor of footnoted history lessons. Looking with all sounds and sights and locations and words projecting and broadcasting between the rooms of Smith's exhibition, with more than eyesight, as an opulent training in receiving. As in getting a message.

Smith often asks how we respond to personal crisis at a social scale, in moments when any number of these personal and social crises might overwhelm. Much as the Shaker community was lost following the death of Mother Ann Lee. Or when spirits overwhelmed Alice Coltrane as the 1960s turned over into the '70s. More on point, Noah Purifoy in the debris filled streets of post-rebellion Watts.

> In the face of racial turmoil that leaves one hurt and hopeless and not knowing what to do, what if something is always done—even if not in direct or clear response—what if something always happens? The comeback, or response, to racial injustice is not predicated on its image-worthiness or whether it is caught on camera.[6]

5. Alice Coltrane-Turiyasangitananda, *Monument Eternal* (Los Angeles: The Vedantic Book Press, 1977), p. 27.

6. Romi Crawford, *Racism and Gestural Disobedience* (Chicago, The Green Lantern Press, 2018), p. 13.

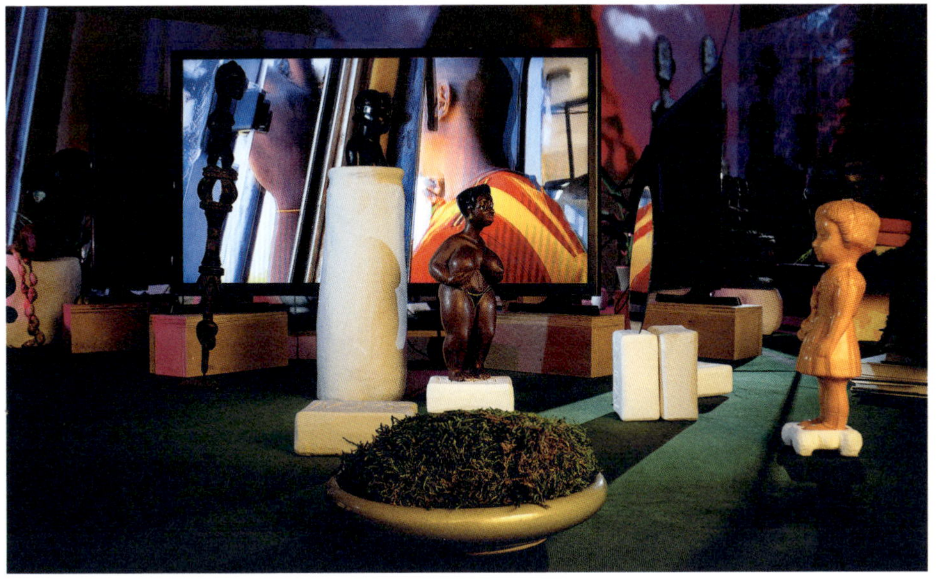

Epistrophe (detail), 2018
Multichannel video (color, sound), four CCTV cameras, four
monitors, projection, custom wood table, taxidermy raven, wood
figures, bronze figures, plastic figures, books, seashells, minerals,
jar of starfish, Magic 8-Ball, maneki-neko, mirror, metal trays,
plaster objects, wood objects, wire object, fabric, glass vase, plants

Later we'll return to Romi Crawford's point. For now, another
series of questions: What is image-worthy, what is not easily caught
on camera, and what appears here an image of worth for Smith?
Gifting. Devotion. Guidance. Blackness. Feminism. Rather than
precisely submitting either herself or us to their demands, she
models them: books stage; a taxidermized raven—Blaer—cares to
a wounded African figure; banners direct the viewer to appreciate
and afflict and comfort. The moving images of *Pilgrim*, *Epistrophe*,
and *Sojourner*—above all else—record the often-elusive gestures
and reflective gifts unfolding in the swirl, whiz, whoosh, float,
submerge speed of an everyday blackness in which *something always
happens.*

Cauleen Smith's entire exhibition moves along a similar-seek-
ing path to Crawford's *something always done—even if not in direct
or clear response.* Smith's never alone in this, which is precisely why
she reads, visits, invites, observes, and begs questions of dazzling
everydayness and barely visible histories. It is why a patterned metallic wallpaper landscape refracts traces of our world within drawn
homages. Mirrored.

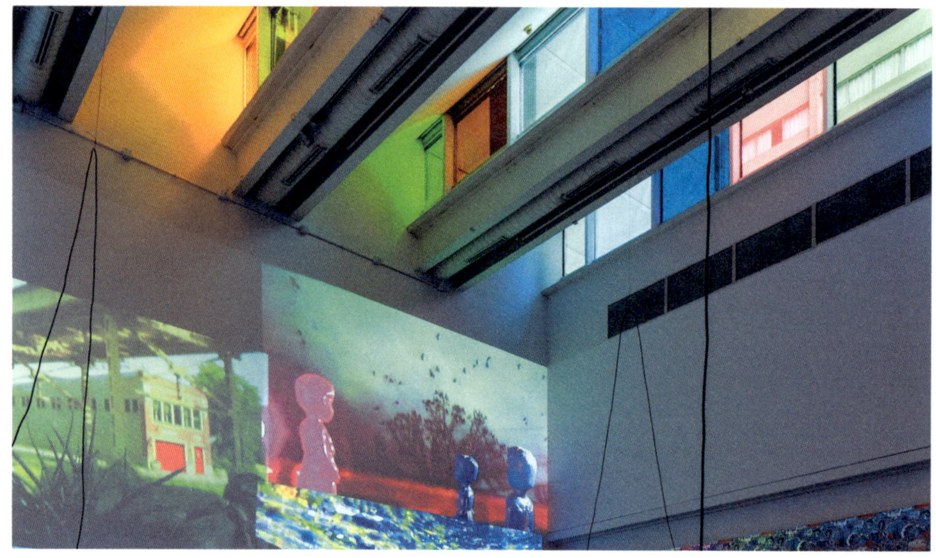

***Sky Learns Sky*, 2018**
Lee Filters film gels, architecture,
eight lawn chairs, and sunlight.
Dimensions variable

We realize that the only people who care enough about us
to work consistently for our liberation are us. Our politics
evolve from a healthy love for ourselves, our sisters and
our community which allows us to continue our struggle
and work.[7]

Epistrophe's four CCTV projections expand across and up the wall,
reaching for largeness of sky not in name of spectacle but in need
to recalibrate a personal feel for scale and scope. Cinematic Lee gel
filters in windows bring in the tricked-out sun, hued to artificial
rhythms of dawn, noon, evening, and midnight—turning every day
into an ongoing film shoot. Doesn't spirit always speak in light? Yes.
Under *Sky Learns Sky*, amidst *Epistrophe*, faced with the peripheral
interjection and minor floral arranging movements of *Black and
Blue Over You (After Bas Jan Ader)*, *Strelitzia Satellite Meditation*,
and *Cotton Plant 187?*, is to be generously intermixed and alive, in
service of making spaces unabashedly black, feminist, and spiritual.
We, how beautiful, asked to turn to spirits of blackness and tune to
visible traces of health and sickness in response. Plants and flowers
here are not all that need arrangement and pragmatic care.

7. The Combahee River Collective,
"The Combahee River Collective
Statement" (1978). Accessed: http://
circuitous.org/scraps/combahee.html.

Time still unfolds in slight lawn chair recline; nouns are still held less rigidly to guard against archival reburial. Consider two potential theoretical contexts for engaging *Give It or Leave It,* neither precisely attuned to Smith's questions, yet each still a guide toward how we might love or write love songs in public: be free or play free. Then replace *or* with *and.* First:

> The emergence of sound in the arts and the specific curatorial problems it generates, forced artists and curators to look for other types of spaces, inside or outside the white cube as defined by [art critic Brian] O'Doherty. This is certainly true, but even if one includes those other types of spaces (such as the black box) in a reflection on the types of sound that are presented and represented in these spaces, one will discover an unmistakable bias, which allows us to say that most alternative spaces are still predominantly 'white cubes', and that even the black box paradoxically remains a 'white cube'.... The chances are high that the 'white cube'—cube or not, white or not— *sounds* white.[8]

Next, the following, by anthropologist Eduardo Viveiros de Castro:

> Our current idea of "culture" projects an anthropological landscape peopled by marble statues, not ones made of myrtle: a classical museum rather than a baroque garden. We think that every society tends to persevere in its own being, and that culture is the reflexive form of that being; we believe that a violent, massive pressure is needed for it to deform and transform. But, above all, we believe that the being of a society is its perseverance: memory and tradition are the identitarian marble out of which culture is made. Moreover, we judge that, once they have been converted into something other than themselves, societies that have lost their tradition have no way back....
>
> But perhaps, for societies whose foundation (or lack thereof) is the relationship to others, and not self-identity, none of this makes the least sense.[9]

Intervals to attend wisely. The above statements can be further interlaced to enunciate the question writer Franya Berkman asked in understanding Alice Coltrane's music:

8. Dieter Lesage and Ina Wudtke, *Black Sound White Cube* (Vienna: Löcker, 2010), p. 17–18.

9. Eduardo Viveiros de Castro, *The Inconstancy of the Indian Soul: The Encounter of Catholics and Cannibals in 16th-Century Brazil* (Chicago: Prickly Paradigm Press, 2011), p. 17.

11. Susan Howe, *That This* (New York: New Directions, 2010), p. 28.

10. Franya J. Berkman, *Monument Eternal: The Music of Alice Coltrane* (Middletown: Wesleyan University Press, 2010). p. 3.

> How do we make sense of these songs? They are at once African American and South Asian. Their histories can be traced to religious revivals spanning India's medieval period, as well to cultural formations that coalesced in the New World among the descendants of African slaves. They form a genre attributable to an individual composer, yet they are also a ritual that belongs to the whole community. Appreciating and understanding Alice Coltrane's sacred music at the ashram—and, for that matter, the other music that she recorded and performed over the course of her prolific career—requires that we move beyond reified categories of musical style and religious practice and honor the open-ended quality of cultural production and the ways we pass on the life of cultures.[10]

While these above passages churn, let's regroup along a detail. Cauleen largely edited the footage of *Pilgrim* not to the melody of Coltrane's composition, "One for the Father," which provides the soundtrack, as would be customary. Instead, she listened for the moments when Coltrane appeared to take her fingers away from the piano. The breathing absences that propel rhapsodic melodic furl. A gallery away from *Pilgrim*, while seated in a jute lawn chair, the rhythmic sway-swell sound of Coltrane's piano interweaves into *Epistrophe* and faintly, perhaps, into *Sojourner*. Intrusion can be reaching, rolling, rotating; one can feel it calling forth in decrescendos and overlaps and silences never silent. Rhythm's breathy curling. What might a pause contribute to Smith's case? Rebecca Cox Jackson, 1795–1871 (hard pause). With overlaps, Simon Rodia, 1902-65 (pause); Noah Purifoy, 1917-2004 (pause); Alice Coltrane, 1937-2007 (pause); Combahee River Collective 1974-80 (pause).

> When we listen to music we're also listening to pauses called 'rests.' 'Rests' could be wishes that haven't yet betrayed themselves and can only be transferred evocatively.[11]

Coltrane and her music loom largest throughout *Give It or Leave It*, in part because the volume and presence of the music in Smith's films *Pilgrim* and *Sojourner*, alongside the possibility that Coltrane now *belongs to the whole community* to *honor the open-ended quality of cultural production and the ways we pass on the life of cultures*. And here, in rest, emerges a way of acknowledging: I don't know what tomorrow looks like and still I know the measure of today just isn't enough to live a culture for we, how beautiful. Pauses allow us to recognize periodic cycles of pattern, and to stake sounding claims in a baroque garden of blackness, including one clearly stated by a preliminary banner at opening of the exhibition, an appreciation of *our* effort's potential: I appreciate you in advance.

Traces and histories and people, though ephemeral, always possess locations that can be filmed, even if that location must be enacted through removals and erasures and cover-ups. Research helps guide Smith where to travel, whom to talk to, and most importantly, where to point the camera. She is well aware of misogyny, and the militaristic and colonial metaphors and structures by which film is traditionally made. Scouting locations. In the field. Shooting. Capturing. Etcetera. Smith wants this undone. Crews and actors as collaborators, process as improvisational responses, structures as questions asked in tandem to find still other questions to share in answering—filmmaking with the strength of a baroque garden of myrtle. Filmmaker as traveler in disregard of marble towers. *Give It or Leave It* unfolds with a beginning and a middle and an end: black men hanging in Watts (1966) moves on to tone-poem pastoral mourning at the Sai Anantam Ashram (2016), then to Chicago activism (2017) and finally to the searching-call sunset of Joshua Tree desert (2018). Setting out as *Pilgrim*, through the swirling variating repetition of *Epistrophe* to gain the strong feminist heart of *Sojourner*. Films that keep opening rather than confirm any one thought-line for blackness and feminism.

In these films, formally sustained extended views all happen close at hand—the gentle pace and frozen calm of an ashram, the stoic architectural distance and cultivated prissy garden of a Shaker village, an organ entombed, a desert sun setting, a vibrant neighborhood, and gathering women. These longer views are periodically interrupted by flashes, or ghostly manifestations—sun shaking the Watts towers spires, cultivated flowers double exposed, adorned humble Arkestra house, playful urban horses, the dilapidated disregard of John Coltrane's Philadelphia residence, a brick wall marking the total physical absence of Rebecca Cox Jackson in her town of gathering. This unfolding and in-shards ghostly visual register is a world in collectively felt discovery and impression and response.

> We are sentimental because we have a sense of time,
> [Anna] Quindlen says, we have a sense of time because
> we can only take in so much of the world, we attend and
> withdraw, attend and withdraw, and that withdrawing
> is the tick we hear, the shutter clicking—time consists of
> our recurrent shutting and knowing that we shut, re-
> gretting what we miss and remembering in images—rank
> sentimentality![12]

12. Lyn Hejinian, *Saga/Circus* (Oakland: Omnidawn, 2008), p. 23.

Give It or Leave It will travel and transform—the exhibition is not site-specific. Individual artifacts placed in *Epistrophe* can be recognized from Smith's past CCTV assemblages, so can an interest in crows, reading, and the rhythms of our planet. Just as banners, disco balls, Alice Coltrane, wallpaper, Sun Ra, and a heavy social heart coupled with the buoyancy of personal spirit can also be recognized from previous spaces, processions, drawings, and films. This said, *Give It or Leave It* was structured by Smith as three places tuned between the melody of her films and the sustained harmonic of ICA's second floor galleries in Philadelphia. *Epistrophe* literally occupied the center at ICA as pivot between the gentle invitation of *Pilgrim* and the slivered arrival of *Sojourner*. When the Shaker community was in crisis, several sister members responded to spiritual manifestations by recording their experiences in "gift drawings." Many of these drawings feature fantastical "heavenly musical instruments" meant to be played only by celestial means to soothe and call the chosen. Consider the way the broadcast visions of *Epistrophe* might be present-day gift drawings responding to present-day crises. The tabletop monitors with landscapes recorded by Cauleen's phone, or NASA and *National Geographic* camera feeds might overlap as a heavenly mouthpiece, or an all-transmitting table top. Since 2015, I have been thinking about the space of the table with Matthew Stadler's *The Table & the Network:*

> A table—unlike a store or a television or a political convention or the street as it is configured in most cities— puts us face to face at close proximity (with no variable purchasing power to mask our sameness), so that we cannot pretend we don't see what is happening to those around us. It does so in a setting where we can be certain that whatever we allow will soon enough come around to afflict (or benefit) us, too. A table is the space of egalitarian, human beings together—of human decency.[13]

With Stadler's table in mind, a description better than heavenly music machine for what's amassed on *Epistrophe's* circular table might be Great Black Objects, Ancient to the Future—a cheeky rewrite of the Art Ensemble of Chicago's motto "Great Black Music, Ancient to the Future." And like the sounds and ceremony of the Art Ensemble of Chicago, here devoutness, humor, mourning, joy and individual mastery, irreverences visual and aural, and dedication to *the space of egalitarian, human beings together—of human decency* intermix as elements of a culture of blackness.[14]

13. Matthew Stadler, *The Table & the Network* (Minneapolis: Wooden Leg Print and Press/Publication Studio, 2015). p. 17.

14. For more on an open notion of Black culture, see Hortense Spillers, "The Idea of Black Culture," lecture at the University of Waterloo (2013). Accessed: <http://www.youtube.com/watch?v=P1PTHFCN4Gc>. For more on the Art Ensemble of Chicago, see Paul Steinbeck, *Message to Our Folks: The Art Ensemble of Chicago* (Chicago: University of Chicago Press, 2017).

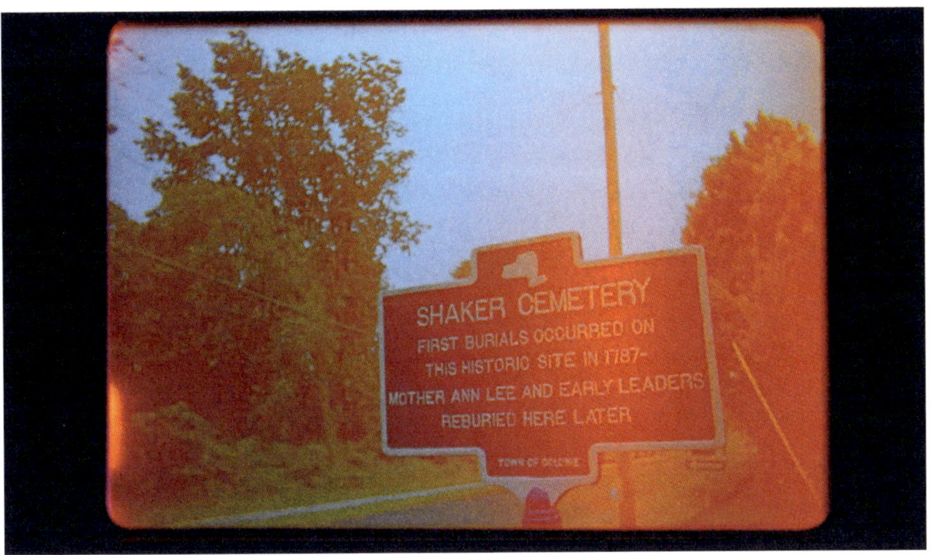

Pilgrim (still), 2017
Digital video and 16mm film,
color, sound, 7:41 minutes

"Great Black Music, Ancient to the Future" physically manifests as extended drifting, pastoral moments, frantic outbursts, and the collective ramifications of individual responses. A key to this balance was the Art Ensemble's decades-long dedication to what they called "little instruments"—including gongs, cymbals, toys, bird calls, sirens, and noisemakers of all shapes and absurdities, from any and all cultures. This approach was developed by bassist Malachi Favors Maghostut, in part to broaden and complicate the sonic, historical, and geographical spectrum for music traditionally associated with or presumed to be the place for African Americans, particularly jazz musicians. It also strikingly affected the visual presence of an Art Ensemble concert.

Similarly, the overlapping soundscapes and collected small-scale sculptures, living plants, and incidental affects populating Smith's CCTV landscapes harken, broaden, and complicate. Just as the Art Ensemble would blend Christian preaching, Buddhist ceremony, African costume, minstrelsy, and heathen pulse, Smith often blends ikebana, Nam June Paik's *TV Buddha* (1974), and other forms of what might mark the black spiritual turn to Eastern religion and traditions during the late 1960s. There are African artifacts and cheap tchotchkes, carved plaster Ivory soap bars, a stacked plaster rainbow, doo-dads, feathers, a two-dollar bill, and the aforementioned taxidermized raven. In this collective culture of relations through an individual connectivity, precedence might likewise be found with the just-so attitude combines, incongruent and stark humor, and the funky seams of artists David Hammons or Betye Saar, for just two examples. Or, closer to home here, Noah Purifoy.

Return to the world at the windows: Black death, class warfare, environmental collapse, siloed divisions, and cynical bureaucracies. In a collective culture of relations, we, how beautiful, need delay quantities and economics, so we can with each step manifest horizons for qualities, feelings, gatherings. This is how I define sentimentality. It is in this way that the assembled Combahee, Cox Jackson, Purifoy, Rodia, Turiyasangitananda, should be tuned to and received.

> The utopian as we know it includes feminist Frances Wright's failed and deeply flawed abolitionist experiment at Nashoba in Tennessee in the 1820s but not one example of any instance of marronage in the entire Americas. Brook Farm and numerous white middle-class separatist communities are part of its known legacy but not the multicultural Combahee River Collective or the many coalitional collectives like them. The utopian as we know it includes Ursula K. Le Guin's off-world anthropology but not Toni Cade Bambara's in-the-here-and-now community studies. The examples can be multiplied.

> After spending a good amount of time in these archives, it became clear that there was an exclusionary zone of tremendous magnitude and that it was precisely in that zone or blind spot where we might find, if we were prepared to or anticipating it, those "fugitive moments of comprehension" that could yield a genealogy of and paradigms for more adequate histories and theories of the many real and imaginary strivings for a livable and human social existence. For in that zone of exclusion, we find a utopian thought and practice which is as transitional as it is local; which is as oriented to the present and the past as it is to the future; which is as comfortable with wild speculation as it is with collective movements; which substitutes complexity for perfection; which privileges diversity over homogeneity; which treats the self and society as equally important objects of social transformation; and which

offers enriched and inclusive notions of freedom, sovereignty, and happiness. In that zone of exclusion, the utopian is a standpoint for the here and now—not only the future—which registers and incites the works, thoughts, and the better worlds inhabited by those who always, as Raymond Williams puts it, "meanwhile carry on."[15]

Berkman, again, reflecting on the arc of Alice Coltrane's life:

> How many people realize their potential to this extent? How many are able to watch their creative imagination unfold so vividly? How many musicians hear their compositions in the hands of master players, and in the hearts and voices of their students as devotional ritual? How many people invent traditions that outlive them?[16]

Frankly, hardly anyone. Nor do we often deserve the few who do, sadly. We too often sit idle and expect messianic moments to arrive via prescribed Messiahs and recognizable spirits. I'm not here to besmirch Turiyasangitananda or Cox Jackson's spiritual devotions, nor the secular dedication of the Combahee River Collective—true, monumental leaders all. But let's consider devotional ritual and traditions that extend without clear leaders. With everyone a leader, as with the Art Ensemble. With the gift of neighborhood, as in Watts. Consider while transfixed by the spiraling disco-slivered cosmos of *Space Station: Two Rebeccas.* This radiant cosmos at 33 and a 1/3, honoring Rebeccas (Cox Jackson and her confidant Rebecca Perot), mirroring other souls whose solace thrives in celestial dance. To merge, to deemphasize individuality and agree to prolong in glittering orbital gravity against the *nothing-ever-was-anyway.*

We, particularly we closely resembling myself—*too male too white too heathen too oblivious too implicated*—accompanying Cauleen Smith here and now need be more attuned to our proximities and not deny real tasks and pains at hand. We, too, need to start carrying on.

> February 8, 1849. I was brought into deep tribulation of soul about our people, and their present condition, seeing the awful event that is at hand. I cried unto God who hears the ravens cry, to hear my cry in their behalf.[17]

Hearing calls. Asking the ground to be level, truly leveled. Freely giving great gifts and efforts. Let's now look to Romi Crawford's *Racism and Gestural Disobedience,* again.

15. Avery F. Gordon, *The Hawthorne Archive: Letters from the Utopian Margins* (New York: Fordham University Press, 2017), p. vii–viii.

16. Berkman, *Monument Eternal: The Music of Alice Coltrane,* p. 110.

17. Humez, ed., *Gifts of Power: The Writings of Rebecca Jackson, Black Visionary, Shaker Eldress,* p. 213.

18. Crawford, *Racism and Gestural Disobedience*, p. 17.
19. Ibid., 19.

20. Coltrane-Turiyasangitananda, *Monument Eternal*, p. 39.

21. The Combahee River Collective, "The Combahee River Collective Statement." See Note 6.

These, what I will call applied forms of resistance, are deep-seated (more than they are radical looking) in the face of racial oppression. Applied forms alter, even reverse, norms of what makes sense. Even more, they are barometers of creative thinking in the moment of despair and paralysis, when one asks, when we all should ask: What should I do?[18]

The quiet sanctity of a Shaker village or the nondenominational embrace of Turiyasangitananda's Vedantic center, the nonplussed chic of black men having their picture taken in Watts, or the slow weathering of Purifoy's Joshua Tree desert museum might all be described as altering, even reversing, what "makes sense." But you won't necessarily see the pathways of rewrite and rejection.

There are also instances of everyday love and loathing that are signs of fighting against, or of not working with, or of "meeting," an unjust system. Most of the time, these gestures are non-eventful so they don't disclose as disobedience or as protest in the customary sense.[19]

This disobedience hangs around. Rests. Withdraws. Expands in everydayness. Tunes in to feminist love and loathing. Remembers. Radiates blackness. Speculates in compound tenses. Where once there were nine unseething men occupying a questionable present tense crafted by photojournalist Billy Ray for the *LIFE* magazine issue "Watts: Still Seething," we now encounter twelve women stoically occupying a future-facing black present at Noah Purifoy's desert museum. These women tune into the Combahee River Collective, also Turiyasangitananda and Cox Jackson. If I too receive the broadcasts, I might find any number of paths.

On another plane of existence, boys and girls appeared to be undifferentiated; that is the girls could sit as free as a boy or child might, without any feelings of indignation or embarrassment. The hair on the heads of some people looked as if it were sprinkled with diamonds. It sparkled like stars in the night.[20]

Or:

This focusing upon our own oppression is embodied in the concept of identity politics. We believe that the most profound and potentially most radical politics come

directly out of our own identity, as opposed to working
to end somebody else's oppression. In the case of Black
women this is a particularly repugnant, dangerous, threat-
ening, and therefore revolutionary concept because it is
obvious from looking at all the political movements that
have preceded us that anyone is more worthy of liberation than ourselves. We reject pedestals, queenhood, and
walking ten paces behind. To be recognized as human,
levelly human, is enough.[21]

Some directions might be as oriented to the present and the past
as they are to the future.

> At dawn, sit at the Feet of Action.
> At noon, be at the Hand of Might.
> At eventide, be so big, that sky will learn Sky.[22]

If quieter, non-eventful applied forms of resistance look like anything in collectivity, they look like horizons for love unanticipated.
These questions are not coercive, however they are disturbed,
knowing that image-worthiness is often defined by who is in power
and where they find comfort in looking. "It is as if everything she
did asked the question: 'Why would anybody want anything else if
this is a possibility?'"[23]

When we all should ask: *What should I do? She* cannot wait any
longer for me to ask: What should I do? *She* isn't just Coltrane, Cox
Jackson, Smith, etc. In simply refusing answers to history's cycle
of indifference *she* meanwhile carries on with horizons of blackness.
"Looking away but with the sides of her mouth turned up again,
she asked, 'Would you rather celebrate the Beautiful One or be the
Beautiful One?'"[24]

23. Berkman, *Monument Eternal:
The Music of Alice Coltrane*, p. 97.
24. Mackey, *Late Arcade*, p. 57.

22. Coltrane-Turiyasangitananda,
Monument Eternal, p. 53.

Sojourner, 2018

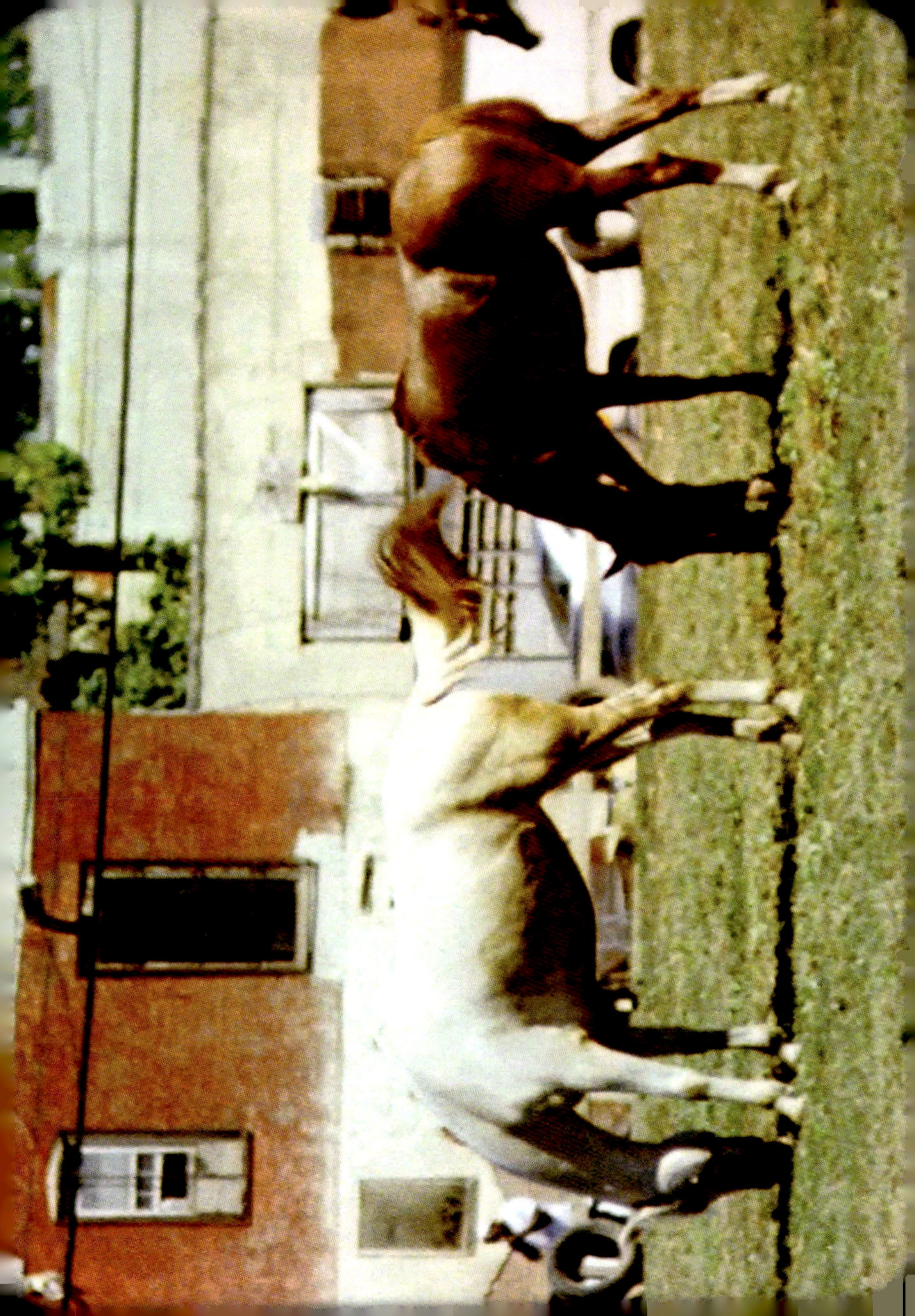

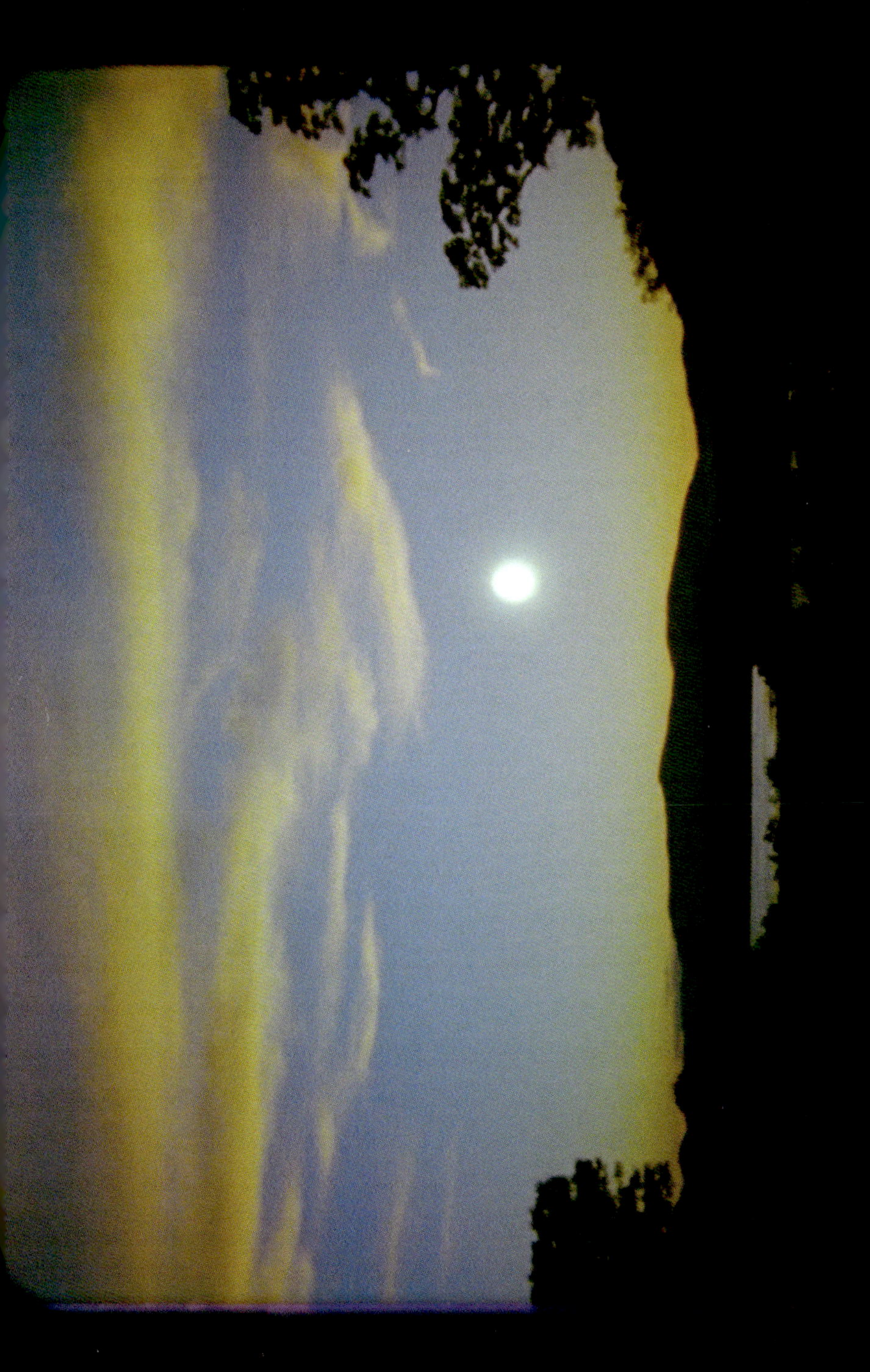

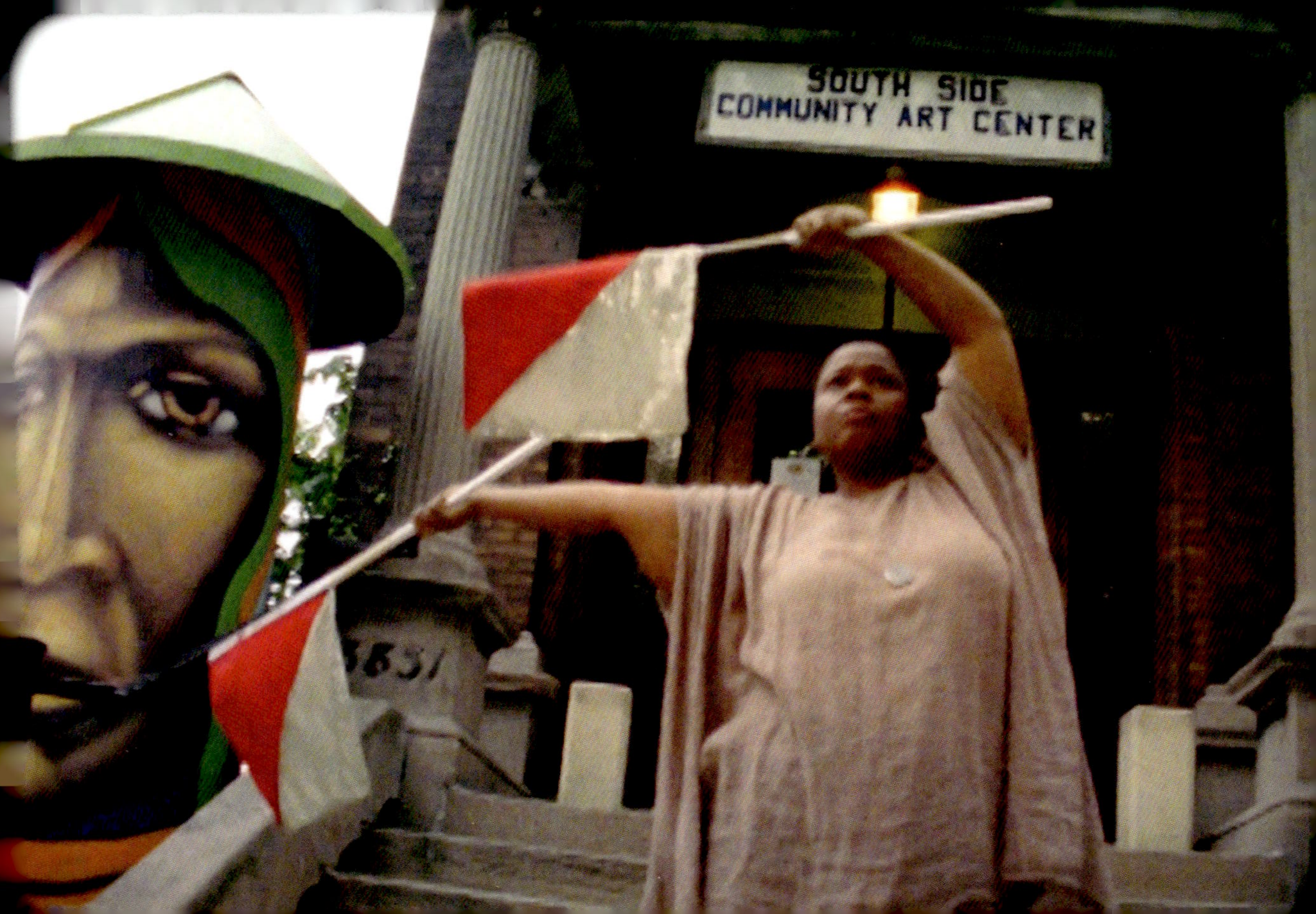

SOUTH SIDE
COMMUNITY ART CENTER

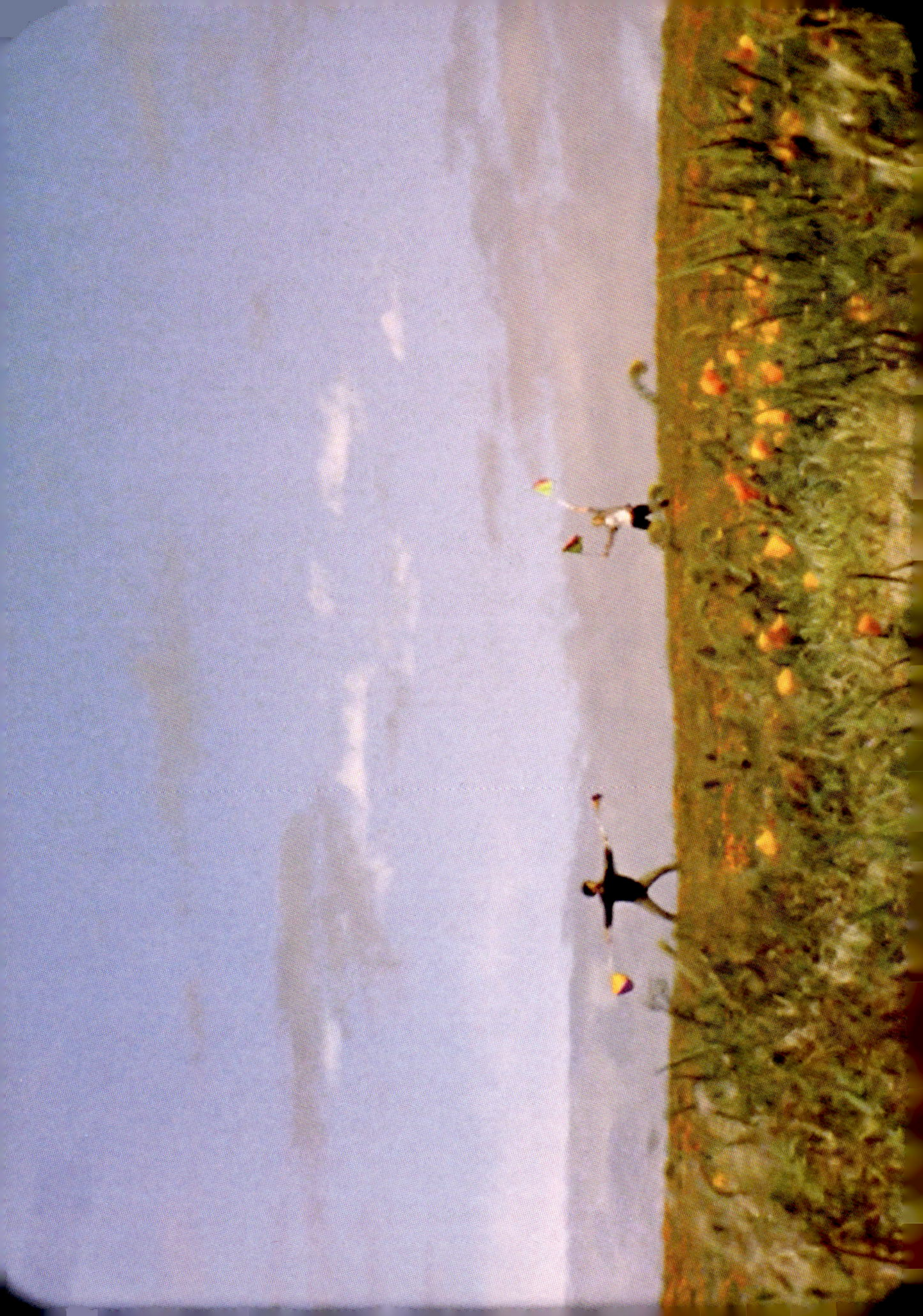

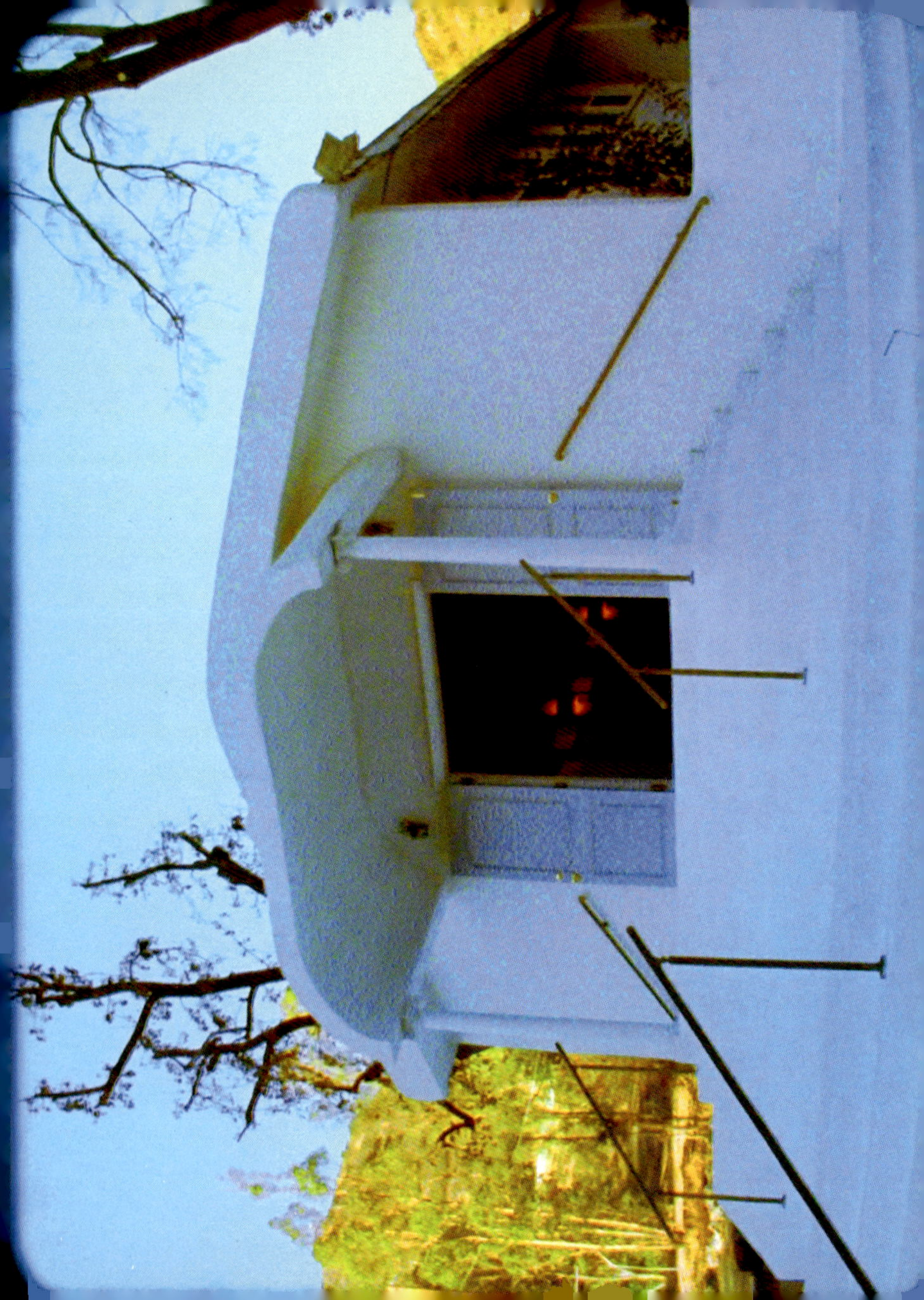

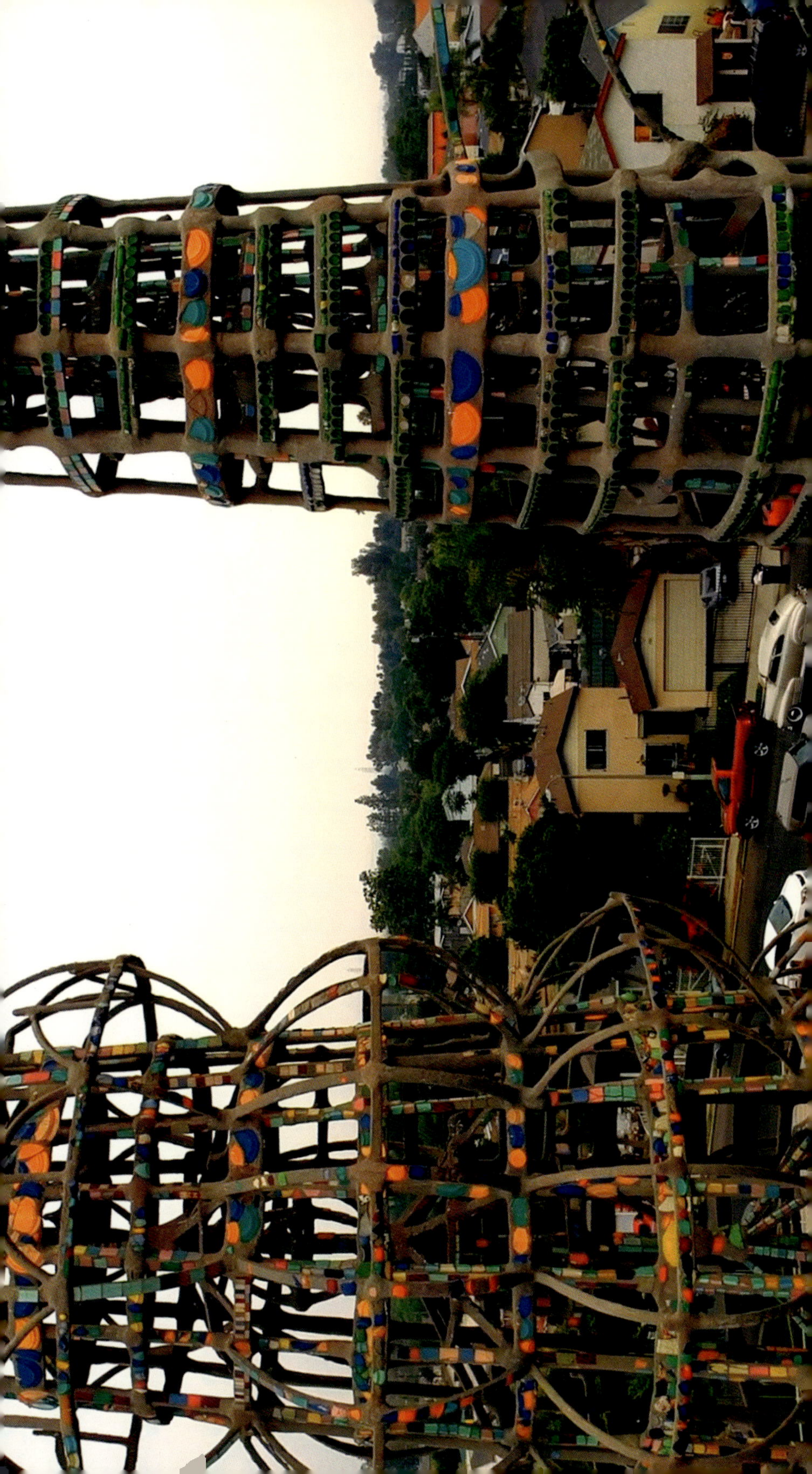

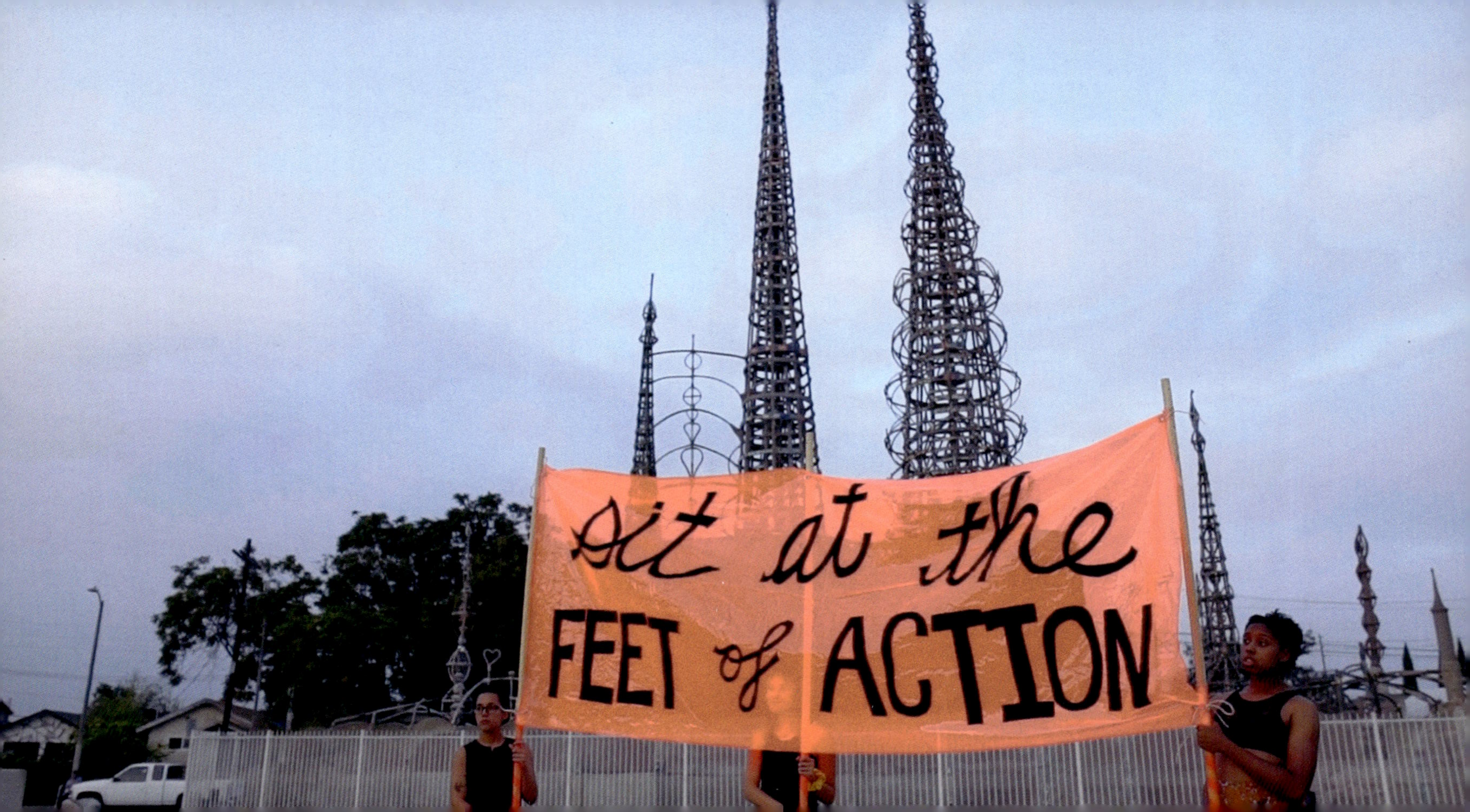

sit at the
FEET of ACTION

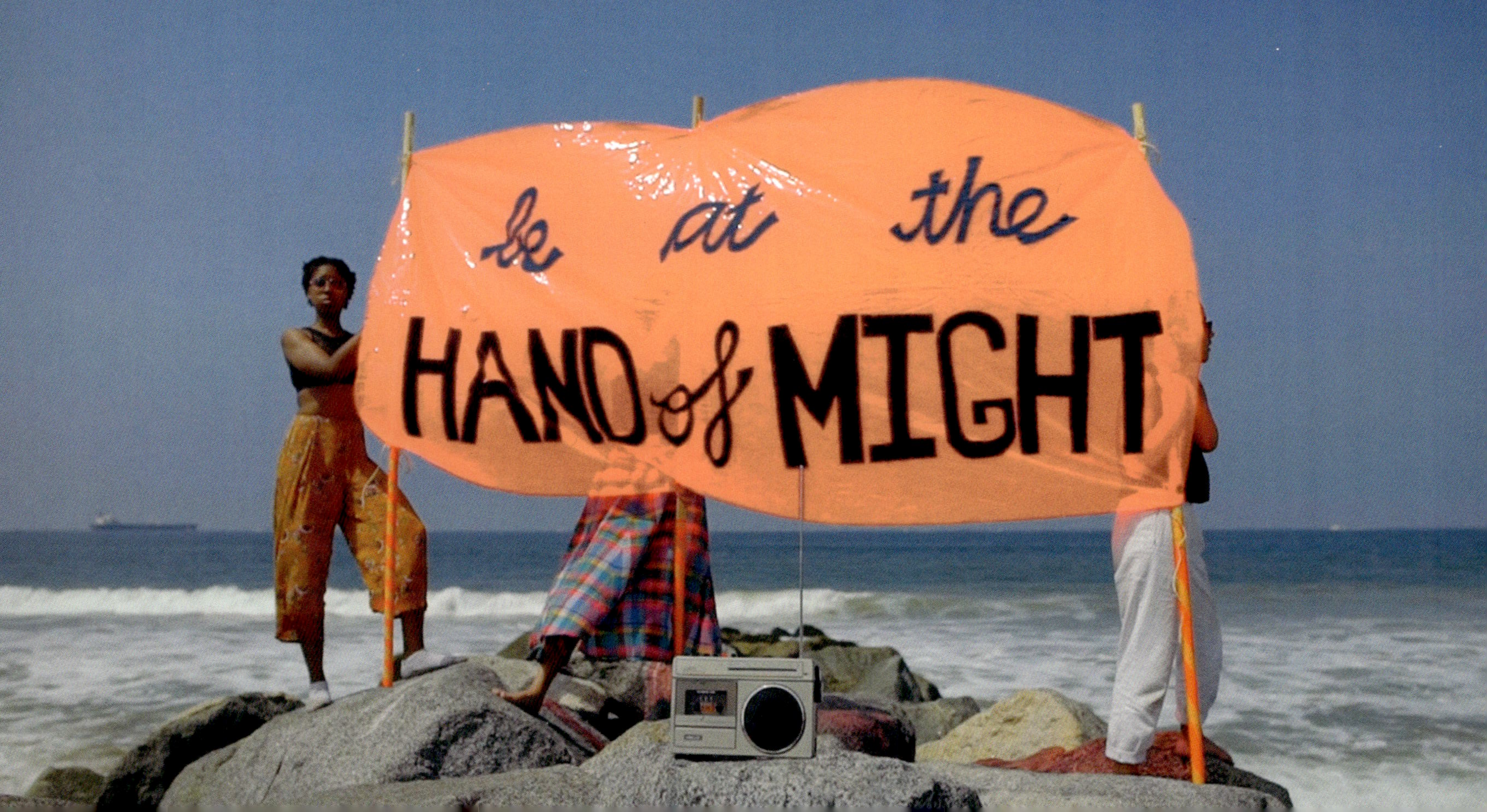
be at the
HAND of MIGHT

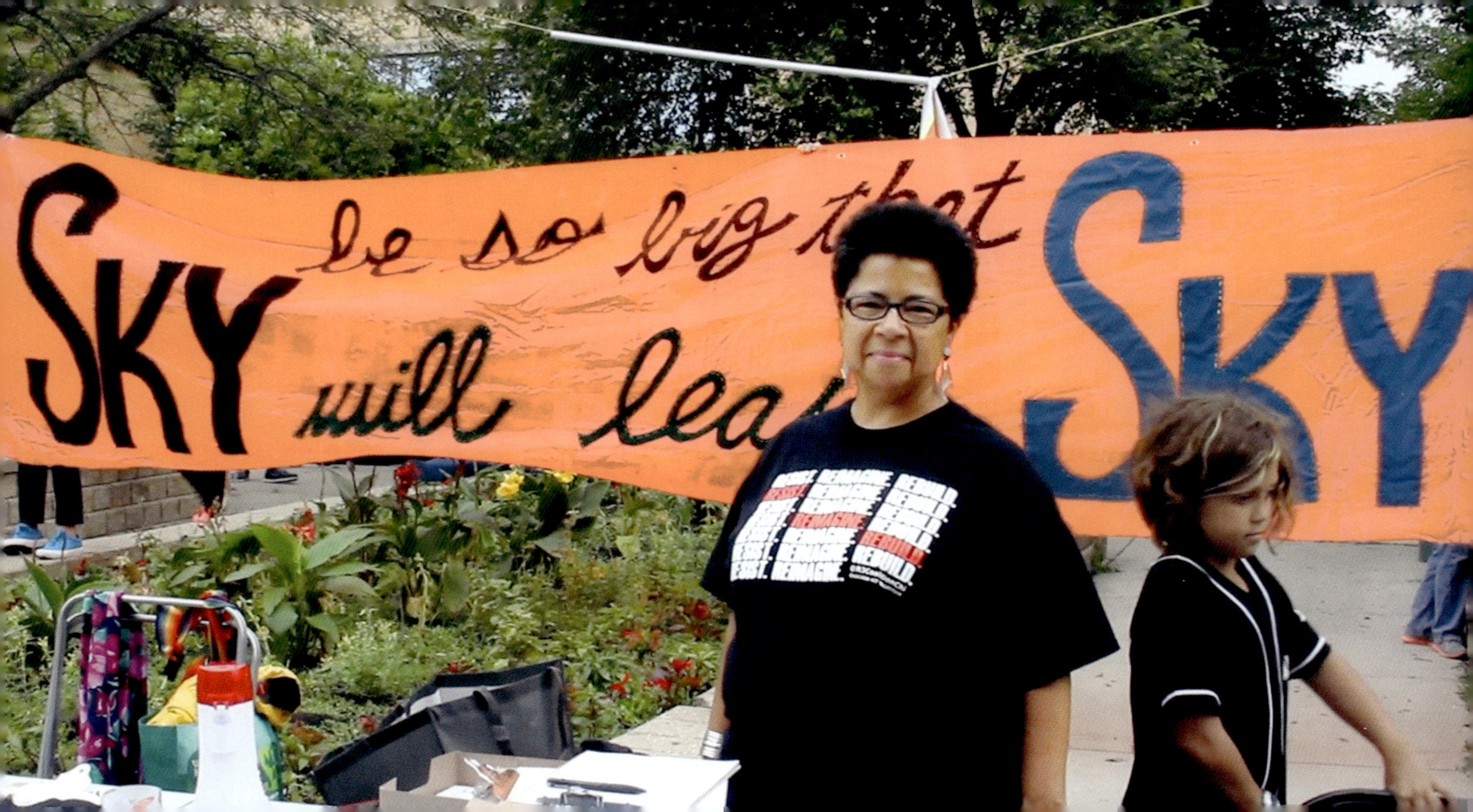
SKY be so big that will lea SKY
REBUILD REIMAGINE REBUILD

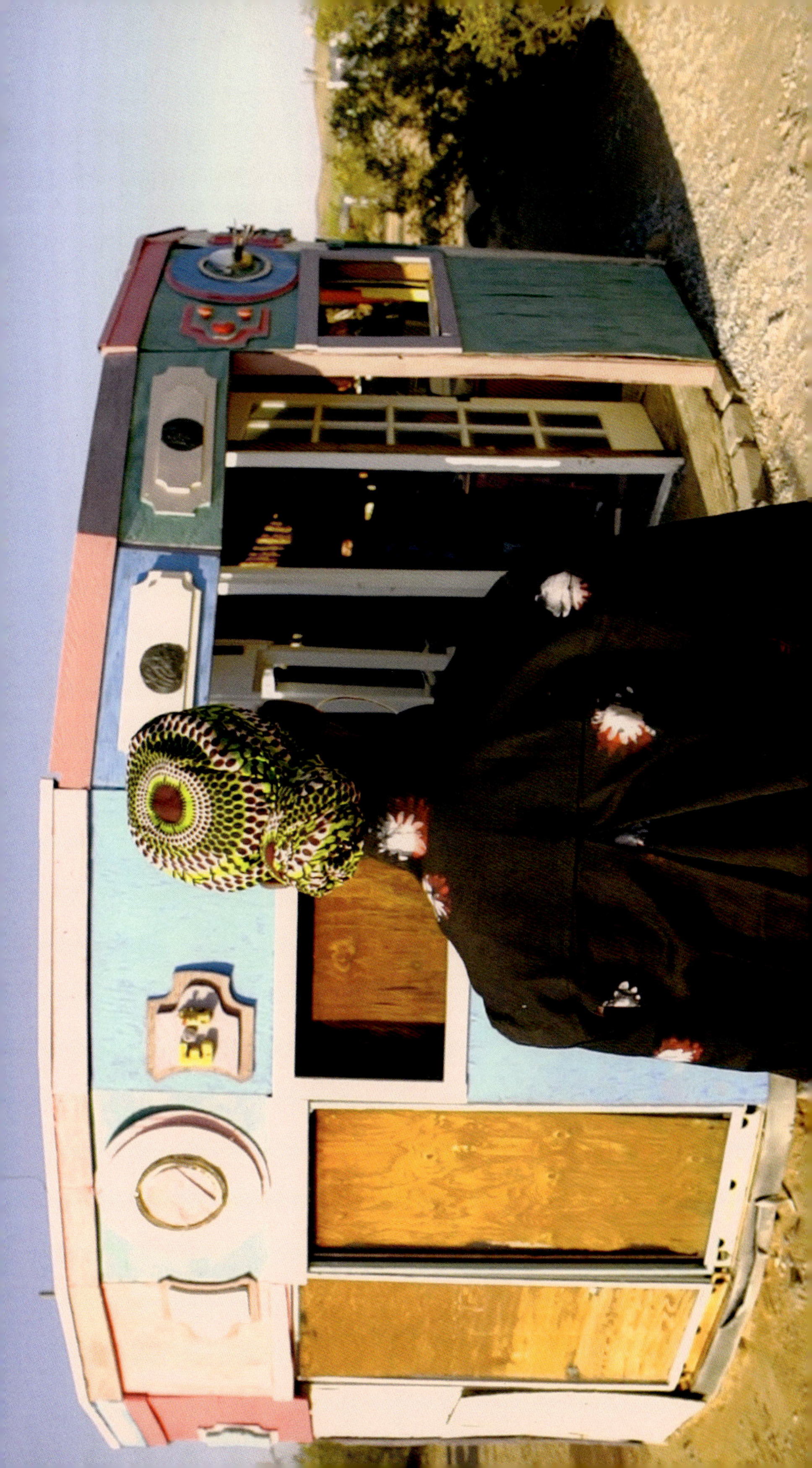

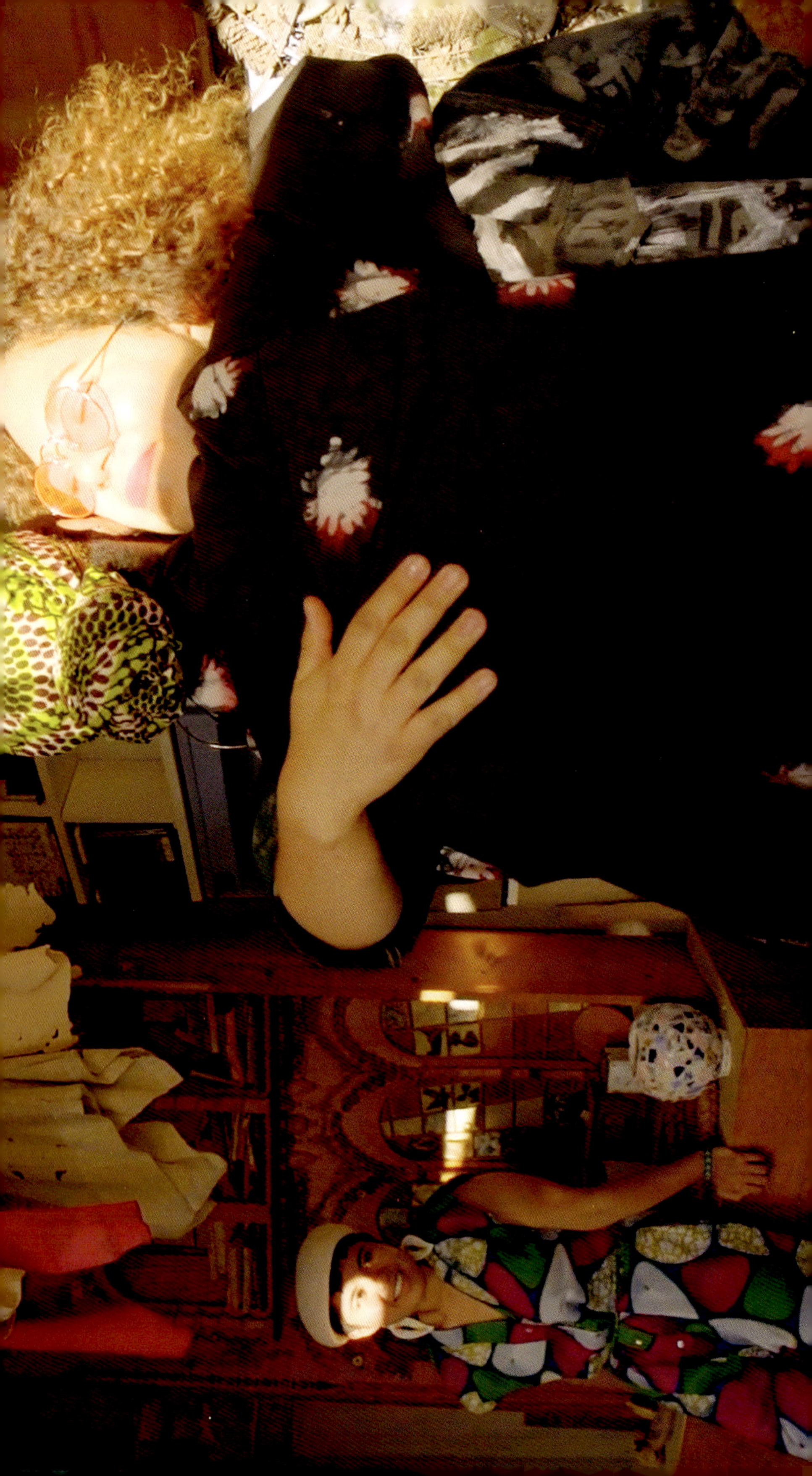

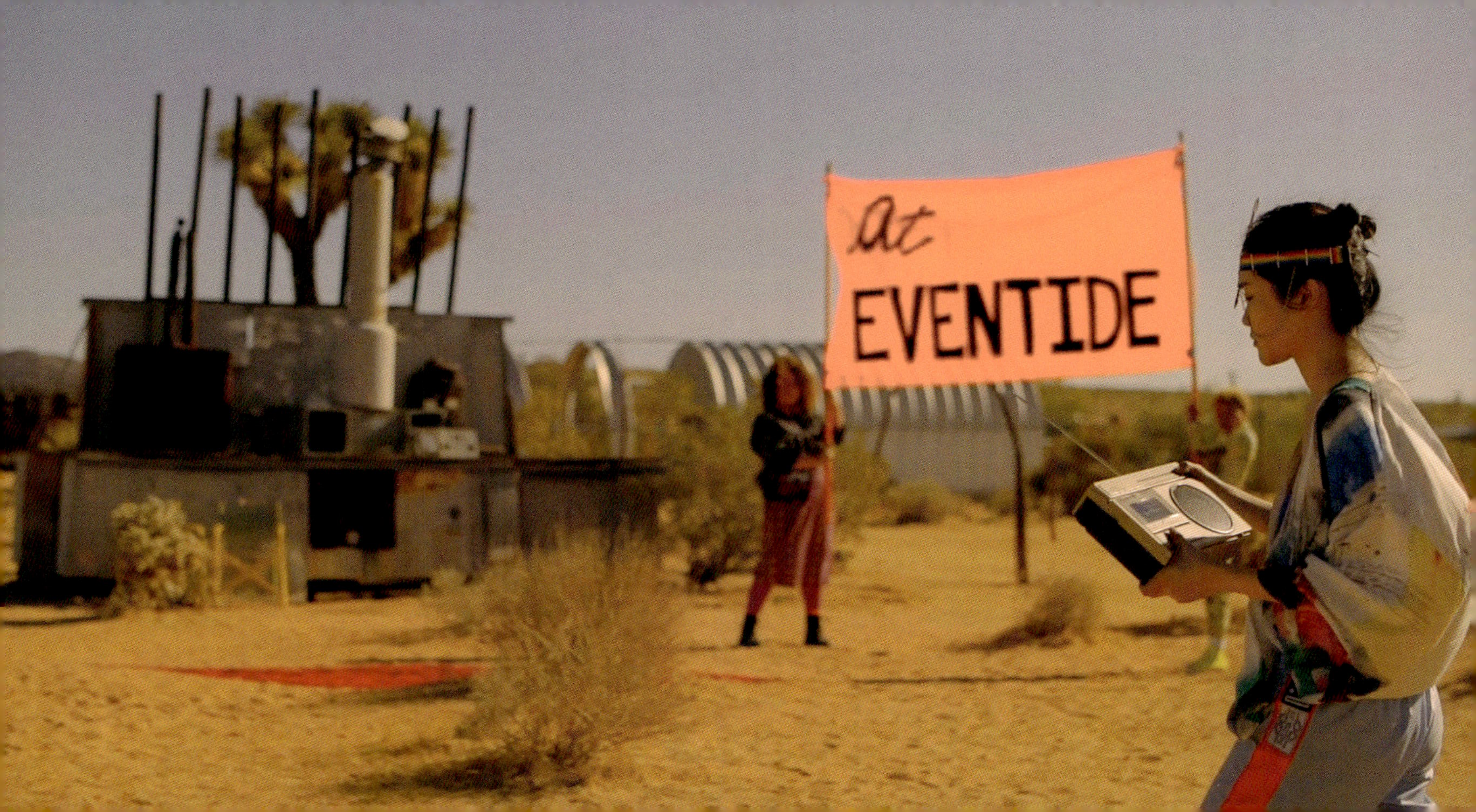
at
EVENTIDE

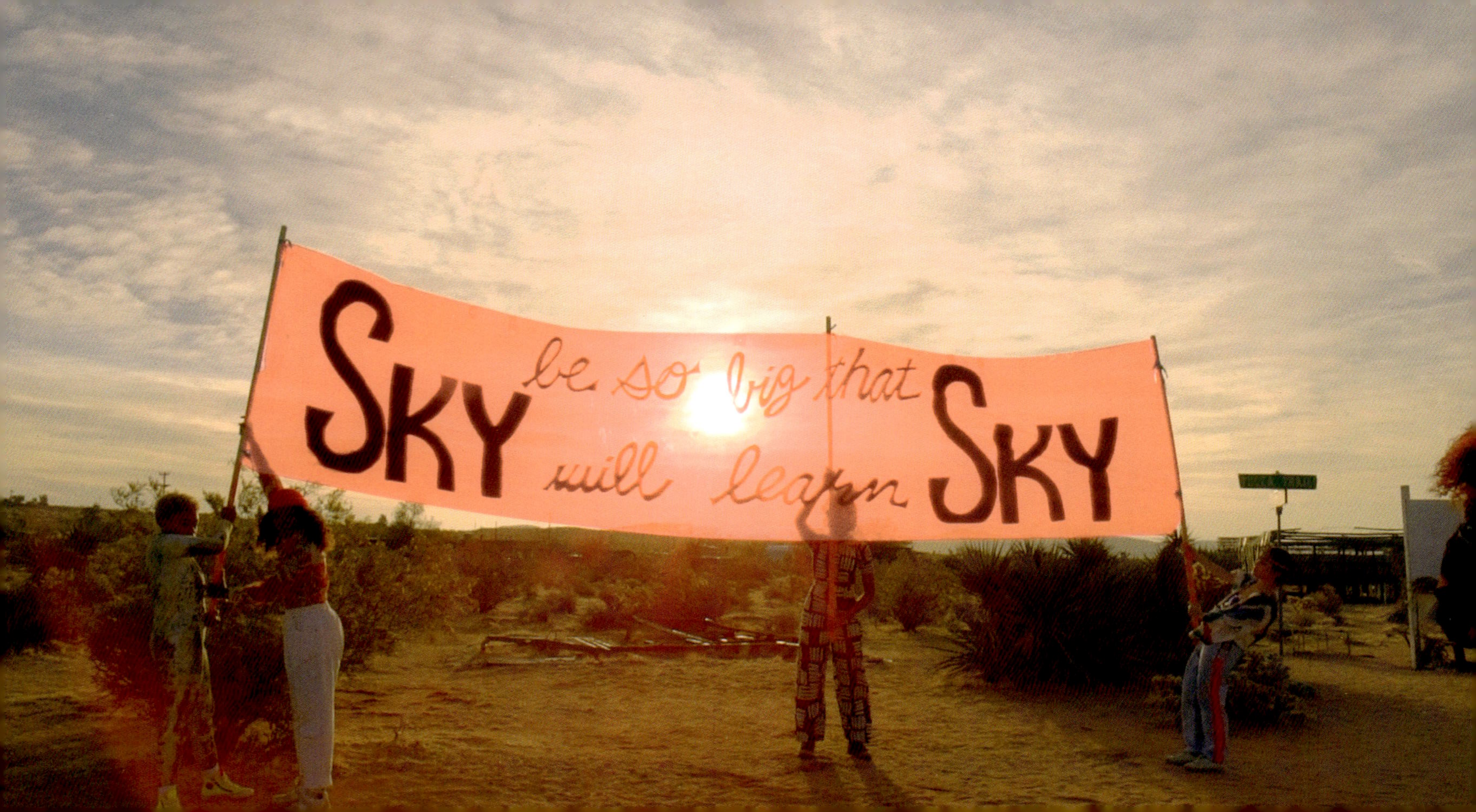
SKY be so big that will learn SKY

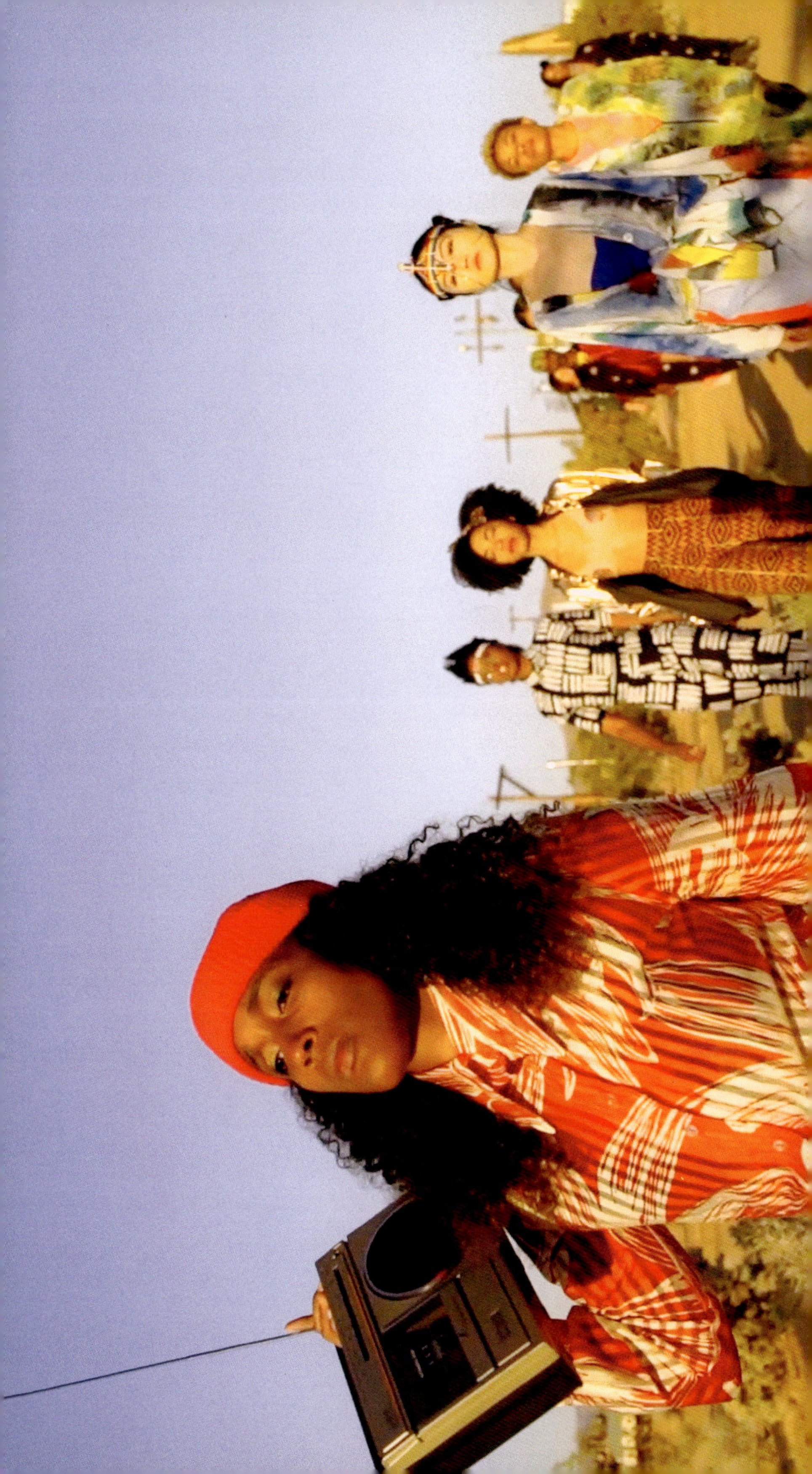

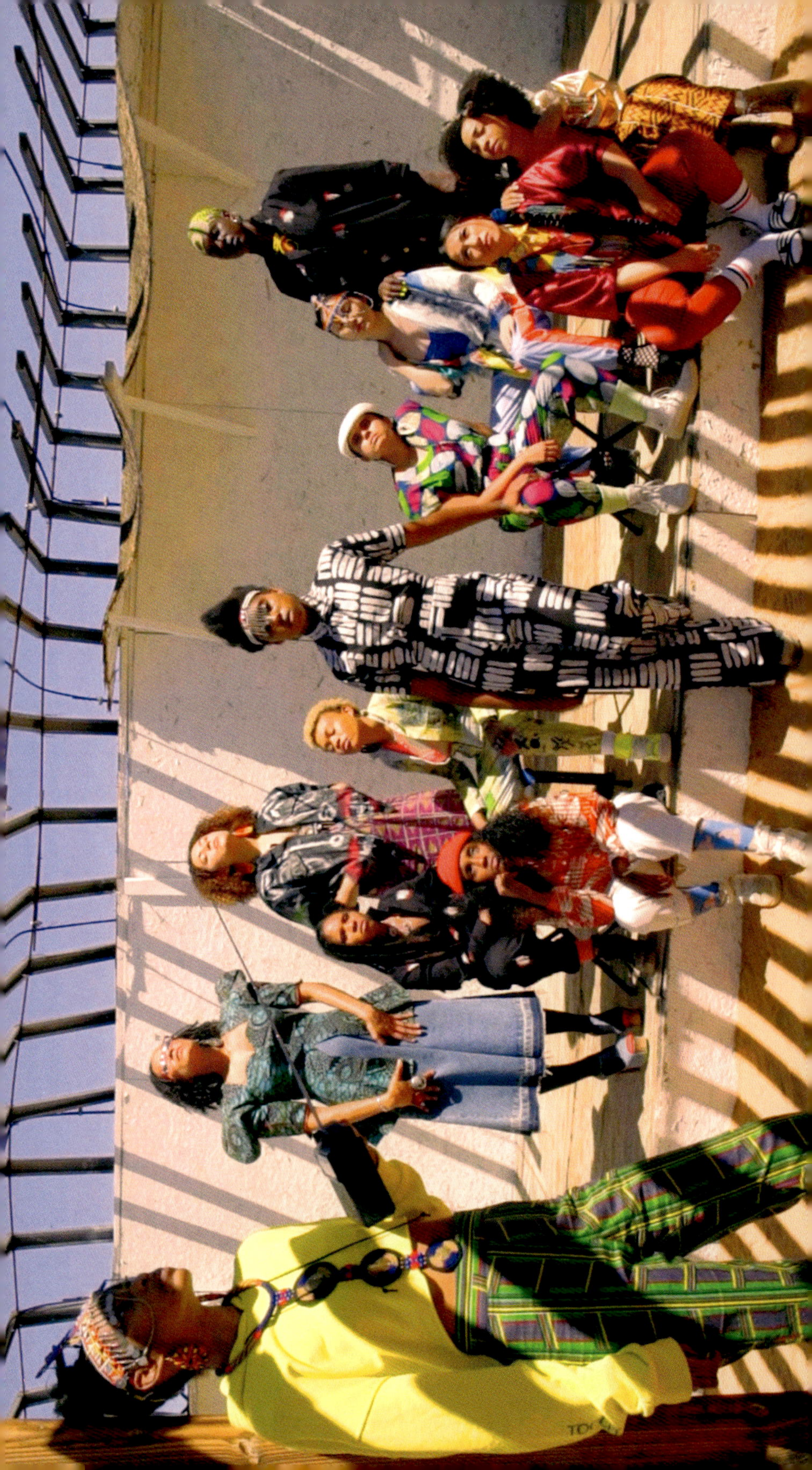

Sojourner, 2018
Digital video, color, sound,
22:41 minutes

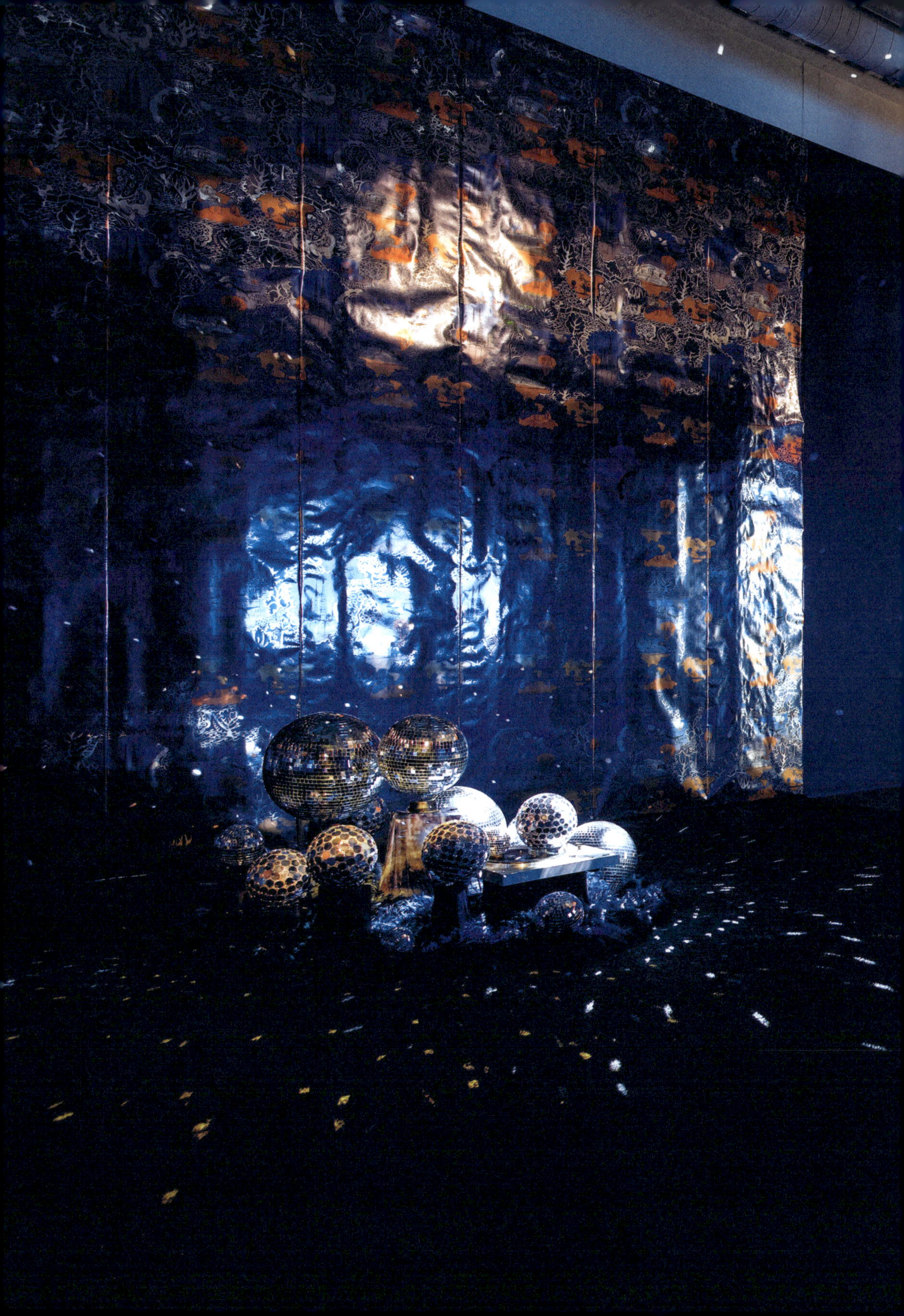

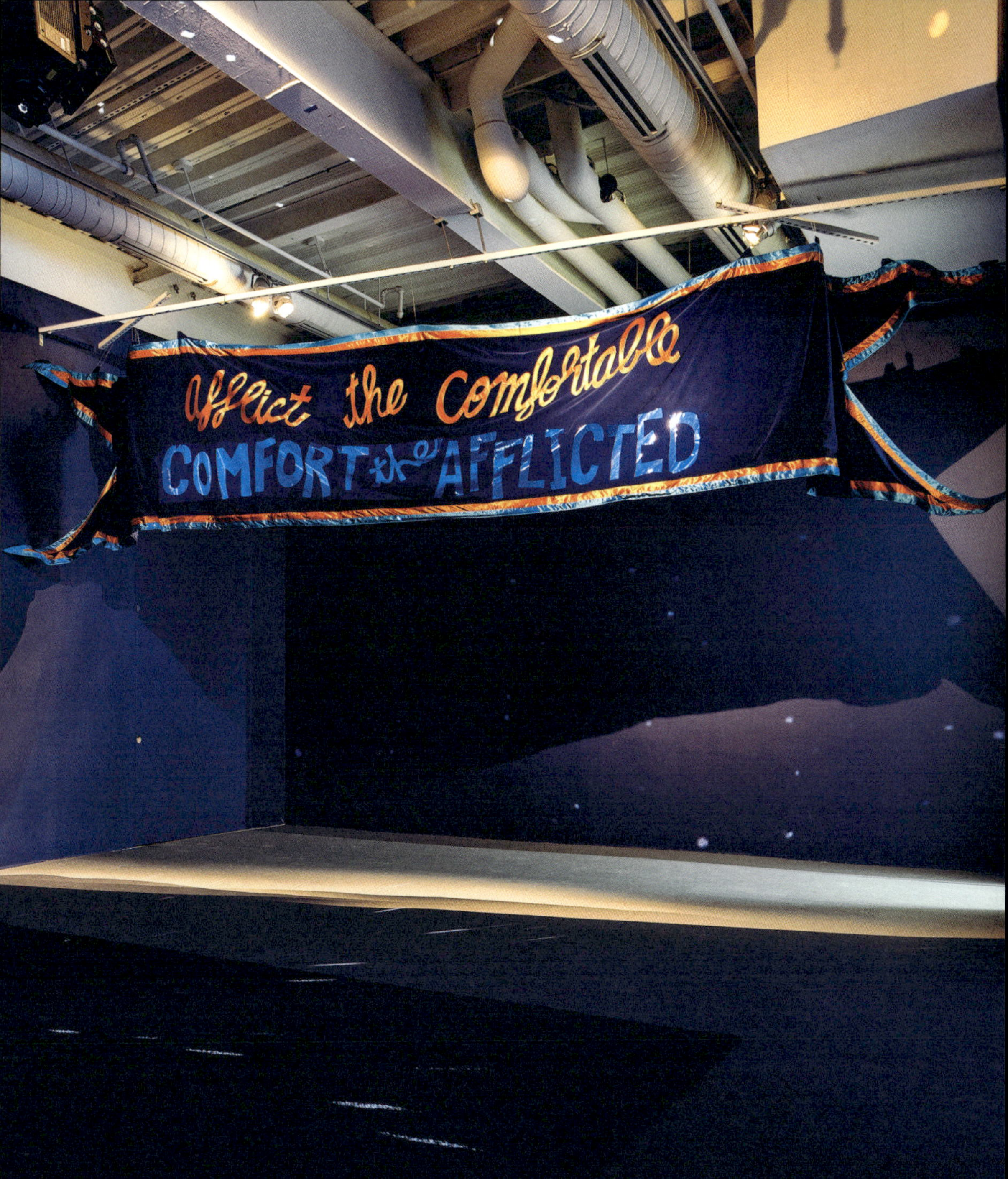
Afflict the Comfortable
COMFORT the AFFLICTED

Rodney McMillian in Conversation with Cauleen Smith

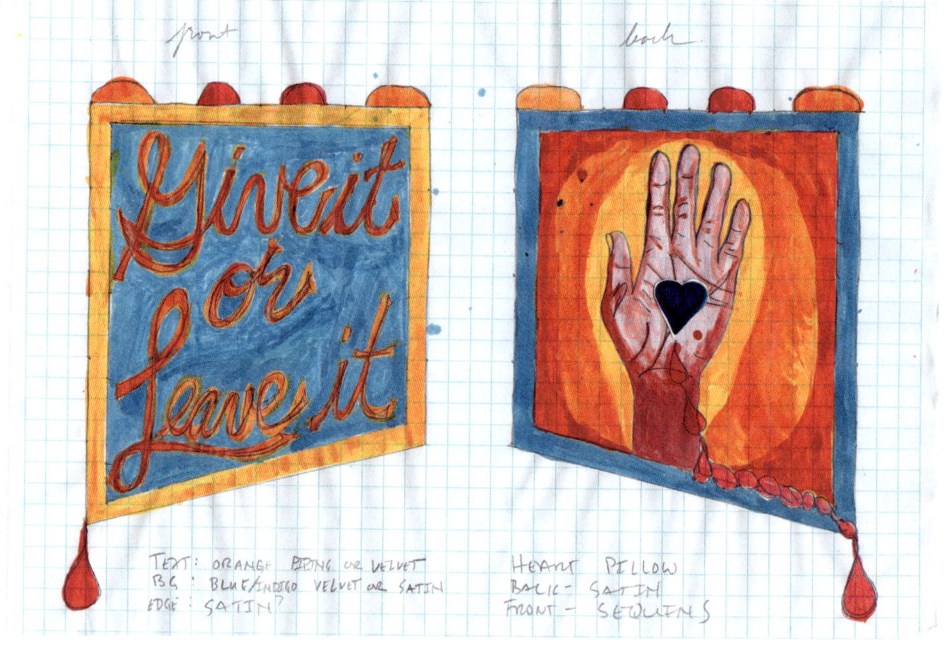

Give It or Leave It Banner, 2018
Production drawing. Graph paper,
graphite, acrylic ink. 9 × 12 in.

Cauleen and I were introduced by the artist Kira Lynn Harris in Los Angeles, over eighteen years ago. In many respects, this conversation does not reflect the often times humorous, spirited, and occasionally contentious nature of our friendship. Over the years, our check-in's have centered on politics, TV, god, race, the moon, aesthetics, and whatever else was or is scratching the edges of an idea, at any given time.

This conversation occurred while Cauleen was at the beginning stages of some of the work for this exhibition, while in the midst of editing her film *Sojourner*. In fact, I mostly saw raw material for the banners and objects and only a few minutes of the film—a scene of women hanging out at Noah Purifoy's Outdoor Desert Art Museum. In many ways, this interview finds me asking Cauleen questions to understand what she intended to show. Thus, my rather direct—and in some cases, flat-footed—inquiries are an attempt to envision what had not yet been produced or completed. This experience also offered the opportunity to pose a few new questions, which have been forming as I've encountered her installations over several years.

————Rodney McMillian, June 18, 2018

Rodney McMillian

Can you talk a little bit about the banners and how you think about these banners for this show?

Cauleen Smith

Well, there are four banners. There are two *Give It or Leave It* banners, which—I think they're gonna just be put away for now. And there's a banner that will be in the main entryway that says "I appreciate you in advance."

Rodney

That's sweet.

Cauleen

And then there's a banner that you'll see on your way out that says, "Comfort the afflicted. Afflict the comfortable." [It's] from a painting by Paul Thek, which is actually a quote from some crazy Chicago newsman.

Rodney

And what does the title mean, *Give It or Leave It*?

Cauleen

To me, this is a kind of challenge. Taking something that's a coercion and a threat, "Take it or leave it," which is all about knowing you have the upper-hand and knowing that someone else has. . . . What do you call that? Not a forfeiture, but—

Rodney

Submission?

Cauleen

Submission, but there's another word for it. When you say, "You win." A forfeit—much more than just walking away and quitting.

Rodney

Surrender.

Cauleen

Yes! Instead of coercion, it's about surrender. Thank you. Surrender. And thinking, "What does anti-capitalism look like?" It doesn't look like communism. It looks like a radical kind of hospitality, which is really difficult, really painful, impossible, and even when it's been practiced, it's not being reciprocated. So this requires a new kind of consciousness. It requires a conversation around how we think and understand ourselves in order to even attempt something beyond what we already know.

Hospitality, Surrender. What if instead of trying to negotiate who gets what. . . . What if the solution was always: give it away? And this is something in my gut that goes against my instincts about black culture. Which is that we *do* fucking give it away, and we also resent the way in which others profit from what we give away.

Rodney

How would you say that we give it away?

Cauleen

We make stuff. We show off how well we do it. We make it completely available and accessible to anybody who wants to absorb our fabulousness, and then we get mad when people try to copy us. But what else would they do?

Rodney

But what do you do with blacks who are part of a system where they sell their works? You're clearly part of this institution. A lot of the women that you reference were participating in institutions or systems or commercial aspects, from music to religion to art to academia and writing.

Cauleen

We are all participating in it all, right? I'm not even proposing that we should pretend as if we can walk away from something that we're a part. Maybe what I'm proposing is just completely impossible. But it's what I want to see.

Rodney

What would you say you're proposing?

Cauleen

What I want to see is: instead of the constant taking and accumulation and need to hoard and need to assign values and give and take in that way, that there is a fundamental flow on every level of needs being addressed by those who are capable of it. In a way that is based on faith, which is why a lot of the women I'm looking at are spiritual women. That crazy idea that Christians have that there's some "Thing" that will provide. That thing isn't out *there*. It's you. It's me. The faith that you or I or some other human being will be there when something is needed is actually what I'm interested in.

Rodney
Fascinating. I remember, maybe several years ago, you were talking about how you were struck by your relationship to Sun Ra and his work and his music. You were struck by the spiritual practices that he and others have, and that you were struggling with that for yourself. This is a really fucked up question in certain ways, but do you see yourself trying to get there through your practice or through these philosophical musings? Is that where your spiritual practice is growing?

Cauleen
I guess. Spiritual practice. . . . I don't have one other than trying to think about these things every day. Maybe art is—and I'm not the first, and I won't be the last artist to say this—maybe art is a particular kind of vocation. But I'm a total heathen. There's no religion I've encountered that I could comply with. I can't say the word "God." I cannot say "The Creator" without smashing up my face and being snarky and sarcastic. I find these terms attached to masculinity. To the patriarchy.

Rodney
Judeo-Christian? Sounds like you can't escape the patriarchy with it.

Cauleen
Can't. So I can't. So I can't. I cannot. I cannot. I can't submit to that. I'm asking people to do something that I can't even do on an intellectual level.

Rodney
You said *Give It or Leave It* is this act of surrender. This kind of radical hospitality. And you said some of the banners might not be in the show. Can you talk about why they don't belong?

Cauleen
The form that they're in, and the way they're made, and everything about the way they're designed comes out of a design for another set of banners called *In the Wake*. In those banners, I was thinking about funerals. I was thinking about the black church very explicitly. Grand hat ladies, and black women in their dresses, and funerals. That particular form is not what's needed here.

Rodney
Those forms—did you invent those forms or did you come up with those associations for the banners?

Cauleen
I came up with the associations.

Rodney
Were the associations legible in those banners?

Cauleen
I don't think so. But I think what's recognizable is a sort of Catholic requiem procession, which I was definitely riffing on. Also [the] military, which is inevitable. Those are the things that are immediately legible. Until you go up close and you see the hand in them and then they look much more like garments. They're made out of materials that you would wear.

Rodney
Those banners, as I recall, they were high up so no one would be able to get that close, and if I'm not mistaken, those banners were also in a parade?

Cauleen
Yeah.

Rodney
I'm curious how you figure out the form. It sounds like there's a personal index that's forming them. Granted there are also larger things like the military and reliquaries and how banners are used. But it seems like there are particular aspects that come out of a personal library of images and also techniques. And those decisions are dictating what you present and how you present it.

So I'm curious about how you come to those kinds of decisions with *Give It or Leave It,* where you're thinking about not putting the banners in because you think that they're—

Cauleen
They're made wrong.

Rodney
They're made wrong?

Cauleen
They're made wrong.

Rodney
[Not only] from a material perspective, but also from a place of intent?

Cauleen
Uh-huh. The form, the shape, the fabrics.

Rodney
How could they be made right?

Cauleen
I haven't figured that out yet for the *Give It or Leave It* banners, but I have figured it out for the other banners, *I Appreciate You in Advance* and *Afflict the Comfortable. Comfort the Afflicted.*

Rodney
How are those made?

Cauleen
They haven't been made yet.

Rodney
Can you describe them?

Cauleen
Yeah. The *I Appreciate You in Advance*

banner is gonna have letters cut out of the banner so that the word, "You," is transparent so light shoots through it, and the "You" becomes a shadow or something. They're both designed as an old- style kind of ribbon. They're more artificial, the kind of ribbons you see on drawings—like that.

I'm kind of an outsider artist in that sense where—I aspire to that kind of clarity that seems to have its own universe. A very legible universe that is not attached to somebody else's dictums about art.

Rodney
Do you think you have that with film?

Cauleen
I think I'm closer to that in film, and it's probably why people don't like my films very much. 'Cause they're much closer to doing what I want to do, which is make this whole other language. I'm trying to use film in really specific ways that movies usually don't do. Movies are very much about pleasure. Even when you're watching tragedy, the way you fall into your sad sentiment is crafted, and really fierce skills go into making those feelings and that view. I'm trying to disrupt that.

Rodney
Do you feel like with the objects, you're trying to do the opposite, closer to the traditional filmmaker's realm with your objects?

Cauleen
No because…

Rodney
I mean, when I hear someone with the background and knowledge that you have say that you're more of an outsider artist, that seems to be kind of romantic. It also seems to suggest a populist desire for many to be able to come aboard.

Cauleen
A desire for many to come onboard? Absolutely. I feel that way when I look at

your paintings. And your paintings are part of a really rigorous intellectual discourse with our history. So just because I want a lot of people onboard doesn't mean that I'm not interested in certain kinds of—

Rodney
No. I was speaking specifically as you described, how your approach is almost like [that of] an outsider artist. I was just thinking about that in relationship to the films that you make, which are so very specific and have such craft, but also have all of these film histories going on and antagonisms toward certain tropes in film.

Cauleen
Well, I don't have the same antagonisms towards objects because we're all surrounded by objects.

Rodney
I get it. I'm not talking about objects that are good or bad. I'm curious about your relationship to object-making within this realm where there seems to be a kind of joie de vivre or less concern for certain types of critical investigations as you have with film.

With film, there are things that you just won't do. I've shared your manifesto in my classes over the past several years. My students have presented that manifesto in class. I've shared your videos with them. They talk about how they're not able—the viewer is not able to sit comfortably and engage. They constantly have to be aware of themselves, be aware of what's going on, and then interrogate both positions in the process of watching.

Cauleen
High compliment. Thank you.

Rodney
And yet, they're along for the ride.

Cauleen
Yeah.

Rodney
But with your banners and other objects—

Cauleen
They don't do that.

Rodney
Why you take such different approaches.

Cauleen
Probably training and lack thereof. Wow. I've never thought of this, Rodney, but when I'm making an object, I'm actually just making a very specific thing. I'm not thinking of them the way that I talk to my students who are sculptors about the objects that they make. All the way through and around them, and the materials, and my alienation and attractions. That's not actually what I'm trying to do with the things that I make. I want you to feel like you know them very, very well. I want them to be intensely familiar. They're more like props than sculptures.

Rodney
That's what I was wondering.

Cauleen
Props that then take on their own aura.

Rodney
You believe in aura?

Cauleen
Through use, yeah. Of props? Sure. It's a whole thing with objects that have been used in films.

Rodney
I was gonna say it sounds like Hollywood.

Cauleen
There's this weird push and pull with props about veracity: How real do they have to be? How fake can they be? What can you get away with? What can't you get away with?

I love that provisional aspect to them. I love the way that the front can be perfect, and then the back can be hollow. For me, that just seems like life. It seems more like my everyday moving-through-the-world relationship to objects.

Rodney
That's an interesting segue because now I want to ask about the raven that you

bought. It's a taxidermy raven. It's clear that it needs to be one that was real, one that wasn't a fake. Can you talk about why it had to be a dead crow?

Cauleen

I've already made films about crows, *The Crow Requiem*, and I'm obsessed with this beautiful and intelligent black bird of North America. The reason I am deeply sympathetic to them is that in Western literature and culture, they're associated with great evil, just on sight, without any knowledge of the animal itself. Only in the past few years, maybe ten to fifteen years, has there actually been scientific study about what crows are, what they do, and how they actually live. What we learned is that they're incredibly intelligent. They have memories. They tell stories. They have family relationships. They mourn their dead. They give people, humans—they like gifts. They have complex relationships with other animals. They're this really marvelous being that is associated with great evil across the board. And also a funny thing with humans and birds—I think I'm not alone—most humans can't tell one bird from another bird. It's a parrot. It's a crow. It's a dove. It's a pigeon. All pigeons look the same. All ducks look the same.

Rodney

But you have five pigeons. You're like, "Oh, five pigeons."

Cauleen

You can't say, "That's Harold. That's Maude. That's…." You can't. They're just pigeons. Also, crows are one of the few birds in North America that isn't really protected. If there are crows on your property and you want to shoot and kill them, you can. There's no consequences. There's no restrictions. You can kill a crow just because it's annoying you. Just because in your mind it's evil. And people do.

Now, crows are a migratory bird, so they are protected under the Migratory Bird [Treaty] Act of 1918. But if you look on YouTube, what you see is a different reality. People hunt crows for fun and they kill as many as they possibly can. They are considered vermin. They are a disturbance; their presence is experienced as a threat. So the law and the actual practice contradict one another mightily. And doesn't that sound familiar?

I did a talk in Chicago and I made my erroneous statement that crows were not protected and [how] that is analogous to black people constantly being in jeopardy. A student, a white woman maybe about thirty-five years old or so, corrected me—which is why I went and looked up the proper law! She said that they were a protected bird. She stated this as if it undermined the reality that black people are fodder for state sanctioned violence— as if my assertions around the irrefutable proof social media offers us, that the job of police is to murder black people, was also wrong. And this is how it works, right? The dominant culture sets the terms for reality. The denial of violence is enforced even while state sanctioned violence is actively cultivated, practiced, and supported by the courts.

Law or no law, it's like I said—you can go on YouTube, and it's really strange, people are avidly acting out their relationship to evil on these birds. They've become this symbol, this metaphor, this avatar for [laugh] blackness and black bodies.

Rodney

Why don't we stop there for now and go watch some films?

Cauleen

Okay.

. . .

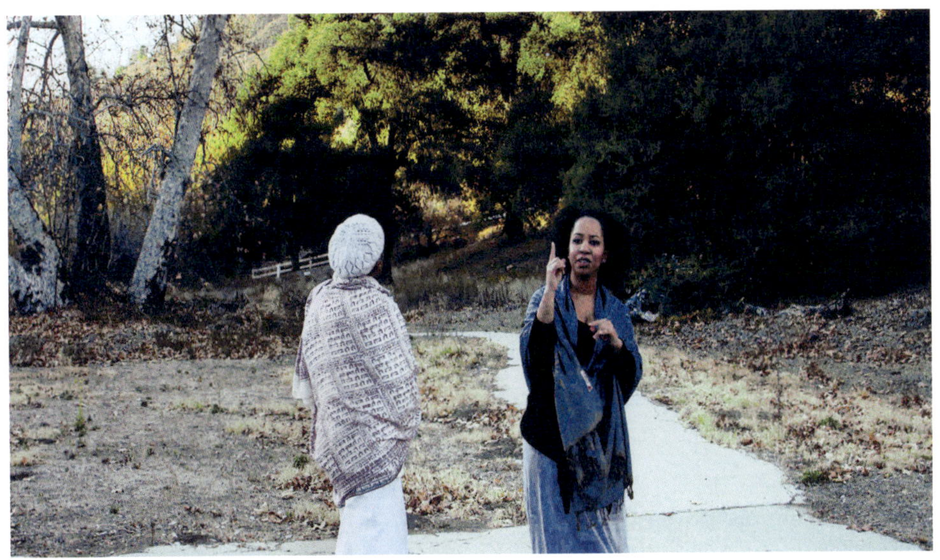

Pilgrim (still), **2017**
Digital video and 16mm film,
color, sound, 7:41 minutes

Rodney
What about the role of the body in this
work?

Cauleen
In this show, one work is about two women
who were lifelong partners, but they were
Shakers. So in theory they weren't engaged
in a sexual relationship.

Rodney
Were they black women?

Cauleen
Black women. Black women Shakers who
lived in Philadelphia. And they lived as
Shakers for quite some time but had to
leave the Watervliet compound. I have been
thinking about the way that they had to
inhabit their bodies at a time when there
was a Fugitive Slave Act on the books and
white people who claimed to be godly but
[who] were in many respects dedicated
capitalists concerned [with] the accumulation of property and wealth, however

communal. This made the Rebecca's
intensely vulnerable.

These two women started their own
commune in Philadelphia together. Now,
both of them have the same first name:
Rebecca. Rebecca Cox Jackson, the
Eldress, and Rebecca Perot, her protégé.
When Rebecca Cox Jackson died, Rebecca
Perot took on her name and became her.
And most of the photographs we have of
Rebecca Cox Jackson are actually Perot.

Rodney
How did you find out about these women?

Cauleen
A scholar who wrote a really beautifully
researched book and [also] Rebecca Cox
Jackson kept a journal for over thirty years.
No one taught her to read. She claims God
gave her the ability to read and write in one
fell swoop. She describes the experience
where she was stricken down; and when she
recovered, she could read and write.

With all these women that I'm looking at—Alice Coltrane Turiyasangitananda, Rebecca Cox Jackson, her protégé Rebecca Perot, and also the women of the Combahee River Collective—there's an alienation from the body within their language that I find really profound. I'm also becoming increasingly sensitive to a general black Judeo-Christian attitude toward our bodies, which applies a kind of shame on the body just out the box. Black women just don't need that on top of being black and women in this world, you know what I mean?

I remember, once, an artist told me that I shouldn't show a young black man and woman making out in a film because it was exploiting their sexuality. It's actually one of the shots that I'm most proud of—this long take of these kids wildly making out.

Rodney
What is the name of that film?

Cauleen
It's called, *I Want to See My Skirt*.

Rodney
I think I showed it in my class. Is this show about these women?

Cauleen
They are the ground, the foundation, but it's much more about a kind of consciousness and a physical space suggesting what is possible. How we might envision a world that actually has already been made over and over and over by black women. How we might actually enact it and embody it.

Rodney
Tell me the three texts that are shaping this video again?

Cauleen
[The] Combahee River Collective Statement, the writings of Rebecca Cox Jackson, and *Monument Eternal* by Alice Coltrane Turiyasangitananda. *Monument Eternal* is Coltrane's first book about

the process of becoming a self-realized Godhead. And Mother Ann Lee, who started the Shakers, was a self-realized Godhead. Now, the women who started Combahee River Collective were Marxists. So I really love the tension between fierce materialism and ecstatic visionaries. The really interesting thing about these extremes, this ecstatic spiritualism and then Marxism, neither actually really speaks to or seems to value a visual culture. In fact, the Shakers were opposed to visual culture and only turned to it when in times of crisis, when they started drawing and making gift drawings to revive their communities.

Rodney
So how do you see your role with[in] visual culture?

Cauleen
Well, this film is a pictorialization, where I gather a group of women in the desert to do a reenactment of a photograph that was actually taken at the Watts Towers.

Rodney
A photograph of whom at the Watts Towers?

Cauleen
A group of boys. I'll show you the picture 'cause it's crucial to this whole situation.

Rodney
Before we go there, in sticking with the question about visual culture, I'm curious about the role of fashion. It seems like you've hired a designer and a stylist for these women. They're all very attractive, and they look very dope.

Cauleen
Yeah. It's funny. It's something I'm gonna have to really take on and find the words for. Fashion is built into this because it's built into our daily lives, you know what I mean?

This photograph is another kind of founding text for me. I stumbled on it researching the Watts Towers, which is also one of the sites I'm looking at in terms of radical hospitality. This was taken in 1966 after the Watts Rebellion. The photographer went there to look for black militancy, you know what I mean? He went looking for something, and the language, the *LIFE* magazine photo captions frequently describe these people, basically like animals. But what you see—

Rodney

Is like a fashion spread. Handsome, stylish brothers who are—

Cauleen

Elegant. This little boy, he's just so elegant. Look at his beautiful hands. Look at these guys. Oh, my God. You know what I mean?

Rodney

A lot of care.

Cauleen

And it's a range of class and orientation. You can tell these guys may be hanging out together here, but they don't really know each other. They're really different. They're a range of ages. *LIFE* magazine did not publish this image. They focused on activism, protest, and gangs.

Rodney

So this was a staged photograph?

Cauleen

It's not staged.

Rodney

Staged as in a fashion spread?

Cauleen

No. I looked into it. They aren't staged. Photojournalist Billy Ray started to accumulate relationships with some of the young men. No young women. He got friendly with them and followed them around. They started following him around. They started making pictures together.

Rodney

Okay. And so this photograph was basis for the assembly of women that you have?

Cauleen

Exactly.

Rodney

And then the fashion the women are donning. . . . Is that in response to how elegant you see these guys?

Cauleen

Yeah. To me, they are dressed for this photographer. I think they showed up looking for him, and then they put on something that looked cool. I didn't want these women in the film to feel like they just came off the street. I wanted it to feel as if they were presenting themselves to each other, to the camera.

So I recast all these boys as utopian role players. This is not a real restaging even though it kind of does work as a restaging.

Rodney

We should watch the film some more. What happened here? There's not gonna be sound?

Cauleen

There will be sound, but I'm putting in all the sound. It's never diegetic sound. The sound is my most direct way of addressing the viewer. When you're saying many of your students go along for the ride, I believe that they're willing to because of the way that I build the sound. I believe that the sound is holding them even while the pictures are maybe alienating.

Rodney

Got it. Can you talk about what you think sound produces in that constructed way?

Cauleen

Healing. Sound waves move through your body. You feel them before you really understand them. The act of hearing is a feeling. It's physical—whereas seeing is a biochemical firing. Sound goes in your body, and therefore, I think it's a really intimate tool, really personal.

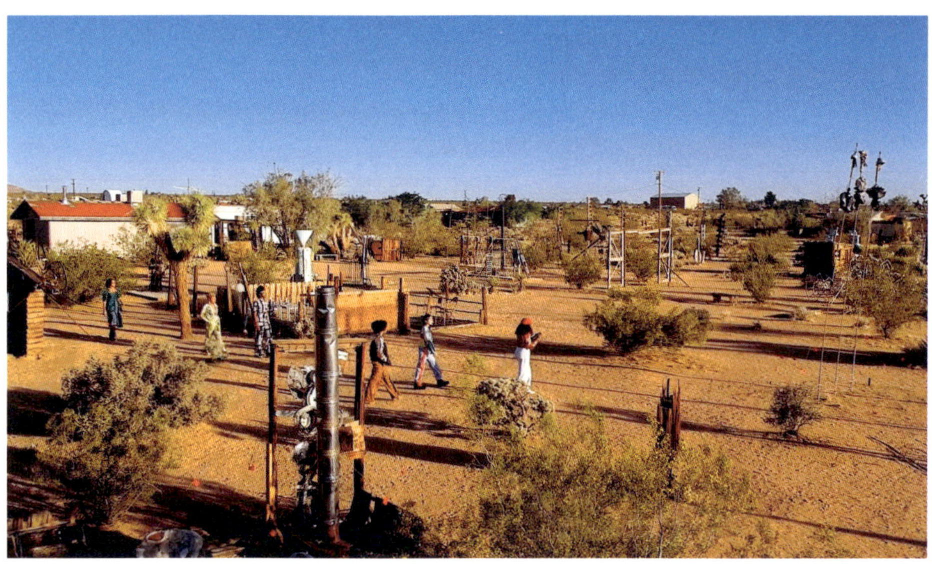

***Sojourner* (still), 2018**
Digital video and 16mm film,
color, sound, 22:03 minutes

Rodney

Why choose this desert location, where Purifoy lived and built all this work?

Cauleen

I chose the desert museum for a site because of Purifoy's relationship to the Watts Towers. He was one of the founders of the art center that's still there, right after the riots. Also, he and several other artists went, combed through all the rubble of the riots, and collected junk and started making sculptures that way. And that shaped the rest of his life. He went from being like a modernist furniture designer to using trash to make work. And he did it there at Watts Towers. And he built something that is there to this day, which is another aspect I'm interested in.

Rodney

"There" being the desert?

Cauleen

The Watts Towers Arts Center. It's still there. It's still functioning. It's still working. It's still part of the community. It's the beating artery of the community, right? This is what attracted me to Rodia's towers in the first place. The radical generosity of building a thing with love and then just giving it away.

Like this, I have been trying to develop a way of working, making films, that goes against the way you're trained to make films. I've been trying to work improvisationally and, this is going to sound really corny, but making through a kind of love and care, because film shoots are the opposite of that. They're very hierarchical. They're very planned out. There are instances of cruelty that are a given in the service of getting a shot. You can mistreat anyone and say anything to anybody. You can abuse anybody as long as you get the shot or as long as you deliver. This is just the culture of film sets. It's some dick-swinging macho patriarchal shit that they actually

teach you how to do in film school. And
I can't do it anymore for a lot of reasons.

Rodney

This is a new way of doing film?

Cauleen

For literally seven years, Rodney, I've been
trying. Every time I do a film shoot, I'm
trying do it differently. A garage band style
of improvisation. So instead of there being
a director and then there's this crew, it's
like the singer, the drummer, the guitar
player, we are in a band together. We're in
the band, playing at the same time.

We're there together. Maybe not like a
rock band. More like: a sextet. We take
solos. We support each other. We have each
other's backs.

Rodney

Are the actors, the characters, also within
that configuration? 'Cause you mentioned
mostly the technical people.

Cauleen

Yes. The actors are crucial in this, because
I no longer work with actual actors. Some
of them are trained, actually, but I don't tell
them what I'm doing. I tell them how I'm
gonna do things. And, look, it's gonna be
improvisational. I'm just gonna shout stuff
out. I want you to listen to me. Just respond
to my voice. Don't stop and interrupt
the flow. We're gonna always keep going.
Pretend like it's live. Pretend like we're
on-stage. Pretend we're singing a song
together and we got to get to the end of the
song. When I say cut, the song is over, but
the song might end before I say cut. You
might know the song is over before I do.
That's the kind of stuff I say.

I gave this whole speech about their
relationships with each other. I was like,
look, your characters don't have names.
You are yourselves, but we are convening.
We are listening to the voices of these
women, and we are following them out to
the desert. We are joining together just
like the Combahee River Collective to
listen, to think, and [to] learn from each
other. That's why we're here.

That's what I'm filming. And they were
like, okay. And because they are who
they are—really, really amazing, creative
women, mostly students at Cal Arts or
artists in their own right, they understood.
It was the first time that my producers,
all the crew, everybody, except for one
person—ha!—understood.

The Association for the Advancement of Cinematic Creative Maladjustment

—

A Manifesto

The following text is from a pamphlet that accompanied the public event, *Skowhegan and Whitewalls Conversation #3: Cauleen Smith and Greg Tate present The Association for the Advancement of Cinematic Creative Maladjustment*, which took place January 15, 2012, at the New Museum, New York.

FRIENDS, I alert you: This manifesto is a
gasconade a non-violent word-grenade

a plushy feral tirade

a bombastic love parade. So, please, walk
with me.

Bang your drum. Blow your horn. Load
your camera. Let us promenade.

— Kelly Gabron
*The third day of January on our two-
thousand-twelfth lap around the Sun.*

CREATIVE MALADJUSTMENT————

*There are certain technical words within every academic dis-
cipline that soon become stereotypes and clichés. Modern
psychology has a word that is probably used more than any
other word in modern psychology. It is the word "maladjusted."
. . . I say to you, my friends . . . there are certain things in our
nation and in the world which I am proud to be* maladjusted
and which I hope all men of good-will will be maladjusted.

*I say very honestly that I never intend to become adjusted to
segregation and discrimination.*

I never intend to become adjusted to religious bigotry.

*I never intend to adjust myself to economic conditions that will
take necessities from the many to give luxuries to the few.*

*I never intend to adjust myself to the madness of militarism,
to self-defeating effects of physical violence.*

*But in a day when Sputniks and explorers are dashing through
outer space and guided ballistic missiles are carving highways
of death through the stratosphere, no nation can win a war.
It is no longer the choice between violence and nonviolence. It
is either nonviolence or nonexistence. In other words, I'm
about convinced now that there is need for a new organization
in our world:*

Cauleen Smith

1. Dr. King repeated this concept in many speeches over the span of several years and in many contexts, including a speech to the American Psychological Association. It seems that this idea was one he reserved for the college circuit and professional associations, which may be why his call for the Association for the Advancement of Creative Maladjustment is less popularly known by and quoted in Civil Rights histories. I have yet to determine how Dr. King came to insert the word "creative" into his programmatic plea. It is this generative qualification that interests me here in the context of discussing a dogma for film-making and a practice of resistance rather than subversion. December 18, 1963. Transcription of a speech given at Western Michigan University, Kalamazoo, MI. Copyright: Western Michigan University Libraries, 2005.

THE INTERNATIONAL ASSOCIATION FOR THE ADVANCEMENT OF CREATIVE MALADJUSTMENT————

> *—men and women who will be as **maladjusted** as the prophet Amos. Who in the midst of the injustices of his day could cry out in words that echo across the centuries, "Let justice roll down like waters and righteousness like a mighty stream." . . . Through such maladjustment, I believe that we will be able to emerge from the bleak and desolate midnight of man's inhumanity to man into the bright and glittering daybreak of freedom and justice. My faith is that somehow this problem will be solved.*
>
> — Dr. Martin Luther King Jr.[1]

THE CINEMA AND THE CREATIVELY MALADJUSTED[2]————

The Pronouncements:

1.

The Maladjusteds say: Images are what we create, but language and its potential for resistance against the over-determination of identity, perception and experience determines the creation of images. Language is the stuff of us. Our debt to language is paid in full. Language is what we have. So we use it now to reshape and control the means, methods, and motivations for the production of time-based media: Moving-Images.

2.

The Maladjusteds know that the spaces in-between words are where the image lives. The arsenal and the pantry of the filmmaker are sited at the in-between space.

3.

The Maladjusteds liberate image from narrative. Narrative is the oppressor of the Moving-Image. The Reader conjures images in her conscious and unconscious mind as she reads. Those images come from some Place. The tasks and demands of the filmmaker extend beyond the mere illustration of the menageries of literature. Yes, it is true that the wild beasts of our literary imagination are painted, dressed, and caged by images the viewer has gleaned from the world around her, but the Moving-Image can and must do more than slave for narrative. The Moving-Image must rise up and reclaim the power it has for so long surrendered to story. The true power of the Moving-Image is its resistance to plot. Images resist.[3]

4.

The Maladjusteds do not seek to destroy (subvert) main-stream commercial cinema. The Maladjusteds create movies that punctuate, highlight, and, indeed (!), capitalize on the ways in which Genre Movies (action, science fiction and horror) potently legitimate sites of radicality within the crusty annals of illusionistic cinema.[4] In Genre (and Genre-Bending) lies the hope and future of commercial cinema. Genre has saved the studio system's flabby ass more than once already.

5.

The Maladjusteds play. We play with all media and materials. We do not mistake the scale of a production nor the source of the production for the value and merit in said production. The Maladjusteds engage works as they are without qualification and without corporate mediations of prowess (box-office rankings, celebrity associations), or the relative evaluations on image quality which reify technology rather than aesthetic and conceptual potency.

2. The Maladjusted are a tribe of creatives who use images in service of time-based media. The Maladjusteds love a good action flick as much as the next person. The writer admires filmmakers who blow shit up, propel objects in space, animate alien creatures, and imbue electromagnetic fields with punishing spiritual malice. However: the Maladjusteds do not require narrative to experience the rewards of time-based media. Narrative is incidental to image. As far as the Maladjusteds are concerned, a filmmaker could tell the same story over and over and it will ever re-new, if the form, materials, and environmental stakes of its subjects are manifested with the love, integrity, and openness that only an amateur can muster. Agape!
3. For over one hundred years, cultural forces, commercial interests, and well-adjusted

consumers have enslaved the moving-image to a an oppressive and insatiable master: narrative. By reducing celluloid's alchemical powers to the servitude of literary constructs, narrative stunted the growth of the most radical material art of the twentieth century, thereby rendering it nothing but a shuffling lackey to theatrical effect and the fetishization of hegemonic and oppressive icons. When contemporary moviegoers discuss cinema, their discussions struggle to travel beyond an analysis of the (usually puerile) plot. The well-adjusted consumer idolizes the storytellers: actors are storytellers, directors are storytellers, writers are storytellers, producers are storytellers. Well, my friends, I say to you that if I wanted to indulge in an intricate story, I would READ A BOOK. I ask you, how many screenwriters in Hollywood are in fact frustrated novelists? Why does the market of

6.

The Maladjusteds project their love of the Spectator onto the screens.

7.

The Maladjusteds resist corporate pressure to fuel the desires of the Spectator. Rather they seek to excavate her needs.

8.

The Spectators of Creatively Maladjusted Cinema do not lack. They do not substitute unattainable longing for the provocations of the mundane. The Maladjusteds seek the destabilization of the familiar and the expansion of the known. They race at the speed of light toward the edge of their seats—toward the screen(s), towards the community of Maladjusteds who understand that economic privilege (or the mimicry of such) is a poor metric for defining the quality of a work.

9.

The Maladjusted Filmmaker has failed the Maladjusted Spectator. Rather than generating and proliferating our own image-language with a vocabulary that enables us to share our tactics, insights, opinions and experiences a with the Maladjusted Spectator, The Maladjusted Film-maker waits for popular culture journalists, art historians, and film theorists to supply these ideas for them. This has left the Maladjusted Spectator with poor translations for their engagement with images. Because of this failure, the Spectator mimics the language of corporate slaves. She compares shit with manure and contrasts mucus and boogers. Because of this famished vocabulary, the Maladjusted Spectator has been forced to register their experience through shareholder values rather than co-operative valences.

10.

And yet, the Maladjusted Spectator perseveres. Like Amos, she resists the indulgences of propaganda in favor the rigors of aesthetic transcendence. The Maladjusted Spectator enters the cinema space as a supplicant enters the cathedral.

11.

The Maladjusted Spectator consumes the flawed-image with as much gusto as she would a flawless one. Like a diner who appreciates collards cooked in salt-fat as much as asparagus wrapped in prosciutto, the Maladjusted Spectator does not mistake the humility of materials and transparency of construction for inferiority. Rather, she recognizes the artifacts of production and the procedural markers of cultures as indicators of conceptual and material integrity.

12.

The Maladjusted Spectator does not expect to be pleased. She expects to be respected.

13.

The Maladjusted Spectator is charged with great power and responsibility. When she watches a Moving-Image, she revels in the freedom of being responsible for her heart and mind, while trusting the filmmaker to expand and enliven both. She grabs hold of the hand that reaches out to her from the screens and she Hangs On! She knows that that those who lean back in their seats waiting for the little spoon to slide pre-digested images into their emaciated imaginations will starve. The Maladjusted Spectator loves to eat.

cinema support mediocrity so well? But Hollywood bears only some of the blame. We well-adjusteds who consume these images have failed the images by submitting to our oppressor's language, internalizing our oppressor's values, and evaluating the viability of moving-image works based on political propagandistic markers of power, like mass agreement (*We all saw 1-2-3.*) rather than individual engagement (*I experienced X-Y-Z.*) Cinema has rules that literature can barely conceive. Like gravity, Time works on an image. What is the science of time and its relationship to movement? Not the description of movement, no! Not the use of movement to get a character from one chapter of dialogue to another, no! For the Maladjusteds, the science of cinematic time wrestles with the movement of objects, bodies, land, and air within the Film-Frame. The ineffable laws of cinema are forever seeking and yet never

14.

The Maladjusteds approach their subjects, materials, and resources with respect, as these elements have their own stakes and sovereignty.[5] The ways in which their autonomy impacts the modes of production, form, and content of a work cannot be subjugated in service of the aesthetic, cultural, social, or political preferences of the market. The Filmmaker must internalize the agency of her collaborators and their environs in order to generate and guide the formal, aesthetic, and conceptual constructs that define the Work.[6]

15.

The Maladjusteds do not privilege radical form over radical content. For what is radical form if all it does is cloak and disguise regressive values and oppressive stereotypes? That is not art. That is placebo-art. Decorative, celebrity-dependent, convoluted theatricality bamboozles the spectator into believing that she has had a culturally-supreme artistic experience; for in spite of the obtuse structural devices and clumsy episodic sequences to which she was subjected, she is encouraged to believe that she managed to access deep-meaning from the work (a deep-meaning which is always attributed to the inherent supreme gifts of the placebo-filmmaker). No doubt, she has extracted meaning from both the radical form and the content of the film. In some cases, though, the primary reason that any coherence can be grafted from such works is because the placebo-film's signs and signifiers are in fact threadbare stereotypes, exoticisms, and clichés.[7] In support of a commercially viable radical form, the placebo-filmmaker relies on the familiarity of minstrelsy for narrative coherence. The semiotics of hegemony are by their very nature a suffocating force that presses true radicality into the margins of culture.

16.

The Maladjusteds do not mistake affect for information. Being moved by an image which claims to document a

expecting to find their Cosmological Constant. The Maladjusted filmmaker simply follows the image into space-time. Film is space is time. And it never stops moving. —K.G.
4. Illusionistic cinema works to conceal the mechanisms and tactics deployed in service of creating seamlessness and forward momentum within the space-time of the film.
5. The chemical elements embedded in film emulsions and computer chips have been unearthed at great and sometimes deadly expense. At some point (surely NOW), the Maladjusteds must face their complicity in the corrosive, exploitative, and violent extraction of resources that enables our access to materials. And once we face it, we must find non-violent modes of active resistance—as is the Maladjusted way.
6. This is why the works of a creatively

social ill is not the same as actually gaining mastery of the concepts and policies that create that social ill. The Maladjusteds are suspicious of "world-changing" agendas in filmmaking, as one might be suspicious of nation-building agendas in war. How can the world be changed by spectral outward projections which abjectify the Other, or reify a singular Hero? Beware of the movie (that claims to be non-fiction) that attempts to titillate then satiate your desire for knowledge in the same way that a video of people having sex titillates then satiates your desire for sexual gratification. A document-airy is not advocacy. It is a tool for Advocates to use in service of their cause. Non-fiction filmmakers must think of themselves as tool-makers in the same way that creative filmmakers must understand themselves as dream-custodians. The cinema-work itself, is merely an object, a tool, a dream. Action, resistance, and change are the realm of humans, not objects, consciousness not sentiment. Beware of televisual narratives that exploit the well-adjusted viewer's ignorance by projecting fantasies of "the abject" as fact and substituting Platonic tragedy for subjectivity.[8]

17.

Knowing what we know about the power of materials which graft, manipulate, and mutate cinematic space-time, the Maladjusteds refuse to patronize the Spectator. This means we're mostly broke, in debt, and desperate for funding. But our profits return to us in the form of emphatic discourse, and creative responses to the destabilizing, empowering, and energizing affects of creative maladjustment. Our bounty is the cornucopia (or vortex) of future-histories.

The Maladjusteds, when all is said and done, travel the cinematic spaceways of ecstatic form because we love our audiences too much.

——————Pronouncements End. Listening Begins.——————

maladjusted filmmaker may not be easily recognizable as being produced by the same maker. The subject, rather than the signature of the maker, determine the applied tactics.
7. Example of placebo-films are the works of David Lynch, in which the 1950's iconography of guileless blonds, silent cowboys, "spooky" little people, and one- legged Voodoo creatures with un-locatable foreign accents manufacture a veil of mystery and suspense. Another example is the Cremaster series by Matthew Barney. However, Mr. Barney should be credited for elevating the lowly televisual genre of the Info-mercial into the realm of high-art, in which his episodic demonstrations of sculptural forms accompanied by celebrity endorsements exploit mass-media channels to convince the viewer of the essentialness and importance of his

objects. Barney makes-believe with his fantastical fabricated devices and thereby demonstrates the potency and desirability of the real (privileged in its invisibility) product that he is peddling: white-masculinity. It slices . . . it dices, it dangles, it spangles! Buy one now!!

8. A short list of works that demonstrate these values would include: *The Wire* (2002–08), *Monster's Ball* (2001), *Training Day* (2001), *Precious* (2009), and *For Colored Girls* (2010). It is so interesting that for films which revel in the abject-i-tude of an imagined blackness, these tendencies are often identified as the best work of the artist who made them. And in the case of *The Wire* and *Precious*, referenced as a document of reality rather than the lush creative fictions that they are. Halle Barry won the Best Actress Award for *Monster's Ball* (only the second such

LOVE AS PRACTICE. LOVE AS PRODUCTION————

For there is another thing about this philosophy that says you can stand before an unjust system and resist it with all your might and yet maintain an attitude of active good will toward the perpetrators of that unjust system. So it goes on to say that the ethic of love can stand at the center of the nonviolent movement. Now when I talk about love at this point, people always have questions to raise. They begin to say, what do you mean, love those who are bombing your home and those who are oppressing you and using any method to keep you in the state of injustice, the state of slavery. How in the world can you love such people? Well, let me rush on to say that when I speak of love, I'm not talking about emotional bosh. I think in so many instances, this whole idea is misunderstood. It is absurd to urge oppressed people to love their oppressors in an affectionate sense. I'm not talking about an affectionate emotion at this point. I think the Greek language comes to our rescue at this point, there are three words in the Greek language for love.

There is the word, "eros." Eros is a sort of aesthetic love, a yearning of the soul for the realm of the divine. Plato used to talk about it a great deal in his dialogues. It has come to us to be a sort of romantic love. So we all know about eros—we have experienced it and read it in all of the beauties of literature. In a sense, Edgar Allen Poe was talking about eros when he talked about his beautiful Annabel Lee with a love surrounded by the halo of eternity. In a sense, Shakespeare was talking about eros when he said, "Love is not love which alters when an alteration finds or bends with the removal to remove. It is an ever fixed mark which looks on tempest and is never shaken. It is a star to every wandering bark." You know, I can remember that because I have [to] quote it to my wife every now and then. That's eros.

The Greek language talks about "philia," which is the sort of intimate affection between personal friends. This is a significant love and on this level, you love people that you like, people that you have dealings with, people that are friends. This is friendship.

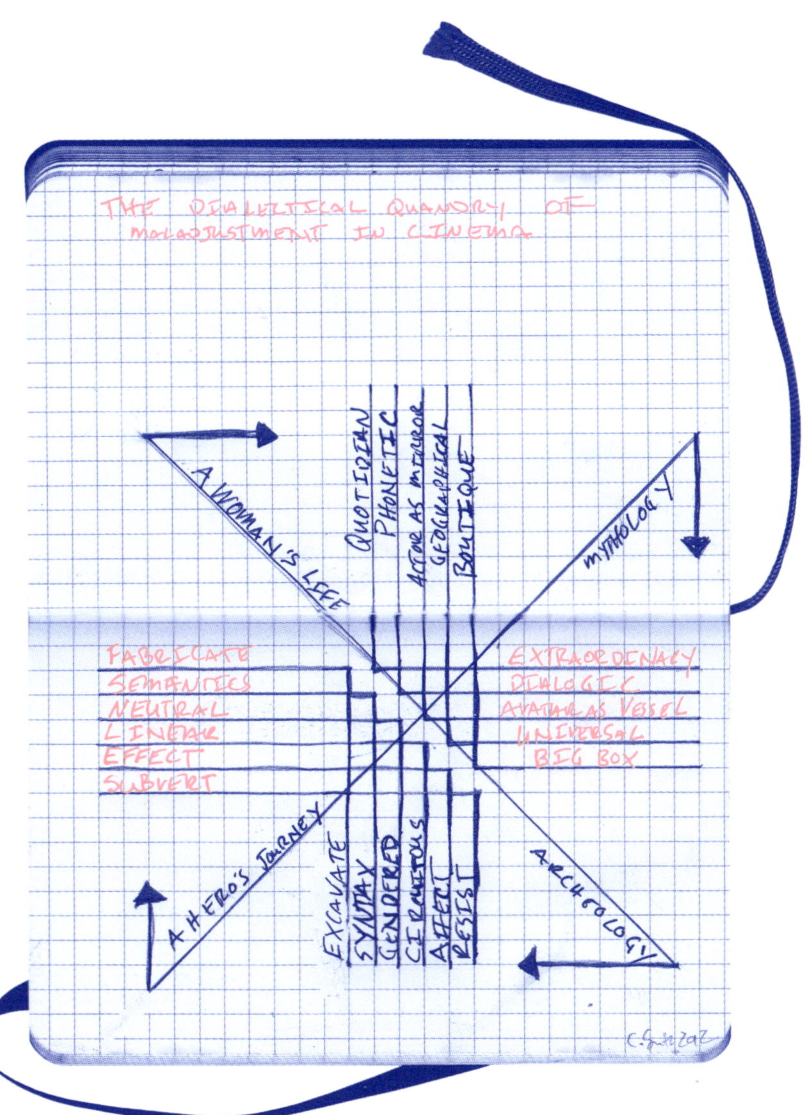

award to go to a black woman in the Academy's eighty-four-year history). African American actor Denzel Washington was overlooked for the Best Actor Oscar when he rendered a slave as defiant and dignified in *Glory* (1989), but won one for playing (quite entertainingly) a thug-stereotype in *Training Day*. Don Cheadle was robbed of the Best Supporting Actor for his complex, unpredictable, and dangerous rendering of a sociopath in *Devil In A Blue Dress* (1995). Such are the priorities of mainstream cinema and the well-adjusted.

9. Ibid. MLK at WMU, 1963.

Exhibition
Checklist

Pilgrim, 2017

Digital video, color, sound.
7:41 minutes

Sojourner, 2018

Digital video, color, sound,
22:41 minutes

Space Station: Two Rebeccas, 2018

Wallpaper, disco balls, turntable,
motor, fur, shag carpet,
two projectors, digital video

Epistrophe, 2018

Multichannel video (color, sound), four
CCTV cameras, four monitors, projection,
custom wood table, taxidermy raven,
wood figures, bronze figures, plastic
figures, books, seashells, minerals, jar of
starfish, Magic 8-Ball, maneki-neko, mirror,
metal trays, plaster objects, wood objects,
wire object, fabric, glass vase, plants

Sky Learns Sky, 2018

Lee Filters film gels, architecture, eight
lawn chairs, sunlight

Black and Blue Over You (After Bas Jan Ader), 2010

Digital video, color, sound. 9:40 minutes

Strelitzia Satellite Meditation, 2012

Digital video, color, sound. 4:44 minutes

Cotton Plant 187?, 2018

Digital video, color, sound. 6:43 minutes

Afflict the Comfortable/ Comfort the Afflicted, 2018

Satin, cotton, velvet, vinyl

I Appreciate You in Advance, 2018

Fiberglass screen, woven metallic
polyesters, woven two-tone silk

Space Station Chinoiserie #1: Take Hold of the Clouds, 2018

Digitally printed wallpaper

Reproduction of archival image by Billy Ray

Black and white photograph on matte
paper. 26.9 × 44 in. Photograph not
published in *LIFE Magazine*. Young men
hang out near Simon Rodia's Watts
Towers. 1966. Time & Life Pictures/
Getty Images.

Page numbers reference full page images
and film inserts. All other images are
captioned below each respective image.

All works courtesy of the artist, Corbett
vs. Dempsey, Chicago, and Kate Werble
Gallery, New York

Contributor Biographies

Anthony Elms is the Daniel and Brett Sundheim Chief Curator at the Institute of Contemporary Art, University of Pennsylvania.

Rhea Anastas (b. 1969) is cofounder of Orchard, and Associate Professor in the Department of Art at University of California, Irvine. Orchard was an artist-run gallery in New York's Lower East Side (2005–2008), a then-transitional neighborhood in Lower Manhattan, started amidst the grim afterhours of George W. Bush's reelection by Anastas, Moyra Davey, Andrea Fraser, R. H. Quaytman, Jeff Preiss—twelve cofounders, nine of whom are artists, in all. Anastas is author, with Michael Brenson, of *Witness to Her Art: Art and Writings by Adrian Piper, Mona Hatoum, Cady Noland, Jenny Holzer, Kara Walker, Daniela Rossell and Eau de Cologne* (Center for Curatorial Studies, Bard College, distributed by D.A.P. Distributed Art Publishers, 2006). She is author of *Double Bind*, a book-length long form dialogue co-written with artist Leigh Ledare (A.R.T. Press, Art Resources Transfer, New York, 2015). Anastas' latest essay, "Property and Community in the Recent Work," considers the work of Louise Lawler as it engages with, and is seen through, the work of three other artists, Andrea Fraser, Cameron Rowland, and Michael Asher. Published in *Louise Lawler: Receptions*, edited by Roxana Marcoci (The Museum of Modern Art, New York, 2017) in conjunction with the exhibition *Louise Lawler: WHY PICTURES NOW*, The Museum of Modern Art, April 30 – July 30, 2017.

Cauleen Smith (b. 1967; lives Los Angeles) is an interdisciplinary artist, whose work reflects upon the everyday possibilities of the imagination. Operating in multiple materials and arenas, Smith roots her work firmly within the discourse of mid-twentieth-century experimental film. Drawing from structuralism, Third World Cinema, and science fiction, she makes things that deploy the tactics of these disciplines, while offering a phenomenological experience for spectators and participants. Her films, objects, and installations have been featured in numerous group exhibitions, including those at the Studio Museum in Harlem; the Contemporary Arts Museum Houston; the Yerba Buena Center for Art, San Francisco; the 2017 *Whitney Biennial; Prospect.4*, New Orleans; the New Museum, New York; D21, Leipzig; and Decad, Berlin. Smith has had solo shows of films and installations at the Kitchen, New York; the Museum of Contemporary Art Chicago; the Art Institute of Chicago; and Threewalls, Chicago. Smith is the recipient of several grants and awards, including the Rockefeller Media Arts Award, a Creative Capital Moving Image Grant, the Chicago 3Arts Grant, the Foundation for Contemporary Arts' Ellsworth Kelly Award, Expo Chicago's Artadia Award, and a Rauschenberg Residency. Smith was born in Riverside, California, and grew up in Sacramento. She earned her BA in creative arts from San Francisco State University and her MFA from the University of California, Los Angeles's School of Theater, Film, and Television. Smith teaches in the School of Art at CalArts.

Rodney McMillian (b. 1969; lives Los Angeles) McMillian received an MFA from the California Institute of the Arts in 2002. He received the Contemporary Austin's first Suzanne Deal Booth Art Prize in 2016, and the resulting solo exhibition *Against a Civic Death* was on view through August 26, 2018. In 2016, McMillian had solo exhibitions at the ICA Philadelphia, the Studio Museum in Harlem, and MoMA PS.1. Each of these exhibitions highlighted a particular set of material and conceptual concerns in McMillian's multivalent practice. Other recent solo exhibitions include "Landscape Paintings," Aspen Art Museum, CO (2015); "Sentimental Disappointment," *Momentum 14: Rodney McMillian*, The Institute of Contemporary Art, Boston, MA (2009); The Kitchen, New York (2008). McMillian's work was featured in the 2015 Sharjah Biennial, curated by Eungie Joo. His work has also been included in group exhibitions at The National Portrait Gallery, London, MASS MoCA, North Adams, MA; the CCA Wattis Institute, San Francisco, CA; the Astrup Fearnley Museet, Oslo, Norway; The Institute of Contemporary Art, Boston; The Institute of Contemporary Art, Philadelphia; the Contemporary Art Museum Houston; the Museum of Contemporary Art, Los Angeles; the Museum of Contemporary Art, Chicago; the UCLA Hammer Museum, Los Angeles; and the Los Angeles County Museum of Art among many others.

Film Credits

Give It or Leave It

Fabricators—
Jinn Bronwen Lee
Karla Canseco
Nizette Krebs
Ariel Navas
Cauleen Smith
Paul Swenbeck

Installation—
Cat Bean
Scott Currie
Hannah Declercq
Emily Elliot
Joy Feasley
Adam Lovitz
Jacob Lunderby
Pat Maguire
Drew Mitchell
Julia Policastro
Jay Roselius
Lydia Smith
Sophie White
Ash Williams
George Wisegarver
Greenhouse Media

Sojourner

Kirby Griffin
Director of Photography

Jamar Jones
Camera and Drone Operator

Candice Majors
Jade Ware
B-roll Camera

Cauleen Smith
B-roll Camera, Director,
Editor, Producer

Amia Yokoyama
Assistant Director

Sami Martin Sarmiento
Costume Designer

Kelly Mock
Assistant to Costume Designer

Indah Datau
Gaffer

James Dii
Set Costumer

Mar Sudac
Line Producer

Pat Brunty
Location Manager

Cast—
Victoria Aravindhan
Laura Bejarano
Khari Blackmon
Charlotte Brathwaite
Lulu Braithwaite
Hannah Cruz
Kiki Green
Lisa E. Harris
Denae Howard
Devin Johnson
Paige McGhee
Naima Noguera
Alicia Piller
Tammie Shui
Billie Soo Hoo
Zurah Taylor
Dr. Barbara Ransby
Chicago activists and Hyde
   Park Chicago community

Voice-over—
Radha Botofasina
Krista Franklin
Lisa E. Harris

Locations—
Watts Towers, Los Angeles
Noah Purifoy Outdoor
   Museum, Joshua Tree, CA
Vasquez Rocks Natural
   Area Park, CA
Antelope Valley California
   Poppy Reserve, CA

Fletcher Street Horse
   Pasture, Philadelphia, PA
Southside Community Art
   Center, Chicago, IL
John Coltrane Residence,
   Philadelphia, PA
Sun Ra Arkestra Residence,
   Philadelphia, PA

Music—
Alice Coltrane,
Turiyasangitananda

Pilgrim

Arthur Jafa
Director of Photography

Appearances—
Shankari Adams
Radha Botofasina
Courtney Bryan

Locations—
Sai Anantam Ashram,
   Agoura, CA
Watts Towers, Los Angeles
Watervliet Shaker Historic
   District, Colonie, NY

Music—
Alice Coltrane,
Turiyasangitananda

Special Thanks

Rhea Anastas
Tiona Nekkia McClodden
Osei-Duro
Jorge Ravelos
Aaron Swanton

This book is published on the occasion of the exhibition *Cauleen Smith: Give It or Leave It*, curated by Anthony Elms, and organized and presented by the Institute of Contemporary Art, University of Pennsylvania, September, 14–December 23, 2018.

ISBN: 978-0-88454-146-2

Institute of Contemporary Art
University of Pennsylvania
118 S. 36th Street
Philadelphia, PA 19104-3289
www.icaphila.org

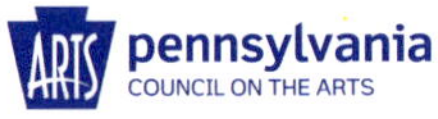

Copy Editor—
Kristi McGuire

Design—
Kimberly Varella,
Content Object

Photography—
Constance Mensh

Color Separations—
Echelon Color

Typefaces—
Graphik, Plantin, and
GT Sectra Display

First Edition
Edition of 1,000
Printed by Verona Libri

Cauleen Smith: Give It or Leave It exhibition tour—

Institute for Contemporary Art at Virginia Commonwealth University, Richmond, VA
February 16–May 5, 2019

Frye Art Museum, Seattle, WA
June 1–September 1, 2019

Los Angeles County Museum of Art, CA
Summer, 2020

(cover and inside cover) *Sojourner*, 2018. Digital video, color, sound, 22:41 minutes

(page 46) Photograph not published in *LIFE Magazine*. Young men hang out near Simon Rodia's Watts Towers. 1966. Time & Life Pictures/Getty Images.

Support for *Cauleen Smith: Give It or Leave It* has been provided by the Ellsworth Kelly Award. The Ellsworth Kelly Award is made possible by The Ellsworth Kelly Foundation and the Foundation for Contemporary Arts. Additional support has been provided by B. Z. & Michael Schwartz, Meredith and Bryan Verona, and Susan Weiler.

ICA is always Free. For All.

Free admission is courtesy of Amanda and Glenn Fuhrman.

ICA acknowledges the generous sponsorship of Barbara B. and Theodore R. Aronson for exhibition catalogues. Programming at ICA has been made possible in part by the Emily and Jerry Spiegel Fund to Support Contemporary Culture and Visual Arts and the Lise Spiegel Wilks and Jeffrey Wilks Family Foundation, and by Hilarie L. & Mitchell Morgan. Marketing is supported by Pamela Toub Berkman & David J. Berkman and by Lisa A. & Steven A. Tananbaum. Additional funding has been provided by the Horace W. Goldsmith Foundation, the Overseers Board for the Institute of Contemporary Art, friends and members of ICA, and the University of Pennsylvania. General operating support is provided, in part, by the Philadelphia Cultural Fund. ICA receives state arts funding support through a grant from the Pennsylvania Council on the Arts, a state agency funded by the Commonwealth of Pennsylvania and the National Endowment for the Arts, a federal agency. ICA acknowledges Le Méridien Philadelphia as our official Unlock Art™ partner hotel.